Computer-Based Testing

Building the Foundation
for Future Assessments

Computer-Based Testing

Building the Foundation for Future Assessments

Edited by

Craig N. Mills
American Institute of Certified Public Accountants

Maria T. Potenza
Microsoft Corporation

John J. Fremer
William C. Ward
Educational Testing Service

LAWRENCE ERLBAUM ASSOCIATES, PUBLISHERS
2002   Mahwah, New Jersey   London

Lawrence Erlbaum Associates, Inc., Publishers
10 Industrial Avenue
Mahwah, NJ 07430

Cover design by Kathryn Houghtaling Lacey

Library of Congress Cataloging-in-Publication Data

Computer-based testing : building the foundation for future assessments / Craig
N. Mills . . . [et al.].
     p. cm.
Includes bibliographical references and index.
ISBN 0-8058-3759-0 (hardcover : alk. paper)
     1. Educational tests and measurements–United States.   2. Educational
technology–United States.   I. Mills, Craig N., 1953–
LB3060.5 .C66   2001
371.26'0973—dc21   2001023575
                                                              CIP

Books published by Lawrence Erlbaum Associates are printed on acid-free paper,
and their bindings are chosen for strength and durability.

Printed in the United States of America
10 9 8 7 6 5 4 3 2 1

Contents

Preface

The decade of the 1990s has been one of significant change for the measurement profession. Much of the change has been driven by the rapid expansion of computer-based testing (CBT). Although CBTs have been administered for many years, improvements in the speed and power of computers coupled with reductions in their cost have made large-scale computer delivery of tests feasible. CBT is now a common form of test delivery for licensure, certification, and admissions tests. Many large-scale, high-stakes testing programs have introduced CBT either as an option or as the sole means of test delivery.

The move to CBT has been, to a great extent, successful. It has not, however, been without problems. As CBT gained in popularity, questions were raised about access to CBT testing centers, the security of CBTs, the reliability of test-delivery systems, the psychometric quality of the tests, and the adequacy of the theoretical models that support them. Traditional concerns about testing, such as item and test bias, continue to be raised with respect to CBTs and have been expanded to include issues such as whether access to technology affects test performance differentially for members of different groups. CBT has been expensive and has placed new demands on test developers to produce more items more rapidly to maintain security in a continuous testing environment.

In contrast to these concerns, many measurement professionals have noted that CBT may have the potential to provide a richer understanding of examinee performance and capabilities. Data that are not available in paper-and-pencil testing programs (e.g., time spent per item) may provide new information to inform the interpretation of performance. In addition, there is some evidence that computer processes may supplement or replace manual processes for test development and the scoring of complex responses and, as a result, render certain forms of testing more economical than has been the case in the past. CBT also allows for substantial reductions in the time between test administration and score reporting, a significant benefit in the eyes of many. Finally, test sponsors are free to offer their tests more frequently, a convenience that many examinees find appealing.

CBT is already a major vehicle for test delivery and could, in fact, become the dominant form of test delivery in the near future. Both the difficulties and the opportunities associated with CBT offer challenges to the measurement profession. Advances in psychometrics are required to ensure that those who rely on test results can have at least the same confidence in CBTs as they have in traditional forms of assessment.

In recognition of the need for rapid, broad-based advances in the psychometric foundations supporting CBT, Educational Testing Service (ETS) sponsored a colloquium entitled "Computer-Based Testing: Building the Foundation for Future Assessments" on September 25 to 26, 1998, in Philadelphia, Pennsylvania. More than 200 measurement professionals from eight countries, 29 states in the United States, and the District of Columbia attended the colloquium. The formal agenda for the colloquium was divided into three major segments: test models, test administration, and test analysis and scoring. Each segment consisted of two or three commissioned paper presentations followed by comments from noted psychometricians.

At the conclusion of the formal presentations in each segment, colloquium participants attended break-out sessions to identify the most important issues raised in the segment and discuss priorities for research. Following the colloquium, the panel of discussant psychometricians used the results of the break-out sessions to develop a CBT Research Agenda. The intent of the Research Agenda is to provide a framework within which the measurement profession can pursue the most critical issues facing CBT in the coming years. We hope it will be useful to researchers, practitioners, students, and funding agencies as they establish their research programs and priorities.

The colloquium provided a unique opportunity for a large group of measurement professionals to focus on a single topic and the issues associated with it for 2 days and to devote a significant portion of that time to collaborative discussions about the research necessary to address CBT issues. We would like to thank ETS for sponsoring this innovative forum and for entrusting us with the responsibility for organizing it. This volume contains the papers presented at the colloquium, the discussant remarks based on those papers, and the Research Agenda that was generated based on participants' discussions in the break-out sessions. We hope the book will provide a useful tool for measurement professionals interested in addressing the challenges of CBT in the coming years.

Many individuals, including the participants, were critical to its success. Within ETS, Ernie Anastasio and Henry Braun provided the financial support for the colloquium and allowed us to rearrange our priorities to work on the colloquium. One other individual, Lisha R. White, deserves special mention. Lisha coordinated all of the logistics of the conference, from initial negotiations for hotel space, through registration processing and materials processing, to on-site event management. Without Lisha's efforts the colloquium would likely have not occurred and certainly would not have been as successful as it was. We owe Lisha an enormous debt of gratitude.

Craig N. Mills
William C. Ward
Maria T. Potenza
John J. Fremer

The Work Ahead:
A Psychometric Infrastructure
for Computerized Adaptive Tests

Fritz Drasgow
University of Illinois at Urbana-Champaign

INTRODUCTION

Computer-based tests (CBTs) and computerized adaptive tests (CATs) have finally become a reality. After many years of research by psychometricians and scholars in related fields, CBTs and CATs have been implemented by several major testing programs. Examples include the Department of Defense's Computer Adaptive Test-Armed Services Vocational Aptitude Battery (CAT-ASVAB), the Graduate Record Examination (GRE)-CAT, State Farm Insurance's selection test for computer programmers, and various licensing and credentialing exams. Clearly, large-scale, high-stakes testing is undergoing a paradigm shift.

The colloquium "Computer-Based Testing: Building the Foundation for Future Assessments," held in Philadelphia September 25–26, 1998, underscores the significance of these new approaches to educational and psychological testing. Seven leading researchers presented papers reviewing current research and practice with respect to several critical aspects of CBTs and CATs. These papers, contained in this volume, integrated current research, including many studies presented recently at national conferences and not yet available in the published literature, and began the task of identifying an agenda for future research. At the colloquium, a panel of noted measurement scholars provided commentary

1

on the papers and offered their ideas and proposals for the research agenda. Colloquium attendees also provided input for the research agenda by participating in small group discussions. A formal report, *Completing the CBT Foundation: A Measurement Agenda*, was written following the colloquium. It summarized key issues identified in the paper presentations, panel commentary, and small group discussions. The research agenda is included as the final chapter of this book.

The colloquium offered a unique opportunity for the psychometric community to shape the future of CBT. Wide-ranging and intense discussions of critical problems clarified various needs for programmatic research. Many ideas for addressing these problems were offered and approaches for theoretical and empirical research were proposed and evaluated. Perhaps most exciting was the opportunity for a community of psychometric scholars and measurement practitioners to lay out a broad framework for the research needed to ensure the success of CBT.

CAT AND CBT: PAST AND FUTURE

Since the 1970s there has been a tremendous amount of research on CAT and CBT. For example, the recently published book, *Computerized Adaptive Testing: From Inquiry to Operation* (Sands, Waters, & McBride, 1997), chronicles the work of the military psychometricians who created the CAT-ASVAB. Countless psychometrician years of effort were required to produce a test that could be used seamlessly with the paper-based ASVAB. Many other testing programs have also devoted great effort to computerizing their assessment instruments.

The efforts devoted to CAT and CBT in the past two decades are reminiscent of the growth of large-scale standardized paper-based testing in the 1940s and 1950s. This growth led to extensive research by psychometricians to ensure that examinees received scores that were fair and equitable. For example, multiple test forms were needed by these large assessment programs so that practice effects and cheating were not an issue. However, the use of multiple test forms creates the problem of placing all examinees' scores on the same scale; thus began the field of test equating.

CBT is having analogous growth today. This growth is creating new technical problems for psychometricians that must be solved for testing programs to operate smoothly. Issues include developing and calibrating large numbers of items, constructing item pools for operational tests, limiting exposure of items to ensure security, designing procedures for scoring tests, and selecting models for characterizing item responses. Furthermore, numerous basic issues have not be adequately studied such as under what conditions should the fundamental unit of analysis be an item or a set of items (i.e., a "testlet"). These issues were addressed in the colloquium; brief summaries are provided in the following discussion.

It is important to maintain one's perspective in the face of the myriad technical challenges to CAT and CBT. Computerization enables a much broader range of measurement advances than just adaptive administration of traditional multiple-choice items. Three avenues for such work are briefly discussed. The first is *visualization*. True color images can be presented with remarkable resolution. Moreover, it is possible to allow users to pan in and out, as well as rotate objects in space. An example is Ackerman, Evans, Park, Tamassia, and Turner's (1999) dermatological disorder exam, which uses visualization to good effect. *Audition* provides a second improvement. Vispoel's (1999) work on assessing musical aptitude provides a fascinating example. Simulations of phone conversations, such as those made to call centers, can also be used to glean information about examinees. What might be called *interaction* constitutes the third area: Full motion video can be presented by the computer and thus it is possible to develop assessments of skills related to human interactions. Olson-Buchanan et al.'s (1998; Drasgow, Olson-Buchanan, & Moberg, 1999) Conflict Resolution Skills Assessment and Donovan, Drasgow, and Bergman's (1998) Leadership Skills Assessment provide two examples. Several other examples of innovative uses of computerization for measurement are presented in Drasgow and Olson-Buchanan (1999).

ISSUES FOR TODAY'S CBTS

Many challenges confront a testing program as it implements and operates a CBT. These challenges, which constitute the raison d'etre for this colloquium, are summarized in this section.

Developing New Items

One of the great virtues of a CBT is the opportunity for walk-in testing where examinees schedule the test at times convenient for them. Walk-in testing is viable when test construction designs reduce the possibility that one examinee can provide information to other examinees about test items they might encounter. To this end, adaptive item selection or adaptive testlet selection can be used.

Way, Steffen, and Anderson (chap. 7, this volume) provide a thoughtful analysis of item writing requirements for a high-stakes testing program. They describe various constraints on item usage that should enhance security. The bottom line on their analysis is that item writing requirements are even more substantial than one might guess.

Calibrating Items

Item response theory (IRT) is the psychometric theory underlying CAT. IRT uses one or more item parameters to characterize each item; estimates of these item parameters must be obtained before an item can be added to the item pool. Perhaps the most common approach to obtaining these estimates before implementing a CAT has been to administer items to sizable samples of examinees using paper-based tests. Parshall (chap. 6, this volume) notes problems with this method.

After a CAT is implemented, new items can be "seeded" into the operational form: New items are administered during the CAT but are not used to compute official test scores. Examinees would not ordinarily know which items are part of the operational test and which items are experimental. Sample size requirements and factors that influence these requirements are also described by Parshall.

Several years ago, the Office of Naval Research funded four psychometricians to work on estimating parameters of seeded items. Both parametric approaches (Darrell Bock; Frederic Lord) and nonparametric approaches (Michael Levine; Fumiko Samejima) were investigated. Despite this initial work, relatively little has appeared in the published literature on this topic. Consequently, we are left with questions: What seeding schemes are effective? What estimation frameworks are superior? What sample sizes are required? What subtle problems can be encountered?

Changes in the Item Pool:
Evolution Versus Cataclysm

Way et al. (chap. 7, this volume) describe the set of available items as the *item vat* and characterize restrictions on item selection for a specific item pool as *docking rules*. They use system dynamics modeling to examine CAT forms assembly given new items flowing into the item vat, old items being removed from the vat, and various docking rules.

In Way et al.'s approach, item pools are taken as intact entities. When an item pool becomes too old, it is replaced by a new item pool. Beyond test security, a critical concern is how new forms are equated to the reference form. Military researchers, for example, conducted careful studies to equate CAT-ASVAB Forms 1 and 2 to their reference form, paper-based ASVAB Form 8A.

A beautiful old hickory tree in my back lawn died recently. I thought about taking down the tree lumberjack style, but instead had an arborist remove it. Rather than felling the tree, he started near the top and cut it down branch by branch. His explanation was, "Small cuts make small mistakes." Way et al.'s treatment of item pools, which might be called item pool cataclysm, seems analogous to the lumberjack's approach; it may allow large equating errors to occur and seriously disrupt a testing program. An alternative would be item pool evolution where only a few items are replaced at a time. Items that are overexposed or items that show evidence of changing characteristics would be candidates. Would such small changes limit mistakes in equating to being small in magnitude? How many items could be replaced before an equating study is required? Alternatively, can item pool cataclysms be designed in ways that guarantee small equating errors? Moreover, is it necessary to replace entire item pools to deter cheating conspiracies? These are questions of critical significance for CAT programs, and they provide opportunities for future research.

Delivering, Scoring, and Modeling

What is presented to examinees affects how the assessment can be scored and drives the psychometric modeling of examinee behavior. Four chapters on this interrelated set of topics are presented in this book.

Test delivery refers to how items are selected for presentation to examinees. In CAT-ASVAB, for example, the computer adaptively selects individual items for administration. Folk and Smith (chap. 2, this volume) describe a number of alternatives to this approach. For example, branching might be based on carefully constructed testlets rather than on individual items. Testlets are particularly prominent in computerized mastery testing where it is essential to satisfy content specifications.

Test delivery affects how a test is scored. Dodd and Fitzpatrick (chap. 11, this volume) first consider scoring CATs with standard item branching (although some of these scoring methods have wider applicability than this delivery method). They focus on scoring methods that may be easier to explain to examinees and other interested parties than the usual maximum likelihood or Bayesian estimates of ability. Dodd and Fitzpatrick then discuss automated scoring methods for performance-based tasks such as the architectural design exam for which Bejar (1991) developed an interesting scoring algorithm.

Scoring, in turn, can be affected by how examinee responses are modeled. Luecht and Clauser (chap. 3, this volume) argue that we should not let currently popular psychometric models drive the type of data that are collected. Instead, they suggest considering more detailed information about the examinee–stimulus material interaction such as response time or the sequence of responses made by an examinee. They note that current IRT models are useful for estimating overall proficiency in a domain, but evaluating qualitative states of learning is beyond their scope.

Continuing in this direction, Schnipke and Scrams (chap. 12, this volume) provide a detailed review of approaches to modeling response time. It seems likely a reasonably large set of models (or considerable flexibility within a given model) is necessary to accurately characterize items that vary in difficulty, processing requirements, and timing constraints. Schnipke and Scrams point out a critical need in this area of research: "No validity studies have been offered that address the utility of the resulting scores."

Item Exposure and Test Security

The convenience of walk-in testing creates a great potential for test compromise; conspirators have many opportunities to steal items. A situation in which a relatively small number of examinees conspire to raise their test scores is unfair to the vast majority of honest examinees, and so testing programs are obliged to take steps to maintain test security. High-stakes testing programs in particular must assume evil intentions on the part of some examinees.

Davey and Nering (chap. 8, this volume) describe methods for item exposure control. Such methods require a delicate balance: They must not let the most discriminating items be overexposed, yet they must maintain the efficiency of adaptive testing. It is probably true in high-stakes testing programs that security needs impose greater requirements on an item pool's size than do psychometric needs. More research is needed on item exposure control and examinees' proclivities for cheating.

Item and Test Disclosure

New York state mandates disclosure of educational tests. The legal status of the New York law is in some question (it has been ruled to be in conflict with United States copyright law), but the educational measurement community seems in reasonable agreement that some degree of disclosure is appropriate.

Item and test disclosure in a CAT setting presents a challenge. If the items presented to individual examinees are publicly disclosed, the item pool will be quickly depleted. Moreover, it will be impossible to write and pretest items fast enough to replenish the item pool. The National Council on Measurement in Education (NCME) convened an ad hoc committee to consider the issues involved; this committee was composed of members from educational test publishers, universities, and the public schools.

After review and debate, the NCME ad hoc committee recommended that testing programs provide the option of what they termed *secure item review*. Here, examinees would have the opportunity to review the items they were administered, their own answers, and the answers scored as correct. This review would take place at a testing site and would be monitored by a test proctor. Examinees would not be allowed to take notes, but some mechanism for challenging items they believe to be miskeyed would be allowed. The committee's recommendations were given in a white paper entitled *Item and Test Disclosure for Computerized Adaptive Tests*, which is contained in the Appendix to this chapter.

STRETCHING THE ENVELOPE

Computerization greatly increases the variety of stimulus materials that can be presented to examinees. As noted previously, we can use the terms visualization, audition, and interaction to classify new assessment tools.

Visualization

Computer monitors are rapidly converging to a true color standard that allows 16 million colors to be presented; this represents the maximum number of colors that can be discriminated by the human eye. Moreover, the cost of monitors has fallen rapidly so that the new generation of large (19-inch and 21-inch) monitors can be purchased by many testing programs. Large screen sizes, true color, and high resolution allow high fidelity displays of images.

Ackerman et al. (1999) exploited these features as they developed a dermatological disorder examination for medical students. Various skin disorders are presented with nearly photographic clarity; examinees can pan in and out to view the disorder. Some information about the case history is also presented, and the student must choose the disorder from a long list.

Assessments in many other domains can benefit from improved visualization. For example, the University of Illinois dendrology course uses visual presentations to test students' abilities to identify trees and woody plants. Identification of rocks in a geology course, paintings in an art course, and molecules in a chemistry course could all benefit from this type of visualization.

Audition

It is theoretically possible to present examinees with high-quality color images in a paper-based exam (but panning and rotation are not possible), but it is prohibitively expensive. Audition is even less feasible for paper-based tests. For computerized assessment, however, examinees can put on headphones and "press enter to begin."

Vispoel's (1999) musical aptitude test provides a good example of the use of audition. Musical sequences of varying complexity are presented, and the examinee must identify a matching sequence.

Again, the use of audition facilitates the assessment of a wide variety of skills. For example, telephone service centers are becoming an increasingly important means of providing service to customers. Simulations of interactions with customers can be presented to job applicants or trainees, and important diagnostic information can be quickly collected.

Interaction

Paper-based assessments of social and interpersonal skills have been difficult to construct. Stevens and Campion's (1994) test of teamwork skills, for example, has been found to be highly correlated with verbal aptitude following correction for unreliability. This high correlation raises serious questions about the construct validity of the teamwork skills assessment. Nonetheless, research on assessment centers (Gaugler, Rosenthal, Thornton, & Bentson, 1987) suggests that social skills are important in the workplace.

Full-motion video provides an assessment medium with much lower cognitive demands than paper-based tests. Olson-Buchanan et al. (1998; Drasgow et al., 1999) used full-motion video to develop an assessment that predicts managers' abilities to deal with conflict in the workplace but is almost perfectly uncorrelated with cognitive ability. Similarly, Donovan et al. (1998) developed an assessment of leadership skills that predicts job performance of managers but is unrelated to cognitive ability. Note that low correlations between cognitive ability and interpersonal skills provides evidence of discriminant validity for the new assessments and provides insights into the structure of human abilities.

The variety of social skills needed by children to interact with their peers seems substantial. Adults also need many disparate social skills to function effectively in the workplace and with their families. Full-motion video presented by a computer seems to be the right way to develop standardized assessments at reasonable costs.

New Models

What kinds of psychometric models will adequately characterize responses to assessments using visualization, audition, and interaction? It is not clear that latent trait models are preferable to latent class models for some of the skills that can be assessed in these modalities. Luecht and Clauser's (chap. 3, this volume) suggestion that we should avoid becoming locked into current psychometric models seems particularly important for these new assessments. Creative work on appropriate models is needed.

DISCUSSION AND SUMMARY

It is now an established fact that CBTs, and CATs in particular, have great value in practical testing programs. Some of these features—walk-in testing, reduced testing time, immediate scoring—are not the focus of this colloquium; we already know they work in practice.

Although the initial generation of CBTs and CATs has been successful in many ways, we need to develop a technical infrastructure so success is not a surprise. The CBT colloquium was designed to develop an agenda for the research needed to ensure success. At the colloquium, participants examined the following questions:

- What do we know?
- What do we need to know?
- How do we get from where we are to where we need to be?

The colloquium was great fun, but it was also a true challenge because it highlighted many difficult questions that must still be answered. The chapters in this book provide a thorough description of these issues and the final chapter summarizes key topics. All of us from the colloquium hope this book provides impetus and inspiration for research that will ultimately create a rigorous psychometric infrastructure for CBT.

REFERENCES

Ackerman, T. A., Evans, J., Park, K-S., Tamassia, C., & Turner, R. (1999). Computer assessment using visual stimuli: A test of dermatological skin disorders. In F. Drasgow & J. B. Olson-Buchanan (Eds.), *Innovations in computerized assessment* (pp. 137–150). Mahwah, NJ: Lawrence Erlbaum Associates.

Bejar, I. I. (1991). A methodology for scoring open-ended architectural design problems. *Journal of Applied Psychology, 76*, 522–532.

Donovan, M. A., Drasgow, F., & Bergman, M. E. (1998, April). *Can a multimedia computerized assessment of leadership skills predict job performance beyond g?* Paper presented at the annual meeting of the Society for Industrial and Organizational Psychology, Dallas, TX.

Drasgow, F., & Olson-Buchanan, J. B. (Eds.). (1999). *Innovations in computerized assessment*. Mahwah, NJ: Lawrence Erlbaum Associates.

Drasgow, F., Olson-Buchanan, J. B., & Moberg, P. J. (1999). Interactive video assessment of interpersonal skills. In F. Drasgow & J. B. Olson-Buchanan (Eds.), *Innovations in computerized assessment* (pp. 177–196). Mahwah, NJ: Lawrence Erlbaum Associates.

Gaugler, B. B., Rosenthal, D. B., Thornton, G. C., & Bentson, C. (1987). Meta-analysis of assessment center validity. *Journal of Applied Psychology, 72*, 493–511.

Olson-Buchanan, J. B., Drasgow, F., Moberg, P. J., Mead, A. D., Keenan, P. A., & Donovan, M. (1998). Conflict resolution skills assessment: A model-based, multi-media approach. *Personnel Psychology, 51*, 1–24.

Sands, W. A., Waters, B. K., & McBride, J. R. (Eds.). (1997). *Computerized adaptive testing: From inquiry to operation*. Washington, DC: American Psychological Association.

Stevens, M. J., & Campion, M. A. (1994, April). *Staffing teams: Development and validation of the Teamwork-KSA Test*. Paper presented at the annual meeting of the Society for Industrial and Organizational Psychology, Nashville, TN.

Vispoel, W. P. (1999). Creating computerized adaptive tests of music aptitude: Problems, solutions and future directions. In F. Drasgow & J. B. Olson-Buchanan (Eds.), *Innovations in computerized assessment* (pp. 151–176). Mahwah, NJ: Lawrence Erlbaum Associates.

APPENDIX

Item and Test Disclosure
for Computerized Adaptive Tests

National Council on Measurement in Education Ad Hoc
Committee on Computerized Adaptive Test Item Disclosure[1]

PREFACE TO APPENDIX

In 1995, Brenda Lloyd, President of the National Council on Measurement
in Education, formed an ad hoc committee to consider issues related to
item and test disclosure for computerized adaptive tests. The committee
was composed of individuals from small and large test publishers, universities, and a public school system. The committee included:

Fritz Drasgow, Chair, *University of Illinois at Urbana-Champaign*
Gage Kingsbury, *Portland Public Schools*
Robert Lissitz, *University of Maryland*
Mary E. Lunz, *American Society of Clinical Pathologists*
Craig N. Mills, *Educational Testing Service*
Mark D. Reckase, *American College Testing Programs*

The committee was charged with analyzing the objectives of disclosure and various means for obtaining these outcomes; moreover, the
committee was asked to consider the perspectives of examinees, test
publishers, and the general public in its deliberations. The committee
found a core set of outcomes that are valued by all parties; conflicts
sometimes arise, however, because the relative priority of these outcomes differs depending on one's perspective.

Analyzing alternative methods for attaining desirable outcomes is
challenging because unintended consequences result from each disclo-

---

[1]This report resulted from the work of an NCME ad hoc committee, but does not constitute official NCME policy.

sure plan as well as the intended consequences. The committee therefore explored a range of disclosure options and evaluated the extent to
which each option could be expected to lead to positive and negative
outcomes.

Testing programs differ so greatly in size, scope, and objectives that
rigid specifications for disclosure cannot sensibly be given. Instead, the
committee believes that disclosure plans must be sensitive to the number of examinees tested annually, the sample size required for statistical
analysis of items before operational use, the number of items in the test's
item pool, examinees' interest in full disclosure, and the cost of a disclosure plan. Note that the cost of disclosure will ultimately be paid by
examinees and so their interest in this service is critical.

In sum, disclosure in the context of computerized adaptive tests is far
more complicated than disclosure of paper-and-pencil tests. Features
that make computerized adaptive tests popular with examinees (test difficulty tailored to the examinee's skill level; tests scheduled at the convenience of the examinee) create great difficulty for disclosure plans. Consequently, disclosure requirements must be crafted with great care to
anticipate all outcomes, including negative outcomes as well as positive.

INTRODUCTION

In a *secure testing program* the items on a test are held in confidence
prior to their presentation to examinees. Often, secure testing programs
continue to preserve the secrecy of the items after use as well. Because
prior information about the specifics of the test items is held constant
across all examinees (i.e., *no information* is available), test security of
this type contributes to test fairness.

This document considers a variety of elements that may be included in
the *test disclosure process*. Among these elements are test familiarization
by examinees, test review and evaluation by scholars, secure review by
an examinee of the items he/she was administered, and public dissemination of some test items or entire test forms from a secure testing program following a test administration. The amount of public dissemination may vary from an occasional item (*item disclosure*) to a complete
test form (*test disclosure*) to multiple forms of entire tests.

Item and test disclosure are not new concepts. Most testing programs
have made sample items, and sometimes entire test forms, available in
their publications for many years. Test items are publicized in this way so
that examinees will become familiar with the format and the types of
questions that are asked. By providing all examinees with a representative set of items, no individual has access to more information about the

test than any other individual and thus the fairness of the test process is enhanced.

With the passage of testing legislation (details are presented later in this report), the requirements for test disclosure have become more formal. For testing programs covered by disclosure laws, full test forms must be made available to examinees on a fairly regular basis, and procedures must be available for checking the scoring of tests.

Test disclosure legislation and many publishers' disclosure practices were developed in the context of paper-and-pencil test administration. This administration model assumes that tests are given to hundreds of examinees at a time in large test centers. Moreover, only a few test administration dates may be available per year and tens of thousands of examinees may be tested nationwide on a given administration date. This paper-and-pencil testing model is very efficient in its use of test questions because a relatively small number of test questions can be administered simultaneously to tens of thousands of individuals. It is, however, inefficient in the sense that many items administered to each examinee are either too easy or too hard and, as a result, do not provide much information about the test taker's skill level. Paper-and-pencil testing is also inconvenient because test takers must arrange their schedules to be available for testing on one of the few days each year that the test is offered.

Computerized testing features two major changes. First, computerized tests are typically administered under a "continuous" testing model. That is, computerized tests are usually offered on many days throughout the year and a relatively small number of examinees take the test on any given day (e.g., a few hundred). Thus, examinees have much more flexibility in scheduling the exam. Second, many computerized tests are adaptive: The items selected for administration are tailored to the skill level of each individual examinee by branching to more difficult items following correct responses and branching to easier items following incorrect responses. As a result, computerized tests can be shorter than paper-and-pencil tests with no loss in measurement accuracy. However, these benefits come at a price. In computerized adaptive testing many more items must be available for administration, both to provide appropriate tailoring of the test and to maintain the secrecy of items. As a result, standard procedures for disclosure of paper-and-pencil tests seem poorly suited for computerized tests

This report focuses on issues pertaining to disclosure of computerized adaptive tests (CATs). We consider both *item pool disclosure*, which reveals all the items in a CAT item pool, and *item disclosure*, which reveals some proportion (e.g., 10%) of items from the item pool.

Due to the important differences between conventional paper-and-pencil tests and computerized tests, current legislation and publisher practices are inapplicable. Computerized adaptive tests require substantial changes to test disclosure legislation and publisher practices.

Goals of Test Disclosure

To provide a sense of the issues that are related to test disclosure, a few frequently mentioned goals of test disclosure will be summarized here. The positive and negative effects of disclosure will be considered in greater detail later, but this summary is intended to provide enough context to clarify the issues.

Four major goals for test disclosure legislation are frequently given. The first is regulation: Legislators view testing as a major industry, which needs regulation as do other industries. The goal is to provide external oversight that will ensure that tests are fair and of high quality.

Second, test disclosure provides examinees with specific feedback about their performance. They can see which items were answered incorrectly and perhaps learn from their mistakes.

The third goal, particularly for high stakes tests (i.e., tests with important implications for examinees), is to provide examinees with an opportunity to check the scoring of the examinations to ensure that no errors have been made. Concerns related to scoring include both clerical or machine scoring errors, and errors in the test items themselves resulting in multiple correct answers or no correct answers. In the past there have been several highly publicized cases of flawed test items that were detected by examinees. These few cases have provided persuasive evidence—at least in the minds of some individuals—of the need for external review of test materials.

The fourth goal of test disclosure is test familiarity. Examinees should arrive at a test session with a clear understanding of the test format, the content of the test, time limits, and strategies for answering items. By making test forms public, examinees can practice on real test forms to determine what will work best for them.

There are certainly many other positive and negative results of test disclosure (see the discussion below for a more extended discussion), but the four reasons for disclosure listed here should provide sufficient context for the initial discussions related to computerized testing.

Types of Tests to be Considered

The immediate concern of this document is how to accomplish the objectives of disclosure for CATs in a way that serves the needs of examinees, test developers and publishers, and the public at large. This issue has become critical because several important testing programs are either currently administering their tests via CAT or are considering a

change to this administration mode. Moreover, a wide variety of interesting research programs focusing on computerized testing and assessment
suggests that this administrative medium is likely to become more prevalent in the future as computers deliver tests assessing proficiencies in areas ranging from musical aptitude to social skills.

In its most common form, a CAT is a computer administered test that
selects test items from an item pool for each examinee during the process of the test in a way that adapts the difficulty level of the test to the skill
level of the examinee. While there may be some overlap in the items that
are administered to different examinees, the overlap is usually kept to a
minimum for security reasons. Thus, the items are selected individually
for each examinee based on his or her responses to previous items and
there is substantial variation in the items presented to different examinees as well as in the order of item presentation.

Future computerized tests may be of a substantially different character
than the current generation of CATs. Extended simulation exercises, writing samples, or other production activities might be administered via
computers and constitute the substance of the exam. The critical feature
of these types of tests is that the activities are longer and more complex,
and fewer items may be administered. Such items may be difficult to create; moreover, procedures for scoring are likely to be time-consuming
and expensive to develop.

In this document, we address the issue of test disclosure for the current generation of CATs. Problems related to disclosure of computerized
tests of the future should be carefully considered at the appropriate time.

Important Features of Computerized Tests

There are a number of important ways in which CATs and other computerized tests differ from paper-and-pencil tests. First, for paper-and-pencil
tests, there is a clearly defined component called a "test form." This is the
set of items in a test booklet that counts toward an examinee's reported
score. Each year, large testing programs produce several test forms composed of mostly unique test items. It is easy to determine how many
items a test form uses, and all items on the form are used the same number of times as the form as a whole. Currently, disclosure legislation and
publisher practice generally assume that entire test forms are released.

CATs do not have test forms of the sort encountered with paper-and-
pencil testing. Instead, items are drawn from the *CAT item pool* by the
item selection algorithm so that items are of appropriate difficulty for
each individual examinee. The CAT item pool contains a large number of
calibrated items; the item pool may include a few hundred to several
thousand items. The items have varying difficulties that assess the mate-

rial specified in a test's blueprint. Calibrating an item involves first administering it to a large representative sample of examinees under nonoperational conditions. Then a statistical analysis is performed to determine characteristics of the item such as its difficulty. Following calibration, items are placed in the CAT item pool; this includes the item's text, the classification of the item vis-à-vis the test blueprint, and the estimated item parameters (including item difficulty).

The item selection algorithm incorporates sophisticated methods derived from item response theory (IRT) to choose items to administer to a particular examinee so that (1) the test is of appropriate difficulty (the item selection algorithm chooses more difficult items if an examinee answers items correctly and easier items if an examinee answers incorrectly); (2) the test provides precise measurement; and (3) all examinees are administered items that span the same test content. Because the test for each individual is created during the process of test administration, there is not a test form in the sense of a conventional paper-and-pencil test.

It has been suggested that the set of items administered to an individual might be considered as a test form. Using this definition, a single CAT item pool would produce hundreds or thousands of different test forms annually. The testing literature has not considered in detail what would constitute the definition of a test form for a CAT or whether the notion of a test form is useful in the context of CAT.

CATs select items from a large collection of items called an item pool. The characteristics of an item pool are critical for a CAT, and the item pool must be constructed very carefully. Because some testing legislation has suggested the release of full item pools, a formal definition of this term is needed so that it can be determined whether an item is in the pool or not.

The manner in which the CAT item pool is revised has important implications for disclosure. Some testing programs use an incremental process. Here, a few old items are removed and a few new items are added; these incremental changes occur several times per year. Other programs leave an item pool intact until it is completely replaced by an entirely new item pool. Item pool disclosure for testing programs that use incremental replacement could have dire implications because many items might still be in use in the operational CAT; for the latter type of item pool revision, the old item pool could be disclosed with much less difficulty because all of its items have been retired.

In the context of paper-and-pencil tests, test disclosure does not require a careful definition of exactly what constitutes an item. However, if disclosure requirements depend on the particular set of items that a person has been administered, the definition of an item becomes important. Recent psychometric literature has included new terms such as "testlet" to indicate sets of items that are scored as a unit. As complex simulations are developed, the definition of the test item will become even more ambiguous. Formal consideration of the definitions of these terms is needed before they are incorporated into legislation.

The purpose of these introductory comments was not to propose new definitions for old terms. It was only to illustrate that commonly used terms with generally clear meanings for paper-and-pencil tests may require new conceptualizations with new meanings for CATs. Once these terms appear in a legal context, it will probably be too late to decide what the formal definitions should be.

Administration Models

An additional area that will need to be considered as test disclosure models are developed is the method of test administration. Currently, large-scale testing programs generally administer their tests to large groups of examinees on a relatively infrequently basis. Computer administered tests are impractical for large group administrations simply because it is difficult to have large numbers of computers in one place at one time. Freeing the test administration model from the large group format has resulted in a wide variety of new options.

Perhaps the most appealing of the many alternatives is individually scheduled testing available on a daily basis. Here examinees reserve a seat in front of a computer for a particular time and take the test at that time. Thus, the test is administered *at the convenience of the examinee* rather than the convenience of the test publisher. Obviously, examinees find this alternative very attractive.

Individually scheduled testing presents significant challenges for test publishers. In this context, maintaining test security becomes a critical issue because examinees take the test serially. Individuals already tested may describe items that they were presented to as-yet-untested examinees. If these latter examinees encounter any of the described items, it is clear that they are provided an unfair advantage. To counter this threat, several methods for exposure control have been developed to minimize the overlap between items selected for administration to different examinees from a given item pool.

Numerous other administration models can be conceived to address security concerns. These include less frequent test administration, multiple item pools, and specific disclosure test dates. Some of these administration models will be more convenient for the examinee than others. It is possible that disclosure legislation will encourage administration models that are less preferred by examinees. Some of these effects of legislation are likely to be unanticipated, but may be a major concern to examinees that are inconvenienced by the administrative models.

Summary

The purpose of this introduction has been to lay the groundwork for a thorough consideration of issues pertaining to disclosure of computerized tests. The lack of clarity of existing definitions for terms used in testing has been highlighted and several new options for test formats and administration models have been noted. It is clear that much work needs to be done to bring coherence to the discussions about disclosure for computerized tests. It is hoped that this document provides a starting point.

In the next section of this report some of the history of disclosure legislation is reviewed. Then the main reasons for item and test disclosure are presented. Practical constraints and limitations on disclosure are described in the next section. A range of disclosure options is described in the following section; these options are analyzed in terms of the extent to which they accomplish the objectives of test disclosure and could be implemented by test publishers. A brief section on research issues follows and this report concludes with a discussion of the main issues, dilemmas, and conclusions.

LEGISLATIVE HISTORY

Test disclosure legislation was initially enacted in California in 1978. However, the first legislation that required full and immediate disclosure of postsecondary admissions tests was enacted in 1979 in New York State. The original legislation required public release of all tests administered in New York for the purposes of admission to higher education. In addition, the law required test sponsors to provide examinees an opportunity to obtain copies of their individual tests, answer sheets, the correct answers, and the manner by which scaled scores were calculated. Similar legislation was considered in about 30 other states over the next several years (McAllister, 1991).

Reaction to Disclosure Legislation

Test publishers reacted to the disclosure legislation in several ways. Most complied with the requirements of the law and offered disclosure services to all examinees (not just those in New York) for those administration dates on which they tested in New York. Test publishers also re-

duced the number of administration dates available in New York in order
to comply with the legislation.

One response to test disclosure was to discontinue testing in New
York. This action was taken by the Graduate Record Examinations (GRE)
Board because the disclosure requirements exceeded its ability to create
new test forms on low volume tests. An amendment to the law subse-
quently provided exceptions in the cases of low volume tests and test
forms. At that point, the GRE Board reinstated testing in New York, but on
a reduced schedule.

A different response was provided by the Association of American
Medical Colleges (AAMC), which filed suit in U.S. District Court claiming
that the New York law infringed on federal copyright law (i.e., a test is
copyrighted and the disclosure requirement is destructive of the value of
the copyright). AAMC sought and obtained a preliminary injunction
against the law and has administered tests in New York under the injunction since that time. In 1990 the district judge ruled that the disclosure requirements of the New York statute are in conflict with federal copyright
law. A permanent injunction against the enforcement of the provisions of
the law against the AAMC was part of the ruling. The state has subse-
quently appealed the decision. Following the AAMC ruling, The College
Board, Graduate Record Examinations Board, Test of English as a Foreign
Language Policy Council, and the Educational Testing Service initiated a
lawsuit against New York.

Exceptions to Disclosure Requirements

In the context of the above litigation, the Attorney General of the State of
New York has entered into a series of stipulations with several testing
programs to allow additional, non-disclosed administrations of tests to be
offered in the state. Under these annual stipulations, testing programs introduced additional administration dates in New York with the result that
the New York test administration schedule matched programs' national
administration schedule.

Several other modifications to disclosure schedules have occurred in
recent years. Both the Law School Admissions Council and the College
Board have modified their disclosure offerings to allow time to build item
inventories following revisions to their exams. The GRE Board has an-
nounced modifications to its disclosure schedule in conjunction with reductions in its offerings of paper-and-pencil tests as it makes a transition
to a fully computerized testing program. Some of these modifications
have come about through stipulations; others have been the result of action in court.

Disclosure and Computer-Based Testing

The situation with regard to computer-based testing and disclosure is, at the moment, uncertain. Testing programs have argued that the current New York statute is incompatible with computer-based testing because the premise of the law is that tests are administered periodically to large numbers of individuals on a single day. Legislation designed to extend the New York law to computer-based tests has been introduced in recent years, but to date it has not passed. A bill currently (1996) under consideration in New York would require programs that administered tests on computer in 1994 to provide copies of the tests administered, answers provided, and correct answers to

- 25% of the test takers in 1996,
- 50% of the test takers in 1997,
- 75% of the test takers in 1998, and
- 100% of the test takers in 1999

within 60 days of the test date.

In addition, the proposed legislation requires that complete CAT pools from which the above disclosure is provided be filed with the Commission of Education. Finally, it requires two years prior notice on the part of test sponsors considering the introduction of computer delivered tests.

Depending on the size of the CAT item pool and the frequency of paper-and-pencil test administration, the proposed CAT legislation may require disclosure of perhaps five to twenty times as many items per year as the current law for paper-and-pencil test disclosure. It is difficult to see how even the largest testing programs could write, edit, and pretest this many additional items.

REASONS FOR TEST DISCLOSURE IN CAT

In adaptive testing, as in conventional testing, it is essential that examinees are administered fair and valid tests. To help accomplish this goal, it has been suggested repeatedly that examinees should be provided the opportunity to examine tests they have taken. Such an inspection allows examinees to detect incorrectly keyed items as well as mechanical errors in the scoring of their responses. The rationale for allowing review and disclosure in paper-and-pencil tests has been discussed rather extensively (i.e., Green, 1981). Many of these arguments carry over to adaptive testing; moreover, some of the features of adaptive testing highlight the importance of disclosure and review.

There are many good reasons for test review and/or test disclosure. In this discussion, four frequently cited rationales for disclosure will receive particular attention. They include: (1) assuring the fairness of the testing procedure; (2) allowing test takers the opportunity to learn from the testing process; (3) providing a mechanism for the evaluation of the test itself; and (4) reducing test compromise. Each of these issues provides a rationale for test disclosure or test review; in the paragraphs that follow, these arguments are presented in the context of a CAT.

Assuring Fairness in the Testing Process

In paper-and-pencil testing, one argument for test disclosure is that test takers should be able to verify that answers that were keyed as incorrect actually were incorrect. To avoid such scoring errors, it has been suggested that test takers should be allowed to review the tests they have taken. It should be noted that the number of items revealed as incorrectly scored since the passage of the New York test disclosure law is very small relative to the total number of disclosed items; however, these miskeyed items have received substantial public attention.

Allowing students an opportunity to check their answers also provides a rationale for disclosure in the context of a CAT. Some related reasons for disclosure include the following.

- Very large CAT item pools may be required to discourage test compromise. More items may be created per year for tests administered via computer, thus providing a greater chance of a keying error.
- If an item is miskeyed on a paper-and-pencil test, all examinees are affected in the sense that they all attempt the item. With an adaptive test, however, different test takers are administered different items and only some individuals will be affected by an incorrectly keyed item. This is clearly unfair to individuals who were administered the flawed item.
- CATs are ordinarily shorter than their paper-and-pencil tests, so an incorrectly keyed item may have a greater relative impact on an examinee's test score. The adaptive nature of CATs causes them to be self-correcting to some extent, but research is needed to determine the magnitude of the effect of incorrectly keyed items on test scores.

A second type of fairness issue can arise in an adaptive testing context: Tests may vary substantially in terms of their content. For example, an adaptive test of mathematics achievement might administer only geometry questions to a particular examinee, even though the test was intended to measure general mathematics achievement. Simple (Kingsbury & Zara, 1989) and complex (Stocking & Swanson, 1993) procedures have been developed to ensure that adaptive tests conform to test blueprints. Clearly, it is important for test publishers to build mechanisms for controlling content into their CATs. Moreover, it can be argued that examinees and independent scholars should be provided an opportunity to examine the substance of tests rather than to trust test publishers to implement correctly content balancing.

Providing an Opportunity to Learn

Particularly in educational testing, it can be argued that a test should include a learning component as well as a measurement component. Two distinct aspects of learning can be identified. The first is familiarity with the form of a test, which teachers facilitate by introducing students to the types of questions contained on a test before it is administered. This allows students to become familiar with complex item formats, so that their performance on the test is not adversely affected by novel question formats. Familiarity with complex item types has been shown to increase performance on the GRE (Powers & Swinton, 1984), and it seems likely to do so for tests that use unique item types.

A second aspect of learning involves learning from one's mistakes. In the context of classroom testing, this type of learning often takes the form of reviewing questions that were answered incorrectly. It is important, however, to distinguish (1) learning how to solve a single instantiation of a principle and (2) learning the general principle. Teaching a student how to reproduce the steps involved in answering a specific item correctly is not necessarily identical to teaching the underlying concepts required to answer similar items. Thus, feedback to students that provides information about their mastery of critical principles may better help them learn from their mistakes than specific items answered incorrectly.

In an adaptive testing situation, these opportunities to learn could be provided to test takers in two ways. First, for the purposes of test familiarization, a representative set of practice items for all of the item types that appear on the test could be conveniently available to test takers. Selecting these items from a previously operational item pool would help ensure their representativeness. Second, to provide an opportunity to learn from one's mistakes, test takers might be offered an opportunity to review the items that appeared on their own test in a setting that does not compromise test security.

Providing a Mechanism for Evaluation

All parties in the testing process agree to the general principle that examinees and test users have a right to know about the quality of a particular test. To this end, informed review of a test by scholars is an important element of the test disclosure process; from such reviews, examinees and test users can obtain a better understanding of a test. It is difficult, however, to devise a process that facilitates evaluations of the merits of a test by independent scholars yet maintains a test's security. Test publishers are rightly concerned about their test copyright and may be reluctant to share information that independent reviewers believe is needed to critique adequately a test's technical characteristics.

By their nature, CATs are technically more complex than conventional tests, and so it is likely that external evaluations may also become more difficult. A review of the content specifications, items, reliability, and validity of a test form would likely be part of such an evaluation. In addition, an evaluation might consider the adequacy of item parameter estimates, item selection procedure, item exposure control, content balancing, ability estimation algorithm, and termination procedure.

In order to make a valid assessment of the measurement quality of an adaptive test, an independent scholar or agency would need appropriate information about all of the elements listed above. A review of at least some individual items would be an important part of such an evaluation. In addition, examples of the sets of items administered to some actual examinees would be enlightening. Ensuring test security and protecting the publisher's copyright would be essential for this review.

Reducing Test Compromise

Consider a high-stakes, adaptive test that uses a relatively small item pool for an extended period of time. A group of test takers with a desire to improve their long-term passing rate might attempt to compromise the test's security. If the members of this group memorized some of the specific questions that they encountered on the test, and then pooled this information, they could build a data base consisting of the test's questions. Perhaps with additional research, the group would be able to identify the correct answers to these questions, and create a study tool consisting of operational items and their answers. This group of test takers could then improve their long-term success rate in a manner unavailable to other test takers.

In this example, the test takers with prior access to test questions might obtain very high scores even though they lack critical skills. Moreover, a test publisher or test user would be unable to determine whether a particular individual was answering the questions with or without access to the data base. Compromise of this sort can raise test scores dramatically and destroy test validity.

It is an untested but plausible hypothesis that test disclosure might reduce collaborative efforts to compromise a CAT. Some of the motivation for developing such a data base might be reduced by providing examinees with a disclosed item pool. Further, the long-term value of such a collaboration is certainly reduced with disclosure because a carefully constructed data base of test items would be rendered moot when the item pool was released.

For item pool disclosure to reduce test compromise, the availability of disclosed item pools should be communicated to the population of prospective test takers.

CONSTRAINTS ON DISCLOSURE

An important goal of test disclosure is fairness to the examinee. It is important to understand how disclosure might affect fairness, and weigh its intended and unintended consequences.

Some testing programs—particularly small ones—may not be able to disclose items on a frequent basis. Testing programs vary greatly in size and resources. The largest programs may develop and pretest a thousand new items and test a million examinees a year. In contrast, small programs may use the same exam for several years and test a few hundred or a few thousand examinees per year. These small programs may have inadequate resources available for writing, editing, and statistically analyzing enough replacement items while holding the per examinee test fee at a reasonable level. Developing a high quality test is expensive and ordinarily it is the examinees who must pay these costs. If the costs are shared by only a relatively few examinees in a small testing program, the administration charge may exceed some examinees' financial resources. Such a situation seems unfair.

Pretesting new items that would be required by test disclosure procedures has other costs. Test centers often charge by the amount of seat time used, and the administration of new items obviously increases test length and testing time. Thus examinees would be subjected to the inconvenience of a longer test and in all likelihood required to pay for the inconvenience.

A second constraint on disclosure is that the examinee flow rate may be too low to pretest enough new items for a new CAT item pool. Suppose a testing program has found, say, that (1) an item must be administered to a thousand examinees in order to obtain adequate item parameter estimation accuracy for its CAT; (2) to ensure test security, a CAT item pool of a thousand items is needed; and (3) each applicant can be administered no more than ten experimental items. In this situation, the testing program could disclose its item pool only after 100,000 examinees are tested (1000 items in the item pool × 1000 examinees per item/10 items per examinee = 100,000 examinees are required). To maintain a secure test for a testing program that assesses 10,000 candidates per year, arithmetic ineluctably demonstrates that the item pool could be released completely once in ten years.

Third, in some domains, the number of possible items may be limited. In relatively narrow domains, for example, there may be only a small population of questions that might be written. Even with broader domains there may be only a small number of items that might be written on a particular topic that is an important part of the test's blueprint. Here regular disclosure might exhaust the population of potential items and result in a test that omits important content area. This would, of course, reduce the test's validity.

Related to the above problem is the nature of the items that would be revealed in some disclosure procedures. Adaptive tests generally attempt to administer items that are maximally informative about the characteristic assessed by the test. Items that are highly informative—that is, with relatively large IRT item discrimination parameters—are usually administered most often in a CAT. For licensing and certification exams, items with IRT difficulty parameters close to the threshold for passing may be the most informative and, therefore, administered most often. Thus, if test developers were to disclose items that were administered most frequently, they would be left with the very difficult problem of replacing many of their most useful items.

For the reasons reviewed above, attempts to disclose items and item pools on a regular basis may degrade the reliability and validity of a test. Thus, fairness would be adversely affected.

For example, test disclosure is not common among certification and licensure boards that test small numbers of examinees annually (e.g., a hundred or fewer). Examinations in this setting serve to protect the public by certifying an examinee's expertise. Using items that have not been adequately field tested might have unacceptable consequences for the public, and therefore it is important to ensure that only high quality items are included in the item pool.

Item disclosure would also increase the difficulty of maintaining a criterion-referenced standard for certification. CATs require rather large item pools consisting of calibrated items; for a criterion-referenced interpretation of test scores, a criterion standard to which tailored examinations have been linked is also needed. Even if costs were no concern, there may be insufficient numbers of subject matter experts available to carry out item writing and insufficient numbers of examinees to pretest the new items.

OPTIONS FOR DISCLOSURE

This section presents a variety of options for the test disclosure process. The extent to which each of these options satisfies the needs of examinees and the public is analyzed. Simultaneously, the implications of the disclosure requirements for the test developer's task of creating reliable, valid, cost effective, and up-to-date products are considered. Each option for disclosure is evaluated in relation to the reasons for providing disclosure that were outlined above: (1) fairness; (2) evaluating the test; (3) opportunity to learn; and (4) reducing test compromise. In addition, the options are examined in light of the constraints on disclosure: (1) resources; (2) examinee flow rate; and (3) limited numbers of experimental items. These considerations include a mixture of practical limitations and ethical considerations. Clearly, the most immediate concern of any testing program is the impact of a disclosure option upon the validity of the testing effort, which includes a concern for issues of test fairness and bias.

Test Familiarization

It is assumed that every testing program provides a detailed description of its test to examinees. This test familiarization documentation is critical for ensuring the fairness of the testing process. It is also the principal source of information, other than the test itself, that an applicant will have to determine the quality of the test.

As part of the test familiarization process, each test taker should be provided the opportunity to prepare effectively for the test taking experience. This means examinees should have access to materials that provide descriptions of the format and content of the examination, its scoring and reporting procedures, and any additional test administration information. This material should inform examinees whether they should guess, how much time is provided, what type of opportunities are available for reviewing items, the likely length of the examination, areas of coverage, and so forth.

These test familiarization materials should be in a form that is consistent with the computerized nature of the test administration. Although a

CAT differs from a paper-and-pencil test in many ways, publishers have the same obligations to examinees that they had when using the older test format. For example, practice on items in the format of the real test is taken for granted with paper-and-pencil tests. To provide a parallel experience, prospective examinees should be able to obtain (perhaps for a fee) a practice form of the test that is also computer adaptive with the same administration protocols used by the actual test. In addition, a large set of representative practice items should be included. As noted earlier, it would be desirable for these items to come from a previously operational form of the test.

The test familiarization materials should provide answers to test takers' questions about the test experience. These materials allow a test taker to develop an informed opinion about the fairness of the test and thus evaluate the test. Test reliability and validity information should also be included in the familiarization effort. The typical test taker may not be able to understand technical discussions of reliability and validity, but some opportunity to know that such material exists and a familiarity with the basic results of such studies would be helpful.

As noted previously, a regular cycle (e.g., annually) of test disclosure may not be feasible for low volume tests when insufficient numbers of examinees are available for pretesting new items. If forced to publicly disclose test forms too often, a low volume publisher might be forced to reuse previously disclosed items. In this case, test compromise resulting from reuse of disclosed items could constitute a serious threat to the integrity of the test. Consequently, test familiarization may provide the only realistic option under these conditions. Clearly, use of test familiarization as a publisher's approach to disclosure for low volume tests has the virtue of reducing the risk of compromising test validity through excessive disclosure.

One issue that has been raised, but is not addressed by the test familiarization process, is the opportunity to verify the scoring of a specific person's test. Historically, there have been very few items that have been miskeyed (roughly, one item in several thousand), but this is a concern for some. Particularly for low volume tests, the test sponsor, test publisher, and examinees should weigh the costs of approaches to disclosure that go beyond test familiarization against the benefits expected to result from providing examinees with an opportunity to verify the test's scoring key.

In summary, test familiarization should form the core of the publisher's response to legitimate demands by the public for test disclosure. This material should help prepare a person to take the test and to do so in a way that facilitates performance. In addition, the disclosure materials should inform the test taker about the publisher's effort to establish a high quality testing instrument. This documentation will do much to satisfy the need for verifying fairness, evaluating the test, and reducing test compromise in a way that does not require excessive resources and recognizes the often limited opportunity to pretest experimental items.

Types of Item and Test Disclosure

Options for disclosure more ambitious than test familiarization do exist for CATs, and, by necessity, differ from the disclosure of paper-and-pencil tests. These options differ from test disclosure for paper-and-pencil tests mainly because

1. CATs are usually administered in low volume on many days per year whereas paper-and-pencil tests are administered on just a few days per year to large numbers of examinees; and
2. Every CAT is uniquely constructed for an individual examinee in contrast to the standard practice of administering a single paper-and-pencil test form to all examinees tested on a given date.

Thus, disclosing a CAT form can be seen as releasing a test taken by only a single person, which should influence the way that we look at test disclosure. Listed below are several options for public dissemination of individual items, entire tests administered to examinees, and complete item pools; they are analyzed according to their potential degree of disruption and threat to good testing practice and test development.

Periodic Item.   In this approach, subsets of items are periodically released from the CAT item bank. The release of these items would be on a schedule such as once or twice a year. A set percentage of the item bank (e.g., 10%) or a minimum number of items (e.g., 50) would be released at each disclosure. Test publishers might select these items randomly, choose to release items that had been administered most often, or use some other thoughtful criterion.

Differences between testing situations, as indicated above, make specific recommendations for the number of items to be released and the frequency of release difficult to determine. For some testing programs (e.g., small certification testing efforts), disclosing 50 items per year and developing 50 new items to replace the disclosed items may represent a substantial challenge for maintaining the validity of the test. Disclosing significant numbers of items may effect the domain definition of the test and degrade the overall quality of the items because of the difficulty of creating new, equally reliable, unbiased, and valid items. As indicated above in the section on constraints, the flow rate of test takers can make calibrating new items a difficult task.

Thus, for some testing programs (particularly ones with low volume tests) it seems likely that heavy requirements for Periodic Item disclosure could pose a risk to validity that would outweigh the risk of misscoring individual items. In other words, it is to the test-takers' advantage, in some situations, to prefer less disclosure and receive higher item quality in return.

Periodic Item disclosure would provide some basis for reviewing the quality of a CAT's item pool. It would also tend to discourage cheating because the item pool would change over time. However, individual examinees would not have an opportunity to review the questions that they were administered and could not learn from their mistakes.

Periodic Form.   Here a set of items that has actually been administered to certain individuals would be released. For example, the test publisher would publicly release a copy of the questions (and correct responses) given to a student who scored at the 75th percentile on the test. Another set of items that was administered to a specific examinee who obtained a score at near the 50th percentile and a set administered to a student at approximately the 25th percentile could also be included.

With Periodic Form test disclosure it is possible to verify the scoring of selected sequences of items that were actually administered. This advantage, as well as providing real examples of testing, may well provide a worthwhile benefit to the public. For most testing efforts, this form of test disclosure would not compromise the validity of the test by revealing an excessive number of items. By replacing part of the item pool on a regular basis, Periodic Form disclosure might serve to discourage attempts to compromise the item pool. However, no opportunity to learn from one's mistakes would be available.

In sum, Periodic Form disclosure may be appropriate for some testing situations.

Public Upon Request.   In this approach to test disclosure, upon request the test publisher would send to a specific examinee a copy of the items that he/she had been administered, the examinee's item responses, and the publisher's scoring of the responses. Consequently, examinees could review the items that were administered to them, verify the scoring key, and learn from their mistakes.

Because items—and the answer key—are publicly available in this option for disclosure, the potential for test validity deterioration is very high. Even large testing firms testing substantial numbers of persons are unlikely to be able to write and calibrate new items at the rate needed to maintain the item pool. Moreover, there is no basis in research that could be used to justify the reuse of previously disclosed items.

Upon Request test disclosure has some attractive features and may be useful under special circumstances (e.g., a CAT with a very limited number of test administration dates). For CATs administered frequently, it may be impossible to create new items at a rate that makes Public Upon Request disclosure practical. Therefore, we strongly recommend against any requirement for Public Upon Request test disclosure. In the future, empirical research should provide evidence about the limited conditions (e.g., infrequent test administrations; very large item pools) under which Upon Request test disclosure is feasible.

Secure Upon Request. Here the examinee could request a copy of the items that he/she was administered, the examinee's own item responses, and the publisher's scoring of the items. The difference from Public Upon Request disclosure is that the examinee's review in Secure Upon Request would be conducted under conditions acceptable to the publisher and would ordinarily ensure the test's security. Thus, examinees would not be allowed to photocopy or photograph the items they review and they might be required to sign a nondisclosure agreement in which they promise to hold the items in confidence.

Secure Upon Request disclosure would accomplish some of the most important goals of disclosure without sacrificing test validity. Examinees would have the opportunity to examine the scoring of their exam and could be provided with a formal procedure for challenging the scoring of an item. By examining incorrect responses, examinees might learn from their mistakes (although insights about general principles might be less frequent).

Because they would be reviewed in a secure setting, the items could continue to be used in the operational CAT. Thus, the overwhelming difficulties associated with Public Upon Request disclosure would be circumvented.

The major challenges for Secure Upon Request disclosure would be logistical: From a procedural standpoint, how could the review process be conducted? Although there are many possibilities, Secure Upon Request disclosure might be conducted via computer in a secure facility together with CAT administration. At the beginning of a session, the test administrator could, for example, invoke software for administering the CAT for individuals scheduled to be tested or invoke the software for reviewing an already administered CAT for individuals scheduled for this activity.

In sum, we strongly recommend that the opportunity for examinees to review the items they were administered, their responses, and the keyed answers should be made available under conditions acceptable to the test publisher. If examinees are charged for the test review, the fee should not be extravagant.

Periodic Test Pool.   In this approach, an entire item bank is released on some periodic cycle (e.g., every 3 years) and thus Periodic Test Pool disclosure can be seen as the special case of Periodic Item disclosure in which all items are revealed. Clearly, disclosure of 100% of the item pool is an extremely high level of disclosure that could be destructive to test reliability and validity if it is required too often.

Ideally, the test familiarization materials would contain a practice exam resulting from Periodic Test Pool disclosure. Specifically, it is desirable for the test familiarization materials to include a practice exam, and a formerly operational form of the exam may be the best type of practice exam. Such a practice exam would allow the test-taker to become familiar with the types of questions contained in the item bank and practice for the test.

The central issue in Periodic Test Pool disclosure is the *frequency of disclosure*. Even the largest test publishers would find it impossible to disclose an entire test pool every three months without dramatically increasing the cost per examinee and the proportion of experimental items administered. On the other hand, disclosing a test pool (or a set of items equivalent to an item pool for programs that use incremental item pool revision) once a decade seems feasible even for low volume publishers.

The chief advantage of Periodic Test Pool disclosure may result from operational forms of the test becoming available for test familiarization. On the other hand, the objective of allowing individual examinees to review the items they were administered, verify the keying of these items, and learn from their mistakes is unlikely to be accomplished with Periodic Test Pool disclosure. Because writing and editing items is a slow, difficult process and because examinee flow rates place ineluctable limits on the introduction of new items, it seems impossible for even the largest test publishers to disclose entire CAT item pools more than perhaps once a year.

We strongly recommend against mandating inflexible timetables for Periodic Test Pool disclosure. While releasing entire forms of tests is important for test familiarization and provides an effective deterrent to cheating, inflexible timetables might require a rate of test pool disclosure that cannot be maintained. The frequency of Periodic Test Pool disclosure should depend on whether the population of potential items is large enough to allow new forms to be developed, the speed of writing new items, the examinee flow rate (which determines how many new items can be calibrated), the requirements for equating the new CAT form to the old form, and cost to the examinees.

Additional Considerations

There are several additional efforts that a test publisher might consider. First, examinees might be given a profile of scores for subparts of the test (and confidence intervals for the scores), thus breaking the overall score into units that would facilitate studying for a subsequent administration. The problem with this approach is that the standard error of measurement (a measure of accuracy) associated with subtest scores may be rather large and consequently some test-takers would be encouraged to study areas in which their skills were already satisfactory. Some intermediate level of diagnostic reporting might be possible for identifiable areas of the test domain, but a testing program should carefully evaluate this matter before it is implemented.

A second effort that might be considered specifically addresses the issue of misscoring. A test publisher could take one of several steps when a miskeyed item is discovered:

- Administrative procedures could be developed to automatically rescore the test and notify all relevant parties of the corrected test score.
- The examinee could be offered an opportunity to take the CAT a second time.
- The consequences of a miskeyed item on test score as a function of test length could be investigated and the CAT could be forced to administer enough items so that a test-taker's reported score would not be substantially affected by a single miskeyed item. In other words, the test would be long enough that a single miskeyed item would have a negligible effect on an examinee's reported score.

Each of these procedures would provide assurance to the test-taker that in the unlikely event of a miskeyed item, his or her reported score would be essentially unaffected.

RESEARCH ISSUES

Item Reuse

Throughout this report it has been assumed that previously disclosed items cannot be reused in an operational test form. This assumption is consistent with the best professional practices for paper-and-pencil tests. Its rationale is that some examinees may have seen previously released items; this is clearly unfair if examinees have unequal access to such items. Moreover, the construct measured by the test may change if items are reused: Rather than proficiency in the domain specified by the test blueprint, the test may measure examinees' memorization abilities.

Suppose that thousands of test items have been disclosed. In this situation, it might be hypothesized that there would be no measurable effect resulting from including a handful of previously released items in the current operational CAT's item bank. However, the only existing study on item reuse found score inflation given the situation it investigated (Hale, Angelis, & Thibodeau, 1983), and therefore caution with respect to item reuse is clearly necessary.

It seems likely that the impact of item reuse would depend on (1) the importance of the exam (i.e., higher stakes would increase examinees' motivation to memorize items and decrease the level of item reuse possible); (2) the number of previously disclosed items (a larger pool of previously disclosed items would allow greater item reuse); and (3) the proportion of the operational test's item pool consisting of reused items (ceteris paribus, a higher proportion of reused items would increase examinees' motivation to memorize answers to disclosed items) and the frequency of selection of previously disclosed items.

The amount of item reuse possible as a function of the variables listed above is at least in part an empirical question. To date, the only study that directly investigated this issue was conducted by Hale, Angelis, and Thibodeau (1983). These researchers found substantial effect sizes with a rather low-stakes test. Modeling the change in item parameters as a function of disclosure might provide an alternative approach to item reuse. Here, a key issue would be dimensionality: Does disclosure change the trait assessed by a test and thereby introduce an additional dimension underlying test performance? Although additional research investigating item reuse following disclosure is certainly needed, it is apparent that this topic should be considered with a great deal of caution.

Learning About Opportunity to Learn

Throughout this report it has been assumed that students value the opportunity to learn from their mistakes on standardized tests. However, this is truly an empirical question: When it is available, do students request copies of the test, their answers, and the scoring key? What do individuals who request these materials do with the information? Do students actually review their answers and study their mistakes? Do they go to teachers, parents, or others to discuss their errors? One study (Stricker, 1984) found that "access to the disclosed material had no appreciable effects on retest performance" (p. 81).

Clearly, additional research is needed on this topic to learn about the value of disclosure. Does it lie in students' preparation for upcoming tests with different questions, in post-test analyses of their mistakes, or both? Answers to these questions would help us design disclosure policies that would most benefit students.

DISCUSSION

A responsible disclosure policy for CATs must be one that (1) provides an opportunity for public scrutiny of actual tests and their item pools; (2) allows future examinees an opportunity to become familiar with the test and to practice in a "nearly real" setting; (3) provides assurance to examinees that their tests are accurately scored; and (4) protects the security, reliability, and validity of the test for future examinees. Throughout this document, we have discussed how the actions required to accomplish the first three of these goals conflict with policies designed to maintain test security, reliability, and validity. Because it is impossible to achieve all of these desirable goals simultaneously, we believe that compromise is necessary so that all objectives can be at least partially accomplished.

What would be the elements of a disclosure policy that would carve out a middle ground and provide a best approximation to simultaneously satisfying all of these conflicting desiderata? We believe that test publishers should take the following actions:

- Samples of actual CATs should be released on a regular basis for public review;
- Large collections of items in the form of practice tests or pools should be released in domains where enough new items can be written to maintain the CAT item pool. The frequency of release should be determined by the test publisher as a function of the flow rate of examinees and the technical requirements of item calibration;
- Research into the technical quality of their tests and pools should be conducted, published, and disseminated;
- Opportunities for qualified independent researchers to conduct additional research should be provided.

Furthermore, test publishers should investigate the level of examinees' interest in reviewing the questions they were administered, their answers, and the correct answers under secure conditions. The review should be useful to students and widely available, at a price they can afford, at an expense to the publisher that is reasonable, and secure enough that the CAT retains its validity.

Test publishers might, for example, annually release tests that represent different levels of performance (Periodic Test) and release item pools on a less frequent basis (Periodic Pool) dictated by the practicalities of creating and calibrating enough new items for a satisfactory CAT item pool. The number of tests released annually and the frequency of CAT item pool release would have to be determined based on the individual characteristics of the testing program—how many examinees take the test, how many items exist, how frequently the test is administered, the rate of new item production (which should exceed the rate of item release), and so forth.

Disclosure requirements that exceed the test publisher's ability to replenish a CAT item pool will cause a test's reliability and validity to decrease. This is bad for examinees and the public, as well as the test publisher. Moreover, disclosure requirements that can only be satisfied by substantially increasing the examinee test fee are unlikely to be viewed favorably by examinees or by test publishers.

In conclusion, this document reviews a variety of important goals for test disclosure and practical constraints that cannot be ignored. It is critical to strike a balance between these sometimes conflicting desiderata. A disclosure policy that considers only part of the total equation could have dire implications for other parts. Only by addressing the needs of all parties—examinees, test publishers, and the public—can a constructive CAT disclosure policy be crafted.

REFERENCES

Green, B. F. (Ed.). (1981). *New directions for testing and measurement: Issues in testing—coaching, disclosure, and ethnic bias*. San Francisco, CA: Jossey-Bass.

Green, B. F., Bock, R. D., Humphreys, L. G., Linn, R. L., & Reckase, M. D. (1984). Technical guidelines for assessing computerized adaptive tests. *Journal of Educational Measurement, 21*, 347–360.

Hale, G. A., Angelis, P. J., & Thibodeau, L. A. (1983). Effects of test disclosure on performance on the Test of English as a Foreign Language. *Language Learning, 33*, 449–464.

Kingsbury, G. G., & Zara, A. R. (1989). Procedures for selecting items for computerized adaptive tests. *Applied Measurement in Education, 2*, 359–375.

McAllister, P. H. (1991). Overview of state legislation to regulate standardized testing. *Educational Measurement: Issues and Practice, 10*, 19–22.

Powers, D. E., & Swinton, S. S. (1984). Effects of self-study for coachable test item types. *Journal of Educational Psychology, 76*, 266–278.

Stocking, M. L., & Swanson, L. (1993). A method for severely constrained item selection in adaptive testing. *Applied Psychological Measurement, 17*, 277–292.

Stricker, L. J. (1984). Test disclosure and retest performance on the SAT. *Applied Psychological Measurement, 8*, 81–87.

TEST MODELS

William C. Ward
Educational Testing Service

In traditional paper-and-pencil testing, with its fixed forms and simple un-weighted scoring, we may not think much about the practices that are followed in creating and administering a test, or what views of the domain and of individual competence are implicit in these choices. Practice has been established by tradition, and sometimes has no rationale other than that longstanding methods seem to have worked well. Test design decisions may be limited to assuring that desired balances in item content and difficulty are achieved for each test form; everything else has been settled.

The move to CBT brings a different level of attention to every aspect of assessment. Increased scrutiny will be found even when the computer is used as nothing more than a device for delivering the same instrument as in paper-and-pencil testing. The newness of the delivery approach ensures that old and new practices will be questioned, both by those looking for any way to discredit the change in medium and by those more positively inclined who still need confirmation that old rules and relations continue to hold.

More important, computerization results in an explosion in the range of possibilities that can be considered in designing, administering, and scoring a test. "One size fits all" across testing programs or across individuals taking an examination is no longer needed for manageable, cost-

effective assessment. It becomes possible to think about what characteristics of measurement are most important to optimize and to develop or
select an approach matched to those goals. The choice of test model is
central to this consideration, and it provides the focus for the four chapters in this part.

The first contribution is by Folk and Smith (chap. 2, this volume). The
authors present and discuss several models within three classes of approach: CAT, in which items are selected to yield accurate and efficient
measurement for individuals across a broad range of proficiency levels;
linear on-the-fly testing (LOFT), which provides for enhanced test security through automated assembly of a unique test form for each individual
examinee; and computerized mastery testing (CMT), designed for accurate separation of examinees into those who meet a proficiency standard
and those who do not. They consider a range of issues, many cutting
across delivery models, that are salient in implementing a CBT program.
Some of these represent fundamental design issues, such as the decision
whether selection and balancing of items should take place at the level of
the individual item or in terms of testlets—groups of items administered
together. Others involve constraints on how examinees interact with the
test, including what is permitted in item review and omission and when
testing is stopped.

The models discussed by Folk and Smith represent the array of
choices that many testing programs are dealing with as they move to
computerized administration from their traditional paper-and-pencil-
based multiple-choice examinations. This is a huge step, but only the first
of several.

The second chapter in this part considers still more radical change.
Luecht and Clauser (chap. 3, this volume) describe highly interactive
computerized simulations in which the examinee must exercise many of
the problem-solving and management skills required in professional
practice. Computerized simulations have had prior use in training settings, but it is only now, as defensible automated scoring becomes feasible, that they are moving to the arena of large-scale, highly consequential
assessments. The National Board of Medical Examiners' simulations of
medical case management and the National Council of Architectural
Registration Boards' simulations of problems in building and site design
are representative of the dramatic change possible in proficiency assessments, most evidently in occupational and professional licensing and
certification contexts.

The focus in Luecht and Clauser's chapter, however, is not on such
simulations alone, but on the broader context within which decisions are
made about the choice of design for a particular assessment. The availability of complex interactive examinations—with their attendant in-

creased cost and complexity in designing, implementing, and scoring—makes all the more salient our general lack of clear principles and criteria for determining what kind of examination is most suitable on a given occasion. The authors address this lack by providing a broad evaluation framework for test design and analysis in which they consider four major factors: the test purpose and use to which information will be put, task complexity and instrument design, data collection and scoring, and modeling and scaling the test results. As they indicate, their goal is not to present solutions to measurement problems, but to provide a way to evaluate information needs and explore possible solutions.

The two remaining chapters in this part offer commentary on these first two. van der Linden's (chap. 4, this volume) chapter is organized around three kinds of complexity that arise in designing CBTs. The first is the complexity introduced in using the computer to present more realistic test items, as discussed by Luecht and Clauser. Although welcoming such innovation, van der Linden notes that the concepts of realism and test validity involve contradictory requirements; the first suggests that as many real-life factors as possible should be represented in the item, whereas the second requires the removal from the test score of the effects of each factor other than the variable the test is intended to measure. He contrasts the chief means for controlling for error variance in classical testing—standardization and randomization—with that employed in modern testing, the statistical adjustment epitomized by the use of IRT.

The second source of complexity in CBT involves the assembly of individual items to make a test. van der Linden reviews five forms of CBT discussed by Folk and Smith, considering the nature and consequences for measurement of the constraints on item selection imposed in each. Greater constraint can ensure better achievement of content balance, but it generally comes at a price, that of a decrease in the statistical information yield of a test.

Third is the complexity that arises in designing and managing the CBT system. Several compelling examples are presented to show how decisions about testing methods can have unexpected interacting effects. For instance, one study found that selecting the first test item based on an initial ability estimate calculated for each individual had the unanticipated effect of improving the exposure rates of items in the pool. It is clear, as van der Linden concludes, that we have far to go to understand the interacting consequences of test configuration decisions as well as we would like.

In the final chapter in this part, Stout (chap. 5, this volume) notes that it is imperative that we find ways to justify and compensate for the increased costs associated with CBT. The use of cognitively complex items such as Luecht and Clauser describe can do this, but it requires attention to both the cognitive psychology of problem solving and the use of IRT models that are sufficiently sophisticated to capture the richness in the data. He cautions at the same time against the danger of overinterpretation of performance; an overly complex model can lead to the misidentification of noise in the data as meaningful information.

Stout suggests that the two chapters he discusses complement each other well. Whether test items are the relatively simple ones traditionally used in multiple-choice tests or the cognitively complex ones described by Luecht and Clauser, an efficient model for item selection and administration is crucial for effective CBT. Thus, the models presented by Folk and Smith and the issues they raise are of utmost importance for the CBT enterprise. Stout comments on several model-related issues, including advantages associated with the use of testlets and the potential value of several item-selection approaches outside the boundaries of those usually considered in test design. He also identifies several areas, such as differential item functioning and the possible dependence of item parameters on the location of the item in the test, that can offer problems for CBT beyond those encountered in traditional tests.

These four chapters—as indeed the whole of the present volume—evidence the exceptional progress made in the 15 years of use of CBT for academic and licensing decisions. When Educational Testing Service (ETS) fielded its first operational adaptive test, the College Board Computerized Placement Test, in 1986, most of the issues currently under discussion were simply not relevant. There was no methodology for controlling exposure of items in the pool, for example; it was necessary simply to throw out of the pool those items that were used too infrequently and sometimes those that were used too often. There was no possibility of dynamically balancing item content in the course of a test; assignment of items to "bins," with the third item in an individual's test always being drawn from the third bin, was all the control over item content and format that could be exercised. The current situation could not be more different. It is now taken for granted that all the constraints and balances expected in a professionally developed, high-stakes paper-and-pencil examination must also be met by the model-based test administered to any individual. And, as these chapters demand, what can be expected in the CBTs of the future goes still farther beyond what has been traditional practice.

Models for Delivery of CBTs

Valerie Greaud Folk
Robert L. Smith
Educational Testing Service

INTRODUCTION

Although operational administrations of CBTs did not begin until the 1980s, CBT is already an acknowledged alternative to paper-and-pencil testing. Diverse testing programs have implemented CBT, including the ASVAB (Green, Bock, Humphreys, Linn, & Reckase, 1984; Sands, Waters, & McBride, 1997), the GRE (Eignor, Stocking, Way, & Steffen, 1993), and Praxis I: Computer-Based Academic Skills Assessments[1] (Eignor, Folk, Li, & Stocking, 1994). Other testing programs, such as the Law School Admissions Test (Pashley, 1997), are researching the practical considerations of CBT implementation.

Various delivery methods have been developed theoretically and many have been implemented in real testing programs. The delivery methods presented in this chapter are CAT, which can be controlled at the item or testlet level; LOFT; and several models of CMT. In addition, various issues with regard to CBT delivery methods will be discussed. Most delivery methods are based on IRT,[2] as described in Lord (1980), although non-IRT models do exist.

---

[1]These assessments are part of the Praxis Series: Professional Assessments for Beginning Teachers.

[2]In early work (Birnbaum, 1968; Ferguson, 1942; Lawley, 1943), this approach was called latent trait theory; Lord (1952) used the term item characteristic curve theory. It is now commonly known as IRT (Lord, 1980).

ITEM RESPONSE THEORY

Before discussing the delivery methods, we provide a brief summary of IRT models and introduce some important concepts in IRT.

IRT Models

IRT describes the relation between observed test performance and an underlying examinee ability, known as theta (θ), usually using a logistic function of one or more item parameters for each item. This function is known as the item characteristic curve (ICC) for the item. Although one- and two-parameter (1P and 2P) models have been implemented, current CBTs are often based on the unidimensional three-parameter logistic (3PL) IRT model (Lord, 1980, Equation 2-1):

$$P_i(\theta) = c_i + \frac{1 - c_i}{1 + e^{-1.7a_i(\theta - b_i)}}, \tag{1}$$

where $P_i(\theta)$ defines the probability of a correct response to item i, given an examinee's ability, θ. The item parameters, a_i, b_i, and c_i, respectively, are known as the discrimination, difficulty, and lower asymptote for item i. IRT models were originally developed from a normal ogive function, which is intuitively more attractive, but the logistic function provided in Equation 1 is a computationally efficient close approximation with the 1.7 scaling. The 1P model includes only item difficulty with a constant item discrimination value, usually set to 1/1.7 using Equation 1 (Rasch, 1960).[3] The 2P model includes difficulty and discrimination values; the lower asymptote is set to zero for both models. Multidimensional models also include multiple examinee abilities and item discrimination parameters (e.g., Li & Lissitz, 1998; Reckase, 1983b, 1985; Reckase & McKinley, 1991; Segall, 1996). Polytomous models can be ordered and allow for partial credit scoring (e.g., Masters, 1982; Samejima, 1969) or be based on a nominal scale (Bock, 1972).

Ability Estimation

Scoring of examinees may be accomplished using any of several methods. A commonly used method is maximum likelihood estimation (MLE). The following likelihood function defines the conditional proba-

---

[3]The original formulation of the Rasch model sets the a-parameter to 1.0, but it does not scale the logistic function to approximate the normal using 1.7.

bility of a particular response pattern given θ, as defined in Lord (1980, Equation 4-20):

$$L(\mathbf{u}|\theta) = \prod_{i=1}^{n} P_i^{u_i} (1 - P_i)^{1 - u_i}, \qquad (2)$$

where $\mathbf{u}$ is the vector $\{u_1, u_2, \ldots, u_n\}$ of scored item responses, where $u_i = 1$ for a correct response, $u_i = 0$ for an incorrect response, and P_i is defined according to any of the IRT models.

In practice, the MLE of ability is obtained by taking the logarithm of Equation 2, setting the first derivative with respect to θ equal to 0, and solving for θ. Iterative numerical methods, using the Newton–Raphson procedure, may be employed to obtain the solution (e.g., Wingersky, 1983). There is, however, a possibility of multiple maxima or of the maximum only being attained as thetas approach positive or negative infinity. For the 3PL model, the formula for calculating the MLE is defined as:

$$\hat{\theta}_{MLE} = \frac{\partial \ln L}{\partial \theta} = \frac{1.7 \sum_{i=1}^{n} a_i (u_i - P_i)(P_i - c_i)}{P_i(1 - c_i)}. \qquad (3)$$

The MLE has desirable asymptotic statistical properties when it is derived from a large number of items (Lord, 1980). A major disadvantage of the MLE is that it cannot be estimated if an examinee provides all correct or all incorrect responses; in practical application, a limiting ability can be defined.

Bayesian ability estimation methods incorporate a prior distribution of ability with the likelihood function (Lord, 1980, Equation 12-5):

$$L(\mathbf{u}|\theta) = g(\theta) \prod_{i=1}^{n} P_i^{u_i} (1 - P_i)^{1 - u_i}, \qquad (4)$$

where $g(\theta)$ is the prior ability distribution. Point estimates of ability can be obtained by taking the mean of the posterior distribution (expectation a posteriori; EAP) or the mode (maximum a posteriori; MAP). The Bayesian approach enables estimation of ability for all possible response patterns; however, the Bayesian estimates have a tendency to be inwardly biased toward the mean of the ability distribution (Hambleton, Zaal, & Pieters, 1991; Lord, 1980; van der Linden, 1998b). Note also that MLE estimates tend to be outwardly biased (Lord, 1983; van der Linden, 1998b).

An estimated number-correct (NC) true score, ξ, can also be obtained from a transformation of the examinee's ability estimate and the item parameters for a reference set of m items:

$$\hat{\xi} = \sum_{j=1}^{m} P_j(\hat{\theta}),$$ (5)

where P_j is defined according to the IRT model. This score is on a more readily interpretable metric, using a constant set of reference items across examinees. It indicates the number of items that an examinee would be expected to answer correctly if the reference set of items had been administered. It may also be easily transformed to a scaled score metric using an existing transformation for the reference set of items.

Another alternative is the equated NC score (Stocking, 1994b). This approach is derived from IRT true score equating (Lord, 1980), which is widely used in traditional paper-and-pencil linear administrations. In IRT equating, estimated NC scores on one form of the test, $\hat{\xi}$, are transformed to estimated NC scores on another form, $\hat{\eta}$, via corresponding theta values on the IRT metric (Lord, 1980, Equation 13-12).

If one test is defined to be the reference form, NC scores on different forms (such as from CATs) may be equated to the reference form NC scale. Although some of the IRT information is lost in this method, it appears to be a fairly slight loss. An advantage of this method (Stocking, 1994b) is that it may be more readily understood by examinees.

Information

An important concept in IRT is information, which reflects measurement precision at each ability level. The information function is defined in general for maximum likelihood scoring as follows (Lord, 1980, Equation 5-9):

$$I\{\theta, u_i\} = \frac{P_i'^2}{P_i(1 - P_i)},$$ (6)

where $I_i(\theta)$ defines the information provided by item i at θ; and P_i' is the derivative of P_i. Equation 1 may also be substituted to provide the information function for the 3PL model:

$$I\{\theta, u_i\} = \frac{1.7^2 a_i^2 (1 - c_i)}{(c_i + e^{1.7 a_i(\theta - b_i)})(1 + e^{-1.7 a_i(\theta - b_i)})^2}.$$ (7)

The test information is the sum of the item information functions, assuming conditional independence of the item responses given theta (Lord, 1980). This definition of information is known as Fisher information or *local* information, and can be contrasted with Kullback–Liebler (K–L) or *global* information (Chang & Ying, 1996). This index is linear with respect to the a parameter, whereas Fisher information has a quadratic relation with the a parameter; thus, the weight given to the discrimination parameter is less for K–L information (Eggen, 1999). Consequently, Chang and Ying (1996) have argued that K–L information is useful for selecting items early in a CAT when ability is not well estimated. More recently, Chang and Ying (1999) have proposed the use of a multistage CAT where the items with low a parameters are administered early when ability is not well estimated, using more discriminating items later in the test to fine tune the ability estimate. These models may have the advantage of making broader use of the item pool while reducing the exposure of the most discriminating items.

Conditional Standard Error of Measurement

Another concept related to information is the conditional standard error of measurement (CSEM), which indicates the amount of error at each ability level, or the standard deviation of the estimated abilities, given a true ability, θ_0 (Lord, 1980, Equation 4-8). It is the square root of the inverse of the test information function.

$$CSEM = \left[\sum_{i=1}^{n} I(\theta, u_i) \right]^{-\frac{1}{2}} = \left[\sum_{i=1}^{n} \frac{P_i'^2}{P_i(1 - P_i)} \right]^{-\frac{1}{2}} \tag{8}$$

COMPUTERIZED ADAPTIVE TESTING

In CAT, the primary goal is to select items for each examinee that are of an appropriate difficulty level. As a result, CATs are psychometrically more efficient, or shorter, than conventional tests, given a specified level of precision, because few items of inappropriate difficulty are administered (Green, 1983; Lord, 1980; Weiss, 1982). The selection of items takes place during the administration of the test on the computer, as a function of each examinee's pattern of correct or incorrect responses to items that have been previously administered. In practical application, the test generally begins with an item of low to moderate difficulty. Examinees who answer the first item incorrectly will be given an easier item (lower b parameter); examinees who answer the first item correctly will be given a harder item (higher b parameter). An interim ability estimate is calculated as the examinee proceeds through the chosen items. Discussions of many practical issues for CAT implementation are presented in Green (1988), Green et al. (1984), Hambleton et al. (1991), Mills and Stocking (1996), Stocking (1994a), and Wainer (1992).

Selection of the First Item

At the beginning of an examinee's test session, there is little direct information about the examinee's ability level, so either a starting point must be defined arbitrarily or it must be based on knowledge about the distribution of ability. Without prior information about an examinee's ability level, it is presumed the examinee is of middle ability; thus, from a psychometric viewpoint, it is optimal to start the test with an item of moderate difficulty for the population of examinees taking the test. Another view is that examinees who are of low ability may be frustrated if the first item in the test is hard for them (Hambleton, 1986; Wainer & Kiely, 1987). To minimize this concern, the starting point could be chosen from items that are slightly easier than middle difficulty for the population. However, to have a sufficient number of easier items to choose from, it might be necessary to supplement the pool with easy items; if these items are not particularly useful for the remainder of the test, this approach may be wasteful of item-writing resources. As long as the test is not too short, it makes little psychometric difference where the test begins (Hambleton et al., 1991).

Adaptive Item Selection

Methods for selecting items generally manage three features of the test: psychometric characteristics, content specifications, and item exposure. In this section we discuss only the psychometric criteria and content specifications; we cover item exposure in the issues section of this chapter.

A review of psychometric criteria for item selection, including those that predate the widespread availability of high-speed computers, is provided in Kingsbury and Zara (1989). Modern item-selection algorithms commonly use maximum information as the psychometric selection criterion (Lord, 1977). Each item is chosen to maximize information (see Equations 6 and 7) about the examinee's current ability level. Use of local information produces efficient CATs; however, this method of item selection tends to overuse psychometrically desirable items. Use of global information, or selection of items with low discrimination values at the beginning of the test when ability is not well estimated, may more effectively distribute item usage (Chang & Ying, 1996, 1999).

A viable alternative is the Bayesian item-selection method described by Owen (1975). Each examinee is assigned a normal prior distribution of ability at the beginning of the test. A posterior distribution is calculated to incorporate the first scored item response. The mean and standard deviation of the posterior is used to define the normal prior for the next item; this normalization of the posterior occurs after each item administered.[4] Each subsequent item is chosen to minimize the variance of the resultant posterior distribution.

All practitioners recognize that psychometric selection criteria generate CATs that are psychometrically efficient, but inadequate, if content specifications also have not been incorporated into the selection algorithm. The following models for automated item selection have been developed to incorporate psychometric and content requirements simultaneously in the item-selection process. These models have additional features, but the focus of our discussion is only on these two aspects.

The weighted deviations model (WDM; Stocking & Swanson, 1993; Swanson & Stocking, 1993) characterizes psychometric and content specifications as a set of desired properties, or target constraints. The goal of WDM is to come as close as possible to meeting all target constraints simultaneously as each item is chosen; this model allows some constraints to have greater importance than others through the assignment of relative weights to all constraints. During a CAT, the WDM selects each item to minimize the weighted sum of positive deviations from the specified target (psychometric and content) constraints.

An alternative to the WDM, known as optimal constrained adaptive testing (OCAT), has been developed by van der Linden (van der Linden, 1998a; van der Linden & Reese, 1998). The OCAT approach seeks to maximize information for the current examinee ability estimate, subject to a set of specified constraints. In addition, rather than selecting a single item at each point in the test, all remaining items are selected for the current ability estimate; at each subsequent point, the remaining items are reselected. This latter requirement is designed to insure that a full test can be constructed to meet the set of constraints. Jones (1997) also presented an approach that is similar to OCAT.

---

[4]Owen's (1975) formulation used the mean and standard deviation of the posterior distribution to minimize computations. With the power of today's computers, this simplifying procedure would be unnecessary. The exact posterior could be used instead.

COMPUTERIZED ADAPTIVE TESTING WITH TESTLETS

Wainer and Kiely (1987) mentioned several concerns about CAT: various types of context effects, the lack of stability of item parameter estimates, minimal capability to order items by difficulty in examinee tests, and limitations in effectively balancing content. Selection of testlets, rather than individual items, has been seen as a possible way to alleviate some of these concerns (see also Thissen, Steinberg, & Mooney, 1989; Wainer & Lewis, 1990).

Testlets are essentially minitests that can be assembled to meet important content specifications, but are themselves selectable entities. Testlets can be constructed in advance, using the knowledge of content experts (either manually or through an automated testlet creation process with review), to insure that no undesirable context effects occur. Items can be placed into testlet positions that are fairly constant across examinees to maintain similar contextual effects. In addition, to the extent that item difficulty ordering is desired, such ordering may also be employed within testlets. A full test consists of the delivery of two or more testlets according to some rules for administration.

Two-stage testing (e.g., Lord, 1980) is an early model that uses a routing testlet with a sufficient number of moderate difficulty items to roughly determine an examinee's ability level. This is followed by a second testlet that contains items at the targeted difficulty level. Although this approach has some utility, it risks routing examinees incorrectly and thus administering an unsuitable second testlet (Hulin, Drasgow, & Parsons, 1983). If several testlets are administered, this concern can be ameliorated.

Wainer and Kiely (1987), as well as Wainer and Lewis (1990), describe several administration designs that permit a greater degree of adaptation. In general, an initial testlet of moderate difficulty is administered; it may be a single screening testlet that is administered to all examinees or it may be chosen at random from a set of testlets. Administration of items within the testlet can follow a linear path or a hierarchical branching scheme. Subsequent testlets can be administered using hierarchical branching. Where branching is incorporated, some of the efficiencies of adaptive testing are gained, but the number of paths is immensely reduced in comparison with item-level adaptive testing. This method allows for better control over the possible sequences, even to the extreme of having all possible sequences determined in advance so that each complete test can be examined before administration.

Testlets may also be useful if the measure assesses a multidimensional ability. Each testlet can be constructed to represent all aspects of the ability domain, so that content is balanced as each testlet is administered. Another possibility is to construct testlets to assess each component of the ability domain; content balance is controlled by selecting the appropriate number of testlets from each of the components. Hierarchical linking is possible with both within- and between-testlet balancing, so that examinee performance on previous testlets dictates which subsequent testlets are administered (see Segall, 1996, for a multidimensional approach to adaptive testing).

If conditional independence exists among the items within a testlet (this can be evaluated using methods described in Thissen et al., 1989, or Wainer & Kiely, 1987), dichotomous item-level IRT methods may be used to estimate parameters and either MLE or Bayesian methods may be used to estimate ability. When conditional independence does not hold, each testlet can be treated as a single item with score categories defined by the response patterns (Wainer & Kiely, 1987) or with scored responses 0 to n, where n is the number of individual items within the testlet (Thissen et al., 1989). One of the polytomous IRT models (e.g., Bock, 1972; Masters, 1982; Samejima, 1969) can be implemented to estimate item parameters and ability estimates. Thissen et al. (1989) provided a compelling argument that the interitem correlations in testlets constructed around reading passages, for example, falsely inflate the information curves if dichotomous item-level IRT models are implemented, in comparison with polytomous testlet-level models. However, in practical application, the inflation may be minimal (Lawrence, 1995).

LOFT TESTING

In LOFT, the goal is to construct a unique fixed-length test for each examinee. This model addresses item security concerns rather than the psychometric efficiency goals of CAT. LOFT can be implemented at the item level or the testlet level (see, for example, Wainer & Kiely's, 1987, description of successive linear administrations of linear testlets). A unique form is assembled for each examinee to meet a target set of content and psychometric specifications. Note that the items chosen do not depend on the examinee's ability level.

The forms can be constructed at the beginning of an examinee's testing session, or each item can be chosen nonadaptively as the examinee proceeds through the test. Many possible forms can even be constructed well in advance of any testing sessions. The assembly procedures can be similar to those employed for traditional paper-and-pencil testing, although automated methods of assembly (e.g., Stocking, Swanson, & Pearlman, 1993) may be required if a large quantity of forms needs to be generated. Preconstruction of forms permits greater control of parallelism and minimizes the degree of overlap among the forms constructed, because in-house reviews can be performed before the test administrations.

In the LOFT model, each form is constructed to meet content and psychometric specifications and to be of comparable difficulty; however, it is necessary to generate equated scores for each examinee. The IRT parameters can be used to calculate ability estimates (e.g., MLE) or equated NC scores (Stocking, 1994b).

LOFT is a desirable delivery method for a measure with rigorous content-ordering requirements. For example, when a set of items pertaining to a reading passage is administered, it may be important for a main idea item to be administered first, followed by more specific items. The items within a set can be ordered as needed according to defined content requirements. The elements in each set or subcomponent of a test can be arranged in a prespecified order, and the administration algorithm can simply choose the required number of sets or subcomponents. There is little mention of the LOFT approach in the psychometric literature. However, it does have many appealing characteristics for handling set-based tests.

COMPUTERIZED MASTERY DELIVERY MODELS

The goal of CMTs is to categorize examinees, as accurately as possible, into mastery and nonmastery groups. Unlike adaptive testing, where all points on the scale are equally important, the primary focus is a limited number of cut scores. CMT delivery models fall into three general categories, those based on the following: the sequential probability ratio test (SPRT), the adaptive mastery testing (AMT) approach, and various models of CMT. Each model is described as it was originally developed, and significant extensions are then discussed.

SPRT

Wald's (1947) SPRT was first developed as a means of testing sequentially to detect whether product lots meet a prespecified quality level. The SPRT is used to decide which of two competing hypotheses is more likely for a selected sample; the hypothesis having a likelihood ratio greater than a prespecified value is accepted and the lot is passed or rejected accordingly. The probability of observing some number of defective lots given that either H_0 (lot is acceptable) or H_1 (lot is unacceptable) is true is described by a binomial probability model. By specifying acceptable levels of Type I error and Type II error, the stringency and asymmetry of the test can be controlled.

The SPRT was first applied in a mastery testing context by Ferguson (1969a, 1969b). This application uses the concept of a neutral region around the "true" mastery–nonmastery boundary. Two states are defined: p_0 (the highest level of nonmastery) and p_1 (the lowest level of mastery). Expert judgment is often used to define the boundaries of the neutral region. Ferguson treated examinees' responses to items as a set of Bernoulli trials. The probability of observing x defective elements in a sample of size n may be described using a binomial probability model (Reckase, 1983a).

$$\frac{L(\mathbf{u}|H_1)}{L(\mathbf{u}|H_0)} = \frac{p_1^x(1-p_1)^{n-x}}{p_0^x(1-p_0)^{n-x}} = \left(\frac{p_1}{p_0}\right)^x\left(\frac{1-p_1}{1-p_0}\right)^{n-x}, \tag{9}$$

where $\mathbf{u}$ is the vector $\{u_1, u_2, \ldots, u_n\}$ of scored item responses, x is the sum of the u_i, p_1 is the probability the examinee answers an item correctly under H_1, and p_0 is the probability the examinee answers an item correctly under H_0. The use of the binomial model implies that the probability of a correct response to an item is the same for all items in the pool, or that the items are sampled at random. However, if the test is adaptive, with items selected to maximize item information at the current ability estimate, an IRT-like probability model is more appropriate.

Reckase (1983a) extended the SPRT to a tailored testing context using IRT. Values on the theta scale of θ_0 and θ_1 define the boundaries of the neutral region ($\theta_0 < \theta_c < \theta_1$) around the cut score θ_c). Generally, narrower regions are associated with higher decision accuracy and longer tests; wider regions are associated with lower decision accuracy and shorter tests. However, these trade off with α and β. The likelihood for the 3PL model[5]

$$\frac{L(\mathbf{u}|\theta_1)}{L(\mathbf{u}|\theta_0)} = \left[\prod_{i=1}^{n}\frac{c_i(2u_i-1)+\exp[u_i 1.7a_i(\theta_1-b_i)]}{1+\exp[1.7a_i(\theta_1-b_i)]}\right] \Bigg/$$

$$\left[\prod_{i=1}^{n}\frac{c_i(2u_i-1)+\exp[u_i 1.7a_i(\theta_0-b_i)]}{1+\exp[1.7a_i(\theta_0-b_i)]}\right], \tag{10}$$

where $L(\mathbf{u}|\theta_k)$, $k = 0$ or 1, is the likelihood based on the responses to the items administered to this point in the test, under H_0 or H_1, respectively; u_i

---

[5]Formula provided by Charles Lewis (personal communication, August 18, 1998).

is the scored response to item i; and a_i, b_i, and c_i are the standard IRT parameters.

The procedure allows flexibility in reflecting the costs of the different classification errors. For example, if the α and β parameters are set equal, both types of errors are considered equally serious. The α and β parameters can be adjusted if one type of error is considered more serious.

The boundaries that define the neutral region around the true cut score are often set using judgmental methods. The model presented by Reckase (1983a) seeks to obtain the best ability estimate for an examinee (information is maximized at the provisional ability estimate). Spray and Reckase (1994) have shown that selecting items at the decision point, rather than at the true (or provisional) ability estimate, results in shorter tests for the SPRT.

AMT

The AMT model is IRT based, adaptive, and uses Bayesian confidence intervals around the ability estimate to determine whether to classify an examinee or continue testing (Kingsbury & Weiss, 1983). Like Reckase's (1983a) extension of the SPRT, the item providing the greatest amount of information at the examinee's present ability estimate ($\hat{\theta}$) is selected for delivery. Unlike the SPRT, boundaries around the true cut score are unnecessary. The scale is continuous with the cut score θ_c, defined at some point along the scale. Kingsbury and Weiss used the 3PL IRT model to describe the functional relation between θ and the probability of a correct response. The ability estimate is based on the method developed by Owen (1975). A Bayesian confidence interval is constructed around the examinee's provisional estimate of ability (posterior mean) given by:

$$\hat{\theta}_i - z_{\alpha/2}(\sigma_i) \ \theta \ \hat{\theta}_i + z_{(\alpha/2)}(\sigma_i), \qquad (11)$$

where $\hat{\theta}_i$ is the posterior mean following the administration of item i, σ_i is the posterior standard deviation following the administration of item i, and θ is the true ability. If the confidence interval excludes the cut score, the examinee is *passed* or *failed*. If the cut score is contained in the confidence interval, *testing continues*. If the cut score is still contained in the confidence interval when the maximum test length is reached, the examinee is classified based on the whether the point estimate is above or below the cut score.

The AMT makes use of symmetric Bayesian confidence intervals, effectively setting the costs of the two error types (α and β) equal (assuming one cut score). This may be limiting when one type of error is more serious than the other.

As with the Reckase (1983a) version of the SPRT, the AMT seeks to obtain the best ability estimate for an examinee (information is maximized at the provisional ability estimate). Spray and Reckase (1994) have shown that selecting items at the decision point, rather than at the true (or current) ability estimate, also results in shorter tests for the AMT.

CMT

The CMT model developed by Lewis and Sheehan (1990) is a sequential testlet-based (Wainer & Kiely, 1987) procedure to determine whether a candidate should *pass*, *fail*, or *continue testing*.[6] The CMT randomly selects each testlet from a pool of parallel testlets for delivery, seeking to minimize test length while obtaining an acceptable level of classification accuracy.[7] The 3PL IRT model is used to define the relation between true mastery status and observed test performance.

Sequential cut score thresholds are defined for the boundaries of the *pass*, *continue testing*, and *fail* regions, on the metric of cumulative number of correct responses. When few testlets have been administered, the boundaries of the *continue testing* region are far apart. As test length increases, the *continue testing* region narrows. At the final stage of testing, any examinees for whom a decision has not yet been made are classified as *pass* or *fail* based on a single cut score threshold. The decision thresholds are obtained by minimizing the posterior expected loss at each stage of testing based on simulations using Bayesian decision theory.

Loss Functions.   In simple mastery decisions, two types of errors are possible: classifying a nonmaster as a master (a false positive) and classifying a master as a nonmaster (a false negative). Classification rates in the CMT are controlled through the use of loss (cost) functions. Losses are real-valued numbers associated with either of the incorrect decisions or the administration of an additional testlet, as the latter increases item

---

[6] Vos (1997) has applied a similar procedure at the item level using a binomial probability model.

[7] Parallel was used by Lewis and Sheehan (1990) to mean that testlets were composed of the same number of items, were equivalent with respect to content coverage, and were equivalent with respect to the likelihood of particular number correct scores at proficiency levels near the mastery–nonmastery cut-off value. Sheehan and Lewis (1992) have shown the procedure to be robust to nonparallelism of testlets with respect to the likelihood of particular number correct scores at proficiency levels near the mastery–nonmastery cut-off value. Testlets are usually built to maximize information (or some other criterion) at the decision point for a single-cut score test.

TABLE 2.1
Simple Loss Function for a Fixed-Length CMT

	Decision Status	
True Status	Fail	Pass
Nonmaster	0	A
Master	B	0

exposure. Table 2.1 shows a simple loss function for a fixed-length test with a single cut score. The losses associated with each decision error may be set equal if each type of error is considered equally serious; alternatively, an asymmetrical loss function may be specified. Observe from Table 2.1 that no loss is incurred when a correct decision is made.

For a variable-length test, the cost of administering each testlet (C) must also be specified. The loss table will include additional rows for the number of testlets that can possibly be administered and, for each stage i, iC is added to the cost in each cell. Loss functions with higher values of A and B, relative to C, generally result in longer tests.

Decision and Stopping Rules.   The unique decision rule at each stage of testing is found by minimizing posterior expected loss at each stage. For simplicity, a threshold loss[8] is used; the same loss is incurred whether an examinee's score is close to a decision threshold or far from it.

The posterior probability distribution of mastery at the ith stage of testing is given as[9]

$$P[\Theta = \theta_m \mid X = (X_1, X_2, \ldots, X_i)]$$

$$= \frac{P(X_i \mid \Theta = \theta_m) \cdot P_{m|i-1}}{P(X_i \mid \Theta = \theta_m) \cdot P_{m|i-1} + P(X_i \mid \Theta = \theta_n) \cdot P_{n|i-1}} \equiv P_{m|i} \qquad (12)$$

where $p_{m|i-1}$ and $p_{n|i-1}$ are the prior probabilities (based on the first $i-1$ stages) for the master θ_m and nonmaster θ_n states, respectively; and X_i is the NC score on the ith testlet. $P(X_i \mid \Theta = \theta_m)$ and $P(X_i \mid \Theta = \theta_n)$ are poolwide average probabilities. All response vectors producing the same NC score are treated the same for efficiency of computation; the probability of observing any particular NC score is obtained from the chosen IRT model for the defined θ_m.

---

[8]Other loss functions can easily be accommodated; for example Vos (1997) has used a linear loss function in a CMT context.

[9]All CMT formulas are based on Lewis and Sheehan (1990).

The posterior expected loss for *passing* at stage i is:

$$E[L(pass|\Theta)\,|\,(X_1, X_2, \ldots, X_i)] = L(pass|\theta_n) \cdot$$
$$P_{n|i} + L(pass|\theta_m) \cdot P_{m|i} = A \cdot P_{n|i} + iC = A \cdot (1 - P_{m|i}) + iC, \quad (13)$$

and the posterior expected loss for *failing* is:

$$E[L(fail|\Theta)\,|\,(X_1, X_2, \ldots, X_i)] = L(fail|\theta_n) \cdot$$
$$P_{n|i} + L(fail|\theta_m) \cdot P_{m|i} = B \cdot P_{m|i} + iC, \quad (14)$$

where $p_{m|i}$ and $p_{n|i}$ are the posterior probabilities assumed for states θ_m (master) and θ_n (nonmaster), respectively, at stage i; $L(\cdot|\cdot)$ denotes the appropriate loss value, either A or B, plus iC, the cost of the number of testlets administered up to stage i.

The decision whether an examinee should *pass* or *fail* includes the option of *continue testing*; thus, the loss associated with *continue testing* must also be calculated. To determine the expected loss associated with *continue testing* at stage i (for $i < k$, where k is the last stage of testing), we need to look ahead to all possible outcomes at stage $i + 1$. For example, if a *pass* decision were made at stage $i + 1$, the loss associated with deciding to *continue testing* at stage i would be equal to the loss of deciding to *pass* the examinee at stage $i + 1$. However, the set of all possible outcomes at stage $i + 1$ includes the option of administering another testlet; therefore, all possible outcomes at stage $i + 2$ must also be taken into account.

The uncertainty associated with future testlet administrations can be accounted for by averaging the expected loss associated with each of the various outcomes in proportion to the probability of observing those outcomes. The predictive probability, $P_{s|i}$, of observing each possible score X_{i+1} at stage $i + 1$, given the item responses to the first i stages, can be calculated as a function of the posterior probability distribution at stage i.

$$P(X_{i+1} = s|X_1, X_2, \ldots, X_i) = P(X_{i+1} = s|\Theta = \theta_n) \cdot$$
$$P_{n|i} + P(X_{i+1} = s|\Theta = \theta_m) \cdot P_{m|i} \equiv P_{s|i}. \quad (15)$$

The predictive probability for X_{i+1} at stage i incorporates the uncertainty about θ, whereas the IRT probability assumes θ is known exactly. It is for this reason that the predictive probability is used. At the final stage of testing (k), the decision options are reduced to *pass* or *fail*, which simplifies the final set of calculations and enables the computations for all previous stages.

The risk function defined by Lewis and Sheehan (1990) specifies the minimum of the expected losses of *passing* or *failing* the examinee at stage i or *continue testing*:

$$r_i(P_{m|i}) = \min \left\{ \begin{array}{l} E[L(pass|\Theta)|X_1, X_2, \ldots, X_i], \\ E[L(fail|\Theta)|X_1, X_2, \ldots, X_i], \\ E[L(continue|\Theta)|X_1, X_2, \ldots, X_i], \end{array} \right\} \qquad (16)$$

$$= \min \left\{ \begin{array}{l} A \cdot (1 - P_{m|i}) + iC, \\ B \cdot P_{m|i} + iC, \\ \sum_s P_{s|i} r_{i+1}(P_{m|i+1}) \end{array} \right\},$$

where the expected loss of *continue testing* at stage i is defined in terms of stage $i + 1$ and $P_{m|i+1}$ is evaluated for each possible value of X_{i+1}. The decision rule minimizes posterior expected loss at stage i for *passing*, *failing*, or *continue testing*, with only the *pass* and *fail* options available at stage k.

Extensions of CMT.   In the Lewis and Sheehan (1990) CMT model, the prior and posterior distributions were only defined for two points θ_n and θ_m. Smith and Lewis (1995) extended the CMT to an IRT-based model that accommodates an essentially continuous ability scale and continuous prior and posterior distributions. In addition, conditioning is performed with respect to the entire vector of observed item responses, as opposed to the NC score. The mode of the posterior distribution is taken as the estimate of ability (theta).[10]   In this case, the posterior probability distribution is given by:

---

[10]For each choice of testlets and each observed response pattern there is a posterior distribution with associated expected losses for each possible decision at each stage of testing. To simplify this situation, simulees are grouped according to their posterior modal values of theta. The expected losses are averaged for each decision over all simulees with the same posterior modal estimate, at a given stage. The decision with the lowest average expected loss is then chosen for every simulee with the same modal estimate. In practice, thresholds are identified in terms of modal estimates. Thus, for example, all simulees with modal estimates below the first cut at a given stage of testing would immediately fail.

During simulations, when the two smaller average expected losses were found to not differ significantly (.05, two-tailed), as determined by a dependent groups t-test, the threshold was moved in the direction that would allow the examinee to continue testing. The result of this process is a table of threshold values for posterior modal theta estimates. Note that this is a simplification and will not make the optimal decision for all simulees. Modal estimates of theta are effectively substituted for the complete posterior distribution of theta in this model.

$$P[\Theta = \theta | X = (X_1, X_2, \ldots, X_i)] = \frac{P(X_i|\theta) \cdot P(\theta|i-1)}{\int_{-\infty}^{\infty} P(\theta|i-1) \cdot P(X_i|\theta)d\theta}, \qquad (17)$$

where X_i is the vector of item responses observed for the ith stage of testing, $P(X_i|\theta)$ is the likelihood function for stage i based on the item response vector, $P(\theta|i-1)$ is the prior distribution (posterior distribution at stage $i-1$), and the denominator is a normalizing constant that makes the total area under the curve equal to 1.0.

The expected loss associated with the *pass* and *fail* decisions can be expressed as functions of the posterior distribution as:

$$E[L(pass|\Theta)|X_1, X_2, \ldots, X_i] = \int_{-\infty}^{\theta_c} P(\theta|i)d\theta \cdot A + \int_{\theta_c}^{\infty} P(\theta|i)d\theta \cdot 0 + iC, \quad (18)$$

$$E[L(fail|\Theta)|X_1, X_2, \ldots, X_i] = \int_{-\infty}^{\theta_c} P(\theta|i)d\theta \cdot 0 + \int_{\theta_c}^{\infty} P(\theta|i)d\theta \cdot B + iC, \quad (19)$$

where θ_c is the cut score, and A, B, and C are losses defined above. Other components of this model are continuous extensions of the Lewis and Sheehan (1990) model (see Smith and Lewis, 1995).

The sequential procedure employed in CMT assesses optimality in stages, but it may not produce an optimal solution over all stages of testing. Consequently, Smith and Lewis (1996, 1997) tried to approach the problem from a different perspective. Still using a Bayesian decision theory framework, the process was turned on its head. Rather than trying to determine the best set of cut points for each stage of testing, a search procedure was developed that (using simulations) examines all possible cut score tables with respect to total posterior expected loss. The cut score table with the smallest posterior expected loss based on simulations is selected for use. However, the optimal cut score table was not found to replicate well in cross-validation because of overfitting of the data; what was optimal for one sample was not optimal for a second sample. When classification consistency (decision status compared with maximum test-length decision status) was incorporated into the loss structure of the CMT model, in addition to classification accuracy and test length, the model proved more robust.

The decision rules (and the cut score tables based on them) in the CMT models are based on point estimates of theta and average losses across examinees. The same point estimate may be produced from different patterns of response and different posterior distributions (Tat-suoka & Tatsuoka, 1997). Because the point estimate approach treats all posterior distributions associated with the same point estimate alike, it cannot be optimal for all examinees. Depending on the shape of an individual's posterior distribution, a point estimate may place an examinee below the threshold (cut score) even though the greater portion of the posterior distribution (and thus greater probability) falls above the threshold, or vice versa. In these cases the simplified point estimate may result in an incorrect decision in terms of the probable status of the individual. One reason point estimates are used is to minimize the amount of online computing needed to arrive at a decision (e.g., Smith & Lewis, 1995). Smith and Lewis (1998) proposed that the decision rule be a function of the full posterior distribution. Because it is impractical to create the decision table of cut points beforehand for all possible posterior distributions, as this number would be prohibitively large, Smith and Lewis proposed constructing individualized decision rules using the full posterior distribution and real-time simulations while the examinee is taking the test. When this is done using a Pentium processor running at 200MHz, there is a relatively long delay (20 seconds) between the end of one testlet and the presentation of the next testlet. As processor speeds increase, this should become less of an issue.

ISSUES WITH REGARD TO CBT DELIVERY MODES

Item Versus Testlet Delivery

One issue independent of the delivery model is whether to administer one item at a time or a grouping of items (testlet) before scoring. In adaptive testing, a testlet approach may be particularly advantageous in situations where violation of the conditional independence assumption is likely. Testlets also provide better control of the content and psychometric features of each test administered to examinees because they can be constructed and reviewed in advance. When tests are constructed dynamically using item selection during the test administration, it is difficult to know whether every test meets all content and psychometric specifications. However, algorithms for item selection that incorporate content specifications have progressed rapidly over the last 10 years and, consequently, may not suffer as greatly from the anticipated concern about failing to meet content requirements. In addition, tests that are adaptive at the item level and effectively balance content are substantially more efficient than tests that are adaptive at the testlet level (Kingsbury & Zara, 1991).

In general, testlet approaches have some practical limitations. Because testlets are by definition shorter than full-length tests, it may not be possible to include details from specifications developed for full-length tests in the testlet specification. For unidimensional tests, the long run average over many tests may show the detailed specifications to be proportionately represented, but it may not be adequately represented on a test for any given examinee. With multidimensional tests this may prove to be a larger problem because each dimension needs to be proportionally represented in each testlet if testlets are to be parallel. One option is to increase the size of the testlet, although there are trade-offs with this approach. Larger testlets usually mean that some flexibility of the variable-length test must be sacrificed; adaptive tests that incorporate larger testlets need to be longer.

For mastery tests, a different issue arises. Mastery tests have two primary goals: to cover the content of the domain and to make accurate mastery decisions. When items are administered one item at a time, these goals compete with each other. A not uncommon result is to reach a point in the test where a mastery decision can be made, but the content coverage is not representative of the test blueprint. Additional items may be required to fill out the blueprint. At this point, the mastery decision may have become equivocal and testing would have to continue. This pattern is most likely to occur with examinees whose true ability is close to the cut score.

Control of Item Exposure

A major practical concern in any form of testing is the security of the items. This is particularly an issue for adaptive testing algorithms that strive to choose the optimal items for each examinee based on the current estimate of the examinee's ability and, if unconstrained, will tend to choose repeatedly the items with the best psychometric and content characteristics. If such adaptive tests were continually administered, over time the security of these items would be quickly compromised. Various methods have been developed to control the exposure of items without radically compromising the efficiency of the adaptive tests. Although the following methods have been developed for item-selection approaches, extension to testlets should be feasible.

A simple approach is the randomized item-selection strategy (Eignor et al., 1993; Fennessy & McKinley, 1991; Lord, 1977). The strategy is to identify the n most informative items at any given point in the construction of an examinee's test, rather than the single most informative item, and randomly choose from the set of n items. If the length of the test is not limited and the pool from which items are chosen has a sufficient number of items at all difficulty levels, this approach works reasonably well.

A probabilistic approach was developed by Sympson and Hetter (1985). This procedure defines the probability $P(S)$ that an item is selected by an optimally functioning item-selection algorithm and seeks to control the overall probability that an item is actually administered, $P(A)$, such that it remains below a target maximum rate of item usage. An exposure-control parameter for each item is calculated as the conditional probability the item will be administered given that it has been selected, $P(A|S)$. These values are determined through a series of simulations (described in Stocking, 1993) using an established test design and simulees drawn from a typical ability distribution. An adjustment to the exposure control parameters is made, by setting a few values to 1, to guarantee that a sufficient number of items and stimuli can be administered to create a complete adaptive test. The original Sympson–Hetter procedure controls item level exposure only. Stocking (1993) modified the procedure to control exposure for discrete items, items within sets, and stimuli.

Stocking and Lewis (1995a) formally defined a method that uses the multinomial distribution of operant conditional probabilities, sorted according to the desirability of the items and stimuli, given some item-selection model (e.g., the weighted deviations model). The operant conditional probabilities are defined as the probability that each item is administered given selection and the probability that the preceding items are rejected given selection. A parameter may also be set to control the degree to which item exposure is managed in relation to meeting the item-selection target constraints. Rather than a post hoc adjustment on the simple conditional probabilities (just described), the operant conditional probabilities are adjusted proportionally by dividing each value by the sum of the operant conditional probabilities. A further modification (Stocking & Lewis, 1995b) controls exposure conditional on ability.

Fixed-Length Versus Variable-Length Testing

The theoretical framework for CAT suggests tests of variable length can be administered to attain comparable score precision across the ability range. However, Stocking (1987) has demonstrated that bias may be introduced for certain ability estimates when variable-length testing is implemented. Most adaptive testing programs in place today have implemented fixed-length CATs, so that the number of items administered to each examinee is the same. This allows for more straightforward control of testing time limits and simpler scheduling of examinees for testing.

The test length is generally chosen to target a specified level of reliability and CSEM or to attain a target CSEM curve.

Time Limits

Although theory states that speeded tests are not appropriate for adaptive administration, time limits must still be set. It is generally thought that reasonable time limits can be set to enable 95% to 99% of the examinees to complete all items. However, even with the most generous time limits, there will always be some examinees who fail to complete the full set of items in the time allowed. If these examinees can obtain unfair advantage by devoting extra time to earlier items, some method of encouraging them to move through the test at an appropriate pace is needed. One possibility is that a specified number of item responses be required to receive a score on the test. Another possibility is to adjust the examinee's score proportional to the ratio of number of items completed to the number of items in the test; however, an adjustment like this could be severe, particularly for speeded tests. A final possibility is to estimate the score that would be obtained if the examinee had guessed at random on the unfinished items (Segall, 1988; Segall, Moreno, Bloxom, & Hetter, 1997).

Item Review and Omits

In a CAT, each scored response of an examinee contributes to the selection of subsequent items. Omits are theoretically undesirable in a CAT environment because they do not add any information to inform the item-selection process and because examinees can choose to omit until they find an item to which they know the answer. Similarly, if review is permitted, an examinee may change the response to a previous item such that the scored response changes, and, thus, the item-selection path that had been followed will become less than optimal. Neither omits nor item review are permitted in most CAT implementations. However, practitioners are aware of the desire by examinees to have these features available and research is proceeding on many fronts in an attempt to incorporate them in a manner consistent with the theory of adaptive testing (e.g., Stocking, 1997; Stone & Lunz, 1994; Wang & Wingersky, 1992; Wise, 1996).

With testlet-based administrations, item review can be readily incorporated within linearly administered testlets. Depending on the length of the testlet and the method of scoring, omits may be problematic but could perhaps be allowed. Omits would have to be scored as wrong responses, but some limit would be needed because it is undesirable to have too great a proportion of omits.

In LOFT, there is no psychometric reason to prohibit either omits or item review. The only consideration might be the reason for which LOFT was chosen in the first place. If item ordering is important for contextual reasons, it would be preferable for examinees to move through the test in the predetermined order. If this not too great a concern, examinees can be provided with control buttons to let them move forward and backward. It may be simplest to permit this level of movement only within a testlet or item block (e.g., a reading passage), although even that limitation is not psychometrically necessary.

For mastery tests that are variable length, a minimum number of testlets is usually required. Any testlets administered before this minimum number could be treated as a unit with review permitted up to this point. Any subsequent testlets could allow review within each testlet.

Multiple Cut Scores

Mastery tests are designed primarily to handle a single cut score, but SPRT (Spray, 1993) and CMT (Smith & Lewis, 1995) have both been extended to a multiple cut score situation. Multiple cut scores pose another challenge to methods that attempt to maximize information at the cut score. As the number of cut scores increases it is unclear where information should be maximized, and the information function becomes less peaked at any given cut point. One possible answer is computerized adaptive sequential testing (CAST; Luecht, 2000), where branching logic is built into the testlet-selection algorithm. The selection of the branching point can sometimes be a challenge, especially if the test is used to select examinees of distinction. In this case, sufficient numbers of difficult items must be administered to gain a stable estimate for a person of high ability. Because item pools usually are weakest in the high ability range, their routine use to assess whether an examinee is at the high end of the scale places exposure pressures on an already potentially overexposed portion of the item pool.

SUMMARY

Models for CBT delivery that have been developed and implemented to date are varied. In this chapter we reviewed three classes of approaches: CAT, which can be controlled at the item or testlet level; LOFT; and several models of CMT. Each has its strengths and challenges. Among the major issues for these models are item versus testlet delivery, control of item exposure, fixed- or variable-length testing, time limits, controls over item review and omit, and management of multiple cut scores in mastery testing. Although CBT is now an acknowledged alternative to paper-and-pencil testing, ongoing research is necessary to develop appropriate variations to meet the diverse, evolving needs of examinees, institutions, and other score users.

REFERENCES

Birnbaum, A. (1968). Some latent trait models and their use in inferring an examinee's ability. In F. M. Lord & M. R. Novick (Eds.), *Statistical theories of mental test scores* (pp. 397–479). Reading, MA: Addison-Wesley.

Bock, R. D. (1972). Estimating item parameters and latent ability when responses are scored in two or more nominal categories. *Psychometrika, 37,* 29–51.

Chang, H., & Ying, Z. (1996). A global information approach to computerized adaptive testing. *Applied Psychological Measurement, 20,* 213–229.

Chang, H., & Ying, Z. (1999). *a*-stratified multistage computerized adaptive testing. *Applied Psychological Measurement, 23,* 211–222.

Eggen, T. J. H. M. (1999). Item selection in adaptive testing with the Sequential Probability Ratio Test. *Applied Psychological Measurement, 23,* 249–261.

Eignor, D. R., Folk, V. G., Li, M., & Stocking, M. L. (1994, April). *Pinpointing Praxis I CAT characteristics through simulation procedures.* Paper presented at the annual meeting of the National Council on Measurement in Education, New Orleans, LA.

Eignor, D. R., Stocking, M. L., Way, W. D., & Steffen, M. (1993). *Case studies in computer adaptive test design through simulation* (ETS Research Report RR-93-56). Princeton, NJ: Educational Testing Service.

Fennessy, L. M., & McKinley, R. L. (1991). *Analysis of the effect of the randomized item selection technique on the accuracy of the θ and number-right estimation for the GRE computer adaptive test* (ETS Statistical Report SR-91-90). Princeton, NJ: Educational Testing Service.

Ferguson, G. A. (1942). Item selection by the constant process. *Psychometrika, 7,* 19–29.

Ferguson, R. L. (1969a). *Computer-assisted criterion-referenced measurement.* (Working paper No. 41). Pittsburgh, PA: University of Pittsburgh Learning and Research Development Center. (ERIC Document Reproduction No. ED 037 089).

Ferguson, R. L. (1969b). *The development, implementation, and evaluation of a computer-assisted branched test for a program of individually prescribed instruction.* Unpublished doctoral dissertation, University of Pittsburgh. (University Microfilms No. 70-4530).

Green, B. F. (1983). The promise of tailored tests. In H. Wainer & S. Messick (Eds.), *Principles of modern psychological measurement: A Festschrift for Frederic M. Lord* (pp. 69–80). Hillsdale, NJ: Lawrence Erlbaum Associates.

Green, B. F. (1988). Critical problems in computer-based psychological measurement. *Applied Measurement in Education, 1,* 223–231.

Green, B. F., Bock, R. D., Humphreys, L. G., Linn, R. L., & Reckase, M. D. (1984). Technical guidelines for assessing computerized adaptive tests. *Journal of Educational Measurement, 21,* 347–360.

Hambleton, R. K. (1986, February). *Effects of item order and anxiety on test performance and stress.* Paper presented at the annual meeting of the American Educational Research Association, Chicago.

Hambleton, R. K., Zaal, J. N., & Pieters, J. P. M. (1991). Computerized adaptive testing: Theory, applications, and standards. In R. K. Hambleton & J. N. Zaal (Eds.), *Advances in educational and psychological testing: Theory and applications* (pp. 341–366). Boston: Kluwer.

Hulin, C. L., Drasgow, F., & Parsons, C. K. (1983). *Item response theory: Application to psychological measurement*. Homewood, IL: Dow Jones-Irwin.

Jones, D. H. (1997, April). *Mathematical programming approaches to computerized adaptive testing*. Paper presented at the annual meeting of the National Council on Measurement in Education, Chicago.

Kingsbury, G. G., & Weiss, D. J. (1983). A comparison of IRT-based adaptive mastery testing and a sequential mastery testing procedure. In D. J. Weiss (Ed.), *New horizons in testing: Latent trait test theory and computerized adaptive testing* (pp. 257–283). New York: Academic Press.

Kingsbury, G. G., & Zara, A. R. (1989). Procedures for selecting items for computerized adaptive tests. *Applied Measurement in Education, 2*, 359–375.

Kingsbury, G. G., & Zara, A. R. (1991). A comparison of procedures for content-sensitive item selection in computerized adaptive tests. *Applied Measurement in Education, 3*, 241–261.

Lawley, D. N. (1943). On problems connected with item selection and test construction. *Recordings of the Royal Society of Edinburgh, 61*, 273–287.

Lawrence, I. M. (1995). *Estimating reliability for tests composed of item sets* (ETS Research Report RR-95-18). Princeton, NJ: Educational Testing Service.

Lewis, C., & Sheehan, K. (1990). Using Bayesian decision theory to design a computer mastery test. *Applied Psychological Measurement, 14*, 367–386.

Li, Y. H., & Lissitz, R. W. (1998, April). *An evaluation of multidimensional IRT equating methods by assessing the accuracy of transforming parameters onto a target metric*. Paper presented at the annual meeting of the National Council on Measurement in Education, San Diego, CA.

Lord, F. M. (1952). A theory of test scores. *Psychometric Monograph, 7*.

Lord, F. M. (1977). A broad-range tailored test of verbal ability. *Applied Psychological Measurement, 1*, 95–100.

Lord, F. M. (1980). *Applications of item response theory to practical problems*. Hillsdale, NJ: Lawrence Erlbaum Associates.

Lord, F. M. (1983). Unbiased estimates of ability parameters, of their variance, and their parallel form reliability. *Psychometrika, 48*, 233–245.

Luecht, R. M. (2000, April). *Implementing the computer-adaptive sequential testing (CAST) framework to mass produce high quality computer-adaptive and mastery tests*. Symposium paper presented at the Annual Meeting of the National Council on Measurement in Education, New Orleans, LA.

Masters, G. N. (1982). A Rasch model for partial credit scoring. *Psychometrika, 47*, 149–174.

Mills, C. N., & Stocking, M. L. (1996). Practical issues in large-scale computerized adaptive testing. *Applied Measurement in Education, 9*, 287–304.

Owen, R. J. (1975). A Bayesian sequential procedure for quantal response in the context of adaptive mental testing. *Journal of the American Statistical Association, 70*, 351–356.

Pashley, P. (1997, April). *An overview of the LSAC CAT Research Agenda*. Paper presented at the annual meeting of the National Council on Measurement in Education, Chicago.

Rasch, G. (1960). *Probabilistic models for some intelligence and attainment tests*. Copenhagen, Denmark: Denmark's Paedogogiske Institute.

Reckase, M. D. (1983a). A procedure for decision making using tailored testing. In D. J. Weiss (Ed.), *New horizons in testing: Latent trait test theory and computerized adaptive testing* (pp. 237–255). New York: Academic Press.

Reckase, M. D. (1983b, April). *The definition of difficulty and discrimination for multidimensional item response theory models*. Paper presented at the annual meeting of the American Educational Research Association, Montreal, Canada.

Reckase, M. D. (1985). The difficulty of test items that measure more than one ability. *Applied Psychological Measurement, 9*, 401–422.

Reckase, M. D., & McKinley, R. L. (1991). The discriminating power of items that measure more than one dimension. *Applied Psychological Measurement, 14*, 361–373.

Samejima, F. (1969). Estimation of latent ability using a response pattern of graded scores. *Psychometric Monograph, 17*.

Sands, W. A., Waters, B. K., & McBride, J. R. (Eds.). (1997). *Computerized adaptive testing: From inquiry to operation*. Washington, DC: American Psychological Association.

Segall, D. O. (1988). *A procedure for scoring incomplete adaptive tests in high stakes testing*. Unpublished manuscript, Navy Personnel Research and Development Center, San Diego, CA.

Segall, D. O. (1996). Multidimensional adaptive testing. *Psychometrika, 61*, 331–354.

Segall, D. O., Moreno, K. E., Bloxom, B. M., & Hetter, R. D. (1997). Psychometric procedures for administering CAT-ASVAB. In W. A. Sands, B. K. Waters, & J. R. McBride (Eds.), *Computerized adaptive testing: From inquiry to operation* (pp. 131–140). Washington, DC: American Psychological Association.

Sheehan, K., & Lewis, C. (1992). Computerized mastery testing with nonequivalent testlets. *Applied Psychological Measurement, 16*, 65–76.

Smith, R., & Lewis, C. (1995, April). *A Bayesian computerized mastery model with multiple cut scores*. Paper presented at the annual meeting of National Council on Measurement in Education, San Francisco, CA.

Smith, R., & Lewis, C. (1996, April). *A search procedure to determine sets of decision points when using testlet-based Bayesian sequential testing procedures*. Paper presented at the annual meeting of National Council on Measurement in Education, New York.

Smith, R., & Lewis, C. (1997, April). *Incorporating decision consistency into Bayesian sequential testing*. Paper presented at the annual meeting of National Council on Measurement in Education, Chicago, IL.

Smith, R., & Lewis, C. (1998, April). *Expected losses for individuals in computer mastery testing*. Paper presented at the annual meeting of National Council on Measurement in Education, San Diego, CA.

Spray, J. (1993). *Multiple-category classification using a sequential probability ratio test* (ACT Research Report RR-93-7). Iowa City, IA: American College Testing.

Spray, J. A., & Reckase, M. D. (1994, April). *The selection of test items for decision making with a computer adaptive test*. Paper presented at the annual meeting of National Council on Measurement in Education, New Orleans, LA.

Stocking, M. L. (1987). Two simulated feasibility studies in computerized adaptive testing. *Applied Psychology: An International Review, 36*, 263–277.

Stocking, M. L. (1993). *Controlling item exposure rates in a realistic adaptive testing paradigm* (ETS Research Report RR-93-2). Princeton, NJ: Educational Testing Service.

Stocking, M. L. (1994a). *Three practical issues for modern adaptive testing item pools* (ETS Research Report RR-94-5). Princeton, NJ: Educational Testing Service.

Stocking, M. L. (1994b). *An alternative method for scoring adaptive tests* (ETS Research Report RR-94-48). Princeton, NJ: Educational Testing Service.

Stocking, M. L. (1997). Revising item responses in computerized adaptive tests: A comparison of three models. *Applied Psychological Measurement, 21*, 129–142.

Stocking, M. L., & Lewis, C. (1995a). *A new method of controlling item exposure in computerized adaptive testing* (ETS Research Report RR-95-25). Princeton, NJ: Educational Testing Service.

Stocking, M. L., & Lewis, C. (1995b). *Controlling item exposure conditional on ability in computerized adaptive testing* (ETS Research Report RR-95-24). Princeton, NJ: Educational Testing Service.

Stocking, M. L., & Swanson, L. (1993). A method for severely constrained item selection in adaptive testing. *Applied Psychological Measurement, 17,* 277–292.

Stocking, M. L., Swanson, L., & Pearlman, M. (1993). Application of an automated item selection method to real data. *Applied Psychological Measurement, 17,* 167–176.

Stone, G. E., & Lunz, M. E. (1994). The effect of review on the psychometric characteristics of computerized adaptive tests. *Applied Measurement in Education, 7,* 211–222.

Swanson, L., & Stocking, M. L. (1993). A model and heuristic for solving very large item selection problems. *Applied Psychological Measurement, 17,* 151–166.

Sympson, J. B., & Hetter, R. D. (1985). Controlling item-exposure rates in computerized adaptive testing. *Proceedings of the 27th annual meeting of the Military Testing Association.* San Diego, CA: Navy Personnel Research Development Center.

Tatsuoka, K. K., & Tatsuoka, M. M. (1997). Computerized cognitive diagnostic adaptive testing: Effect on remedial instruction as validation. *Journal of Educational Measurement, 34,* 3–20.

Thissen, D., Steinberg, L., & Mooney, J. A. (1989). Trace lines for testlets: A use of multiple-categorical-response models. *Journal of Educational Measurement, 26,* 247–260.

van der Linden, W. J. (1998a). Optimal assembly of psychological and educational tests. *Applied Psychological Measurement, 22,* 195–211.

van der Linden, W. J. (1998b). *Bayesian item selection criteria for adaptive testing.* Unpublished manuscript.

van der Linden, W. J., & Reese, L. M. (1998). An optimal model for constrained adaptive testing. *Applied Psychological Measurement, 22,* 259–270.

Vos, H. J. (1997). *Applications of Bayesian decision theory to sequential mastery testing.* (Research Report No. 97-06). Enschede, The Netherlands: University of Twente.

Wainer, H. (1992). *Some practical considerations when converting a linearly administered test to an adaptive format* (ETS Research Report RR-92-13). Princeton, NJ: Educational Testing Service.

Wainer, H., & Kiely, G. L. (1987). Item clusters and computerized adaptive testing: A case for testlets. *Journal of Educational Measurement, 24,* 185–201.

Wainer, H., & Lewis, C. (1990). Toward a psychometrics for testlets. *Journal of Educational Measurement, 27,* 1–14.

Wald, A. (1947). *Sequential analysis.* New York: Wiley.

Wang, M. M., & Wingersky, M. (1992, April). *Incorporating post-administration item response revisions into a CAT.* Paper presented at the annual meeting of the American Educational Research Association, San Francisco.

Weiss, D. J. (1982). Improving measurement quality and efficiency with adaptive testing. *Applied Psychological Measurement, 6,* 473–492.

Wingersky, M. S. (1983). LOGIST: A program for computing maximum likelihood procedures for logistic test models. In R. K. Hambleton (Ed.), *Applications of item response theory* (pp. 45–56). Vancouver, BC: Educational Research Institute of British Columbia.

Wise, S. L. (1996, April). *A critical analysis of the arguments for and against item review in computerized adaptive testing.* Paper presented at the annual meeting of the National Council on Measurement in Education, New York.

Test Models for Complex CBT

Richard M. Luecht
University of North Carolina at Greensboro

Brian E. Clauser
National Board of Medical Examiners

INTRODUCTION

During the early part of this century, the move to paper-and-pencil tests based on fixed-format item types defined a highly focused context for psychometric research. The result has been the proliferation of test models that provide evaluators with important analysis and psychometric scaling tools. These tools have, however, been developed in a specific, limited context where items are produced in mass quantities, inexpensively published, efficiently delivered, and accurately scored using scanner technology. These large-scale test production capabilities and features have affected the nature of the test models used. For example, the predominance of multiple-choice items has led to the development and study of IRT models for scaling and equating dichotomous data (e.g., Hambleton & Swaminathan, 1985; Lord, 1980; Lord & Novick, 1968). By comparison, psychometric models for polytomous data have received considerably less attention—at least before the recent proliferation of performance and writing assessments—and models for other types of data or information are rare, indeed.

There seems to be a significant lack of research into methods for extracting valid and reliable data from complex interactions between examinees and tasks. With multiple-choice items, there is little need to extract and score anything beyond the response to each item (i.e., matching the response against a single answer key). Holistic scoring and other applications of partial credit or polytomous scoring schemes have been devised to contend with more complicated data. Unfortunately, the development of reliable and discriminating scoring protocols, rater inconsistencies, and other problems with human judgment are continual concerns. It is not clear how successful these holistic approaches are in extracting the optimal measurement information from complex interactions between examinees and elaborated response performance tasks.

Little attention has been devoted to understanding how aspects of test construction and instrument design directly affect outcomes for particular examinees (e.g., exploring and experimentally manipulating the antecedents of item and task difficulty and complexity). Instead, we seem content to rely on the response data to tell us everything about the characteristics of the items, such as, how difficult each item is and what the test measures indicate. For example, when building multiple-choice tests, it is common to select the items to meet a particular aggregate statistical criterion such as a target item average difficulty level or a minimum reliability coefficient. We may further control for certain surface features such as content balance, word counts, or other categorical features. However, we seldom understand enough about the items to select items that would alter certain context effects for a target group of examinees, nor do we have sound research advice about ways to alter the task complexity to discriminate between different knowledge states or processing strategies of learners. Targeting task difficulty and task complexity is a systematic and powerful way to optimize measurement information (an argument similar to those recommending CAT; see Weiss & Kingsbury, 1984).

In this chapter we focus on complex computerized exercises and tasks as potential sources of measurement information. What we need to develop are ways to exploit that information. Complex exercises may appear less economical to design and produce than multiple-choice items, on the surface. They are more time-consuming to administer, leading to the occasional criticism that tests made up of these types of exercises are too short to yield reliable scores. If we limit ourselves to extracting trivial information from these exercises or information that could be equally well obtained from multiple-choice tests, their implementation will seem wasteful from a production perspective and an inefficient use of examinee testing time from a reliability perspective. The challenge is to effectively gather, codify, and use the different kinds of information the computer can produce.

Throughout this review, a recurrent theme is the importance of appropriately considering the purpose of testing within the context of test design, data collection and transformation, and psychometric scaling to produce outcome measures or decisions. The principal consideration is developing an assessment to support the intended inferences and interpretations. The design of the computerized exercises, the methods used for data collection and scoring, and the selection of an appropriate psychometric scaling model should directly relate to the test purpose.

Another recurrent theme is the importance of considering each item or exercise as an experiment. The examinee is the subject in the experiment. Good experimental design requires careful decisions about which aspects of the experiment can and should be controlled, which aspects should be measured and used as covariates in analysis, and which aspects should be randomly sampled in large quantities and treated as residual error. A stronger research agenda seems necessary to understand the conditions of measurement that lead to different outcomes for individuals who are at different levels of proficiency or who are at qualitatively different states of understanding or development. Cognitive psychology has provided a start, but more work is needed.

A computerized assessment can be a potential source of vast amounts of information. Complex interactive exercises—including virtual reality simulations and multimedia applications—provide a wide range of possibilities for actively engaging the examinee in the assessment process. Every keystroke or mouse click, every referencing action, every response, and every elapsed unit of time is a possible source of valid information. Furthermore, the computer is an accurate and relentless data recorder. However, complex computer exercises can be expensive to develop and time consuming to administer. The challenge is to find ways to maximize or at least target the amount of dependable information gathered from a limited number of computerized exercises for a particular measurement purpose.

Maximizing or targeting information implies going beyond traditional psychometric theories and models that adopt a strictly statistical view of information (e.g., CAT, which selects items to provide the maximum score precision at a provisional estimate of the examinee's latent trait score, or CMT, which maximizes score precision in the region of the pass–fail cut point). Statistical information implies precision. The variance of a scoring function (Birnbaum, 1968; Lehman, 1983) and the cumulative nature of statistical information over independent items or tasks lead to the sometimes equivocal conclusion that adding more tasks or items is the best way to optimize the amount of information obtained. Here we suggest there is a challenge to assume a broader view of information as a valuable commodity that can be systematically gathered and creatively used to optimize the accuracy of measurement decisions. Complex computerized exercises only become excessively expensive or time consuming if we gather trivial information or mistargeted information, or limit the potential information obtained through our test development, scoring, or scaling procedures.

AN EVALUATION FRAMEWORK FOR TEST DESIGN AND ANALYSIS

The remainder of this chapter provides a framework for evaluating information needs in a comprehensive sense. We present four aspects of test design and analysis that affect the nature and use of information: (a) the test purpose and use of outcomes, (b) task complexity and instrument design, (c) methods of collecting and codifying the raw data, and (d) structural modeling and procedures for psychometrically scaling the raw data. There appears to be a need for greater integration between how information is perceived during test development and instrument design and how it is ultimately analyzed and used.

The Test Purpose and Use of Outcomes

The test purpose defines the nature of the information gathered and its use. Tests are often called on to fulfill a myriad of purposes, many of which far exceed the original intent of the test designers. Sometimes we need scores or score profiles; other times we only need discrete mastery or competency decisions. Sometimes the examinee population is limited to a well-defined homogeneous group; other times the population is expansive and may extend across multiple grades, cultures, and so on. Each new or altered test purpose or use of the test outcomes makes increasing demands on the available information.

The data constitute a finite information resource that can only be stretched and pulled in so many ways before something has to give. For example, when a policy mandates that proficiency scores have to be reported on a CMT, designed to have maximum score precision in the region of the pass–fail cut point, there are predictable trade-offs that can affect test design and the precision of the outcome indicators, or both. If the test is designed to maximize score precision at the pass–fail cut point, scores farthest from the cut point may be poorly estimated, especially if the test is relatively short. Altering the design of the targeted statistical characteristics to spread out the score information over a wider range of proficiency may sacrifice some precision at the pass–fail mastery cut point.

We also need to consider purposes other than producing gross proficiency scores, ability profiles, summative achievement levels, or global competency decisions (Glaser, 1963, 1973). Computerized exercises and simulations are powerful measurement technologies for conducting formative assessments and exploring modern theories of cognition and learning. Cognitive psychology, in particular, has challenged us to create assessments that uncover what the learner understands to guide instruction (Anderson, 1983, Mislevy, 1989, 1993, Ragosa, 1991, Siegler, 1986, Snow, 1989; Snow & Lohman, 1993; Sternberg, 1984). For example, a gross proficiency score on a 100-item fourth-grade mathematics test is less useful to instruction than understanding specific deficits or faults in students' attention, knowledge, rules, schemas, or problem-solving strategies. Information needs for cognitive assessments often extend to distinguishing between qualitatively different states of the learner, given differential task requirements and experimentally controlled conditions of measurement (Mislevy, 1989, 1993; Snow & Lohman, 1993).

The implication for developing complex computerized testing seems straightforward. If we keep the test's purpose focused on a well-defined, singular set of assessment outcomes, we may be able to target our test and exercise design efforts, our methods of gathering data, and our procedures for psychometrically scaling the results toward maximizing the precision of those outcomes. The focus needs to stay on maximizing decision-making information in a particular measurement context. In some contexts, information needs defined by this focus will call for collecting additional information of the same type. In other contexts, the demand will call for collecting additional kinds of information (Cronbach & Gleser, 1957; van der Linden, 1998). There is nothing in this perspective that is incompatible with traditional psychometric thinking. However, the operationalization of what constitutes "information" may need to be broadened to encompass validity as well as reliability considerations.

Task Complexity and Instrument Design

Task complexity generally refers to the item or exercise difficulty and other factors that directly or indirectly affect the performance of examinees. This definition implies more than an unconditional proportion correct statistic or a vector of IRT item parameter estimates (Hambleton & Swaminathan, 1985; Lord, 1980). A computerized exercise or simulation is essentially a set of experimental conditions that can be knowingly or unwittingly manipulated to elicit one or more responses or actions. The responses or actions may vary as a function of one or more underlying abilities or proficiency states, and the difficulty and task demands may be different for different examinees.

Within the computerized environment, we can systematically increase the nature and amount of interaction to present more than a simple stimulus–response relation. For example, it makes sense to use the computer as far more than an electronic "page turner" to display multiple-choice or short-answer items and collect responses. We can further provide opportunities for examinees to transition through different pathways in the exercise and may even engage the examinees in auxiliary actions such as using online reference materials or creatively manipulating a "toolbox" to solve a series of problems. The potential repertoire of interface and stimulus materials seems almost limitless. It is also within our purview, as test designers, to manipulate time as a condition of difficulty or complexity (i.e.,we can induce speededness, where speed is determined to be a critical component of performance) or to simply monitor time or response latencies. Finally, we can create highly interactive and complex performance simulations involving virtual realism to submerge the examinee in the task environment (e.g., a flight simulator).

An example of a complex computerized assessment is the Primum® Computer Case Simulation (CCS) Project (formerly known as CBX), developed by the National Board of Medical Examiners[1] (NBME; Clyman, Melnick, & Clauser, 1995). The simulation exercises require the examinee to clinically manage a patient's case starting with only a set of presenting symptoms. For example, an individual case may present as follows: "A 65-year-old man comes to your office complaining of chest pain and is having trouble breathing." The examinee, as the physician, has control over ordering diagnostic tests, treatments, and therapies. Each case takes about 20 minutes to complete. The physician/examinee enters orders and initiates actions using various user interfaces, including a free-format text input "order sheet" (see Fig. 3.1) and a "history and physical" order sheet form (Fig. 3.2). In addition to real testing time, the system simulates chronology within the case and the physician/examinee can decide when to see the patient again or when to initiate various actions (e.g., to schedule a follow-up office visit in one week). Finally, the physician can respond to or ignore certain events that occur as a natural part of the case; for example, at some point, the system informs the examinee/physician the patient is having more trouble breathing. There is no cued sequence of events. Therefore, the physician/examinee can misdiagnose a case or mismanage a case and perform unexpected or dangerous actions.

The Primum CCS cases are complicated and highly interactive problem-solving exercises. The test's purpose to assess clinical patient management proficiency is reflected in each exercise by presenting a case and requiring the examinee to manage it. Although multimedia and virtual reality components and capabilities have not yet been added to the software, expansions of this sort seem inevitable.

---

[1]Primum is a registered trademark of the National Board of Medical Examiners.

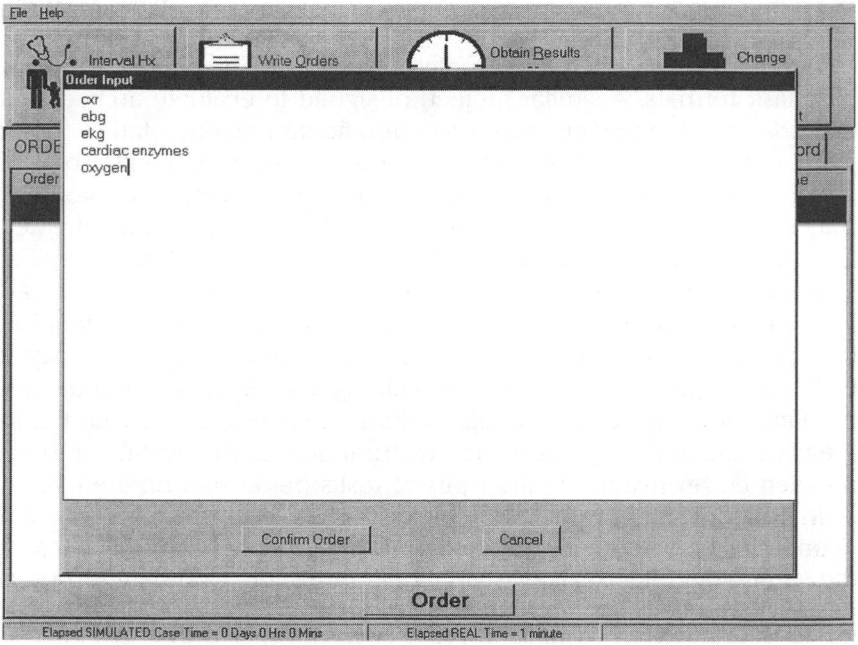

FIG. 3.1. A sample Primum CCS order screen.

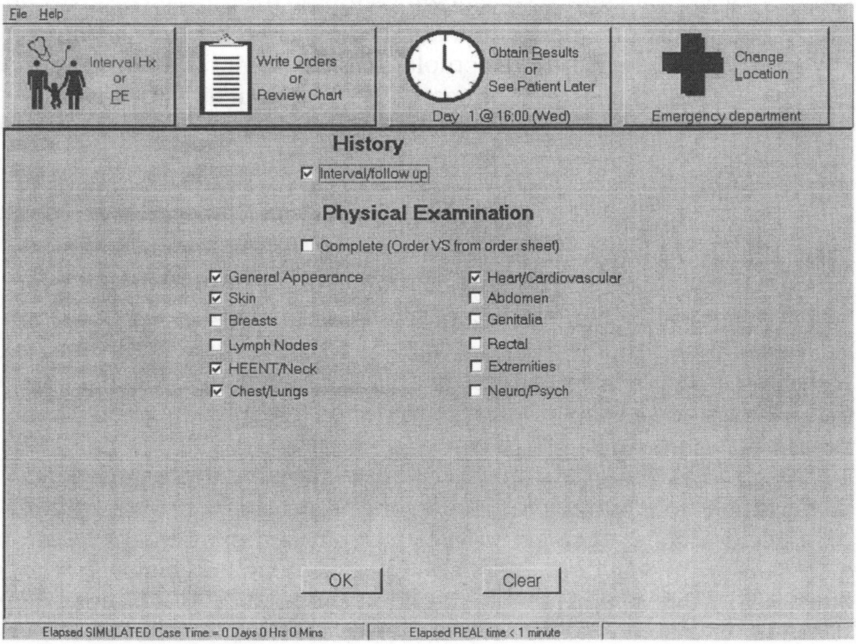

FIG. 3.2. A sample Primum CCS screen for ordering history and physical test results.

73

Primum CCS is only one example of using computers to deliver complex task formats. A similar project, designed to evaluate architectural candidates, has recently moved to operational implementation (Bejar, 1991, 1995). With this assessment, the examinee is called on to solve architectural problems online using a computer interface. The problems may require the examinee to design a layout for buildings and other features (e.g., swimming pool, parking lot, etc.) to fit within a specified space and meet stated constraints (e.g., the swimming pool must be adjacent to the club house). Alternatively, the examinees may be required to design a floor plan, again meeting specified constraints, or they may be called on to grade an area around a building to allow for appropriate run-off. One attractive feature of this evaluation system is that with the increasing use of computers in architectural design, the evaluation bears an even closer relation to the types of tasks performed on the job.

In designing these types of complex exercises or simulations, practical economics need to be considered. Creating complexity simply because the technology allows it is wasteful of either test development resources or the examinee's time, or both. It is important to continually re-evaluate the task complexity within the context of the test's purpose. This re-evaluation needs to be more than a cursory consideration of the face validity of the test or vaguely matching the task components and case features to a list of categorical specifications for the exercises. The task complexity should provide the appropriate information for the test's purpose.

As exercises become more complex, it seems important to determine and manipulate, if possible, the features and characteristics that govern difficulty and task complexity. Although the challenge may seem daunting, consider a simple, real-life example. In many computerized video games, changing the quantity, speed, and weaponry of the attacking "aliens," while simultaneously altering the player's protection and weaponry, effectively allows the game to serve as a criterion-referenced, skill mastery test. The entry level is usually selected by the player and the criteria for success or failure are plainly spelled out. Were it only that simple in educational or other testing situations to design computerized tasks with easily manipulable features of task difficulty and complexity to attain a prescribed level of mastery or to denote a particular level of understanding. Perhaps it is.

It is not that we are incapable of understanding the antecedents of task difficulty, but rather, we seem to choose not to invest in the effort of carefully designing each exercise as a controlled experiment meant to distinguish between competent and incompetent individuals, between qualitatively different states of examinee preparation or learner understanding, or between levels of proficiency or achievement.

The dilemma is that when we design items or tasks with no knowledge of the measurement conditions or processing requirements imposed by the experiment, we ultimately may need to determine those conditions in an ad hoc manner and use them to statistically control for the task difficulty and other performance characteristics of the items. This leads to the traditional view of item difficulty as a simple, ordinal function of the scored responses to the item by a sample or population of examinees (Horst, 1933). An IRT item calibration is also an example of this type of statistical control. The item difficulty and discrimination parameters are estimated from the raw data, ignoring any prior information about the experimental conditions that each item introduces for different examinees. The cost of estimating the item statistics from the data is lost information, manifest in the estimation process itself (IRT parameter invariance assumptions notwithstanding).

In some exceptions methods of predicting item difficulties directly or indirectly from item features have met with some success (e.g., Chalifour & Powers, 1988; Drum, Calfee, & Cook, 1981; Mislevy, 1987; Scheuneman, Gerritz, & Embretson, 1989). However, the normal psychometric approach requires a matrix of dichotomous or polytomous scored responses as the exclusive source of information to estimate the characteristics of the items or tasks and the performance characteristics or state of the learner. By empirically investigating other sources of relevant information about task complexity and difficulty (e.g., Chalifour & Powers, 1988; Drum et al., 1981; Embretson, 1984; Fischer, 1983; Fischer & Pipp, 1984; Flavell, 1984; Kirsch & Mosenthal, 1988; Mislevy, 1987; Scheuneman et al., 1989), we can accumulate additional information useful in designing tests or in scaling the data to obtain outcomes appropriate to the test's purpose.

Data Collection and Raw Scoring

Maximizing measurement information presumes that all of the potential sources of dependable and valid information have been considered. There are many types of raw data that can be acquired by the computer. Some examples include the following: (a) examinee selections from option lists, reordering lists, or clicking the mouse on displayed objects or areas of the screen (including "drag-and-drop" alternatives); (b) open-ended examinee responses to questions or prompts (including short answers or long essays); (c) graphical entries such as drawing lines, circles, and so on; (d) speech entries or other sound sources such as a musical keyboard; (e) series of transitional events or actions tracked by the computer (e.g., a log of screens or menus used to initiate some activity or the process of rotating on-screen a three-dimensional image for some purpose); (f) creating and running programs or other software applications; (g) countable auxiliary actions such as the number of times the examinee consults an online reference or uses an online calculator; and (h) response latencies or elapsed time. There are many other possibilities.

The challenge is not necessarily in gathering and storing data (with the exception of pragmatic concerns such as file size storage or transmission limitations for certain types of raw data). The real challenge is how to filter, encode, smooth and raw score the data to retain as much information as necessary for subsequent use, that is, to be combined to produce the outcome results. It is during this data encoding, transformation, and raw scoring phase where information can be lost through arbitrary or careless data reduction or error added (e.g., by using fallible human judges to rate score performances).

To date, most psychometric and technological testing research has focused on scoring or encoding simple responses. Multiple-choice item formats provide a simple one-to-one relation between item responses and item scores. Many computer-delivered, constructed-response item types fit this approach well. Even when the superficial characteristics of the response is unspecified, the computer may be used to evaluate underlying forms and match the response to a key (Bennett, Steffen, Singley, Morley, & Jacquemin, 1997). Incremental polytomous scores are also popular with constructed-response items and certain simple types of performance assessments. The formulating-hypothesis item type presented by Kaplan and Bennett (1994) provides an interesting example of an item type scored with this approach. The examinee is presented with a scenario and is asked to provide credible hypotheses that might explain the described conditions. The hypotheses are entered as free text using the keyboard. The computer then reduces the entries to a form that can be matched to a key and sums the number of matches for the examinee within each scenario.

For more interactive exercises and where the universe of important actions can be defined, binary vectors (i.e., strings of zeros and ones) can be used to denote which actions were triggered. Options on this encoding scheme include storing a vector of sequence numbers (default = zero) to indicate the order in which actions occurred and storing frequency counts to indicate how often particular actions were performed, or both.

More complex responses require either complicated scoring rules and algorithms or human intervention in the scoring process to provide appropriate raw performance scores or ratings (e.g., polytomous holistic scores assigned by some rubric on a five- or seven-point scale). Here, the reliability of applying the scoring rules needs to be considered across potential sources of error (e.g., judges, occasions). For example, using human judges to holistically score performances can be time consuming and costly and can add error to the data. Recently, promising gains have

been made in automated scoring of open-ended responses and essays
(e.g., Breland & Lytle, 1990; Burstein, Kaplan, Wolff, & Lu, 1997; Page &
Petersen, 1995). Automated, analytical scoring using "policy capturing"
to approximate the holistic scoring rules and weights of expert human
raters has demonstrated promise as an effective way of jointly scoring
open-ended examinee responses and actions for the NBME's Primum
CCS Project (Clauser, Margolis, Clyman, & Ross, 1997). Bejar (1991, 1995)
has reported similarly promising results in encoding expert policies to
evaluate responses to architectural problems. Assuming the automated
scoring process maintains the validity of the information, these techniques will help improve the reliability of the data-encoding and raw-
scoring process.

Event sequence data related to examinee processing or problem-
solving strategies, countable auxiliary actions, and response-time information have received less research attention, especially in relating these
quantities to test purposes and incorporating the measures in psychometric scaling. (However, sequencing of actions and placement of actions within a time reference is an important aspect of scoring Primum
CCS [Clauser et al., 1997].) It is difficult to codify complicated and possibly interdependent data. The signal in the data can be difficult to filter
from the noise. In fact, future research may need to explore fast Fourier
transforms (FFTs) or other filtering and smoothing techniques to process
some of these types of data streams.

One of the inherent challenges in developing complex exercises and
scoring protocols is understanding the trade-offs between task complexity and scoring simplicity. Potentially informative exercises or tasks can
be made artificial or oversimplified to facilitate scoring. Information can
also be selectively ignored to simplify scoring. Table 3.1 provides a summary of 11 existing computerized exercises that illustrate some of these
challenges and trade-offs. From the combined perspective of task complexity and scoring simplicity, these exercise formats provide examples
of the integrative challenges needed in designing realistic tasks and feasible scoring methods. The first column in Table 3.1 lists the general skill
measured by each exercise, followed by a description of the stimulus
provided to the examinees, the nature of the task or problem presented,
the type of response(s) elicited from the examinees, the type of scoring
used, and the original research citations.

The first two exercise formats in Table 3.1—writing and computer programming—are examples in which task complexity was artificially constrained to simplify scoring. In the computer programming example, the
authors stated the format was developed to approximate the challenge
presented in the unconstrained programming task originally described
by Bennett et al. (1990). The constrained version—that is, the version that

TABLE 3.1
Examples of Computerized Tasks (With Citations)

Skill	Stimulus	Task	Response	Scoring	Citation
Writing	Essay containing usage errors	Correct embedded errors	Select section containing error and choose from correction choices provided	Match to key identifying correct changes and incorrect changes to correct passages	Davey et al., 1997
Computer programming	Program containing errors	Correct embedded errors	Modify text using keyboard	Match to key identifying correct changes and incorrect changes to correct passages	Braun, Bennett, Frye, & Soloway, 1990
Mathematical reasoning	Written description of a relationship	Produce mathematical expression representing the relationship	Manipulate a palette of numerical and mathematical symbols to create expression	Reduce expression to a common form and match to key	Bennett et al., 1997
Mathematical reasoning	Written description of conditions	Produce example that meets conditions	Manipulate palette or keyboard to enter expression of numeric values	Sequentially check example against enumerated conditions	Bennett, Morley, & Quardt, 1998
Mathematical reasoning	Written description of conditions	Produce graphical representation that meets conditions	Manipulate graphical interface to produce example	Sequentially check example against enumerated conditions	Bennett et al., 1998

Construct	Stimulus	Task	Response mode	Scoring	Reference
Hypothesis formulation	Written scenario	Formulate hypotheses to explain the scenario	Free text entry	Reduce expression to a common form and match to key and count matches	Kaplan & Bennett, 1994
Patient management	Description of patient including dynamic feedback following examinee actions	Manage patient	Make entries on order sheet using standard keyboard	Complex algorithmic scoring designed to approximate expert judgment of overall performance	Clauser et al., 1997
Architectural problem solving	Description of architectural problem	Create design to meet problem specifications	Use computerized drafting equipment to create design	Complex algorithmic scoring	Bejar, 1995
Writing skills	Prompt describing topic for essay	Write essay	Free text entry	Complex algorithmic scoring	Burstein, Kukich, Wolff, & Lu, 1998
Computer programming	Description of required computer program	Write program	Free text entry	Complex algorithmic scoring	Bennett et al., 1990
Quantitative representation	Prototype and sample quantitative problems	Match sample problems to prototypes based on features such as principle required for solution or form of equation required for solution	Enter sample numbers in box associated with appropriate prototype	Match entered numbers to key	Bennett & Sebrechts, 1997

required correcting errors instead of independently developing a computer program—was created because of the difficulty of producing a computer scoring mechanism to accurately evaluate the unconstrained problem. Merely correcting errors in existing computer program code (i.e., debugging computer code) and writing a program are different tasks. Although debugging existing computer code might be another proficiency of interest, in this case, assessment of the desired proficiency was sacrificed to simplify scoring.

The writing assessment presented by Davey, Goodwin, and Mettelholtz (1997) appears to be a similar case. The desired proficiency of interest is essay writing. The surrogate task is a proofreading exercise that greatly simplifies scoring but sacrifices information relevant to measuring writing proficiency. The free-format writing exercises and algorithmic scoring research described by Burstein et al. (1997) attempt to avoid that type of trade-off.

The five mathematical reasoning and hypothesis formulation tasks described in Table 3.1 represent examples of exercise formats developed to measure abstract, quantitative reasoning proficiencies. The exercises allow the examinees to engage in a complex interaction to produce a particular result or product (e.g., an equation). The scoring mechanisms use a type of pattern-matching protocol to convert the responses into exercise-level scores that provide information about the proficiency of interest. However, some information is still intentionally ignored, namely, the process information related to arriving at the final result or product. That is, the scoring mechanisms selectively reduce the available information to one or more numerical scores derived from pattern matching the result or product against a list of conditions.

The medical patient-management and architectural problem-solving exercises compromise by using simulations to mimic work sample exercises and simplify scoring by attending to selective information. That is, these exercise formats allow the examinee to demonstrate proficiency, but the tasks themselves are abstracted. Patient-management simulation is meant to capture one aspect of the knowledge and reasoning required of a physician. As such, it represents only certain aspects of the real-life activity of the physician (e.g., the examinee does not have to conduct a physical examination to acquire physical findings). Similarly, the architectural problems represent only part of the overall design task that the architect may be called on to perform on the job. Scoring is likewise simplified to attend to critical components within the entire task (e.g., predetermined, critical actions omitted by the examinee in managing the patient).

It is not our intent to be critical of any of the examples described in Table 3.1. Each new attempt moves us closer to better exercises and scoring. Rather, it is important to realize that when trade-offs are made for the sake of efficiency, cost, or simplicity, we often sacrifice or selectively constrain our acquisition of important and useful data or even alter the nature of the assessment or the intended proficiency.

Data collection, transformation, and raw scoring can be further constrained by the psychometric models used for scaling the data (discussed in the following section). Limitations in the estimation capabilities or restrictions on the structural complexity of a psychometric scaling model should not preclude mixing or combining different types of dependent measures, nor should the models impose arbitrary information reduction such as requiring integer scores as the input data. Unfortunately, the reality is that our current psychometric models, especially models for which reliable analysis software exists, often impose restrictions on the type of data that can be handled.

Structural Complexity and Psychometric Scaling

It is interesting to note how much research has been devoted over the past several decades to designing an impressive array of mathematical models (e.g., van der Linden & Hambleton, 1997) as the almost singular focus in developing a comprehensive theory of testing. As Goldstein and Wood (1989) have noted, however, there is little substantive theory—other than statistical theory about the asymptotic behavior of large amounts of data or properties of large sample estimators—relevant to most of the common IRT or latent trait theories. These models are mathematical functions for estimating a particular statistical representation or structure of a data set. The information is in the data set, not in the model. For example, the well-known unidimensional 2P IRT model (e.g., Birnbaum, 1968) characterizes the expected number of correct responses to a dichotomously scored item as a function of some unobserved latent trait, denoted θ, if the structural parameters, which characterize the item's difficulty and discriminating power, are known. In practice, the structural parameters are not known and must be estimated along with the latent traits from a data set of zeros and ones.

The caution here is to avoid ascribing any theoretical substance to a model or to let psychometric modeling completely drive measurement. There are serious implications when models are allowed to restrict the types of data collected or items measured. Complex computerized tests potentially yield a great deal of dependable raw information. Some of that data is response based; other data may be related to process activities, such as time on task or response latencies. In short, the data are there or can be acquired by the test administration software. The question is, can we codify and scale them?

Our intent is not to be critical about the current array of psychometric models, where complex computerized tests are involved. New models will evolve. However, it seems important to point out that the information is there, even for current complex computerized tests, to support a wide range of measurement decisions and contexts. But that information is a valuable commodity and we need to decide how to extract and use it wisely (i.e., we may need to become diamond cutters instead of rock crushers).

If the purpose of testing is simply to produce global proficiency scores, ability profiles, score summative achievement levels, or gross decisions about competency or mastery, simple, unidimensional IRT models like the 1P, 2P, or 3P models may be highly utilitarian (Mislevy, 1993). These types of IRT models are generally economical to implement, are relatively robust to common misfit problems (as far as rank ordering examinees is concerned), have parameters that can be estimated with reasonably small sample sizes, provide clear mechanisms to equate results over time, and can be tied into traditional standard-setting techniques to implement mastery or competency testing. Perhaps most important, convenient computer software is available to carry out the necessary calibrations.

Similarly, if the data can be reliably reduced to a set of ordered integer ratings or polytomous scores, any number of IRT models for polytomous data can be applied (e.g., Andrich, 1978; Masters, 1982; Muraki, 1992; Samejima, 1969, 1972; Thissen & Steinberg, 1986), assuming a test purpose involving measuring global proficiencies or reporting gross competency decisions In fact, by including both a guessing parameter and a scoring function in the generalized partial credit model, Muraki & Ankenmann (1993) have managed to devise a model that makes the 3P model a special instance and that handles both dichotomous and polytomous data. Their model has been effectively implemented in jointly calibrating sets of dichotomously and polytomously scored items on the Test of English as a Foreign Language (TOEFL; Tang & Eignor, 1997).

Modeling raw data other than discrete integer item, task, and exercise scores has been more challenging. Approaches such as Thissen's (1983) model for response times or Schnipke and Scrams' (1997) mixture model seem promising for scaling examinees or making gross competency decisions when speed is a critical factor in the assessment.

For broad-based, nomothetic profiles of ability, it may be advantageous to exploit the explainable covariance (i.e., shared information) in a data set to estimate a multidimensional vector of abilities (e.g., Bock, Gibbons, & Muraki, 1988; Glas, 1992; McDonald, 1982, 1997; Reckase, 1985). Segall (1996) and Luecht (1996) demonstrated variations on using multidimensional modeling to improve the reliability of subscore profiles in CAT contexts. One important caveat is needed: As we add structural parameters, realize the psychometric model becomes more information intensive (Luecht & Miller, 1992; Miller, 1991). There may be identifiability and rotational issues to consider (McDonald, 1982). We further need to confirm that a particular multidimensional psychometric model is the most appropriate structural parameterization of the data for the stated purpose of the test and, if so, whether the model parameters can be estimated accurately enough to support consistent decisions or uses of the outcomes, possibly over time. As a counterexample, estimating a complex multidimensional structure for a CMT that only reports pass–fail outcomes seem grossly inefficient.

In a related vein, but from a cognitive psychology perspective, Embretson (1984, 1993), Fischer (1983, 1993), and Samejima (1995) have introduced models that allow skills, knowledge, or processing strategies to be profiled as components associated with subtasks or subprocesses in a complex exercise. Embretson's model, which is an extension of the Rasch IRT model, allows the complexities to be decomposed from an overall performance score and separately weighted for each component subtask or subprocess. Similarly, Samejima's model incorporates an acceleration parameter that likewise weights the subprocesses or subtasks. Wilson's (1989) Saltus model is another extension of the Rasch model that allows for discontinuous change, based on substantive theory as to where the discontinuities occur.

Finally, there appears to be a resurgence of interest in uses of latent class analysis (LCA; e.g., Luecht & DeChamplain, 1998; Yamamoto & Gitomer, 1993). Latent class models (Bergan, 1983; Clogg & Goodman, 1985; Dayton & Macready, 1976, 1980; Goodman, 1974, 1975) can be used to distinguish between two or more qualitatively different (i.e., discontinuous) latent states. Applications to mastery and CBT are clear; however, LCA has also shown promise in representing salient latent categories denoting a learner's state of understanding, given a particular set of tasks (e.g., Yamamoto & Gitomer, 1993). LCA tends to require few modeling assumptions about the nature of the underlying class structures or about the relations among the responses and improved estimation methods. The primary limitations in implementing LCA have involved technical estimation complexities, but promising solutions are on the horizon (e.g., Hanson, 1998).

Within any scaling approach, there are model fit and estimation considerations. When a model misfits the data, it seems reasonable to evaluate both how the model was constructed and how the data were sampled and produced (or reduced). Selecting the best psychometric scaling model is an empirical, not theoretical, issue. The rule of parsimony dictates that one choose the least complicated model that gets the job done.

When information is at a premium, there may be practical benefits as well from selecting simpler models (e.g., fewer parameters to estimate), provided the outcomes directly relate to the test's purpose.

CONCLUSIONS

Complex computerized assessments provide some potential to test examinees for many purposes. There are too many possibilities to catalog. One thing is clear. Some of these exercises and simulations are expensive to produce and time consuming to administer. If exercises are poorly or ambiguously designed, or if the information provided by the exercises is improperly managed, this type of testing can appear less reliable than conventional multiple-choice testing.

We provide a simple framework that considers four aspects of test construction and analysis and that argues for the need to: (a) become more focused in our test purpose(s) and needs for information, (b) design these complex exercises as precise measurement instruments targeted to produce precise information and conditions of measurement applicable to a specific purpose, (c) ensure that we can gather and score and transform the raw data without losing too much valid information, and (d) scale the data to produce the necessary outcomes. It appears that more concentrated effort and research are needed on both the test-development side and the psychometric side to complete the required synthesis.

This framework does not present solutions. It provides a general way to evaluate information needs and to explore solutions. As we move into computerized testing, there will be an information explosion. The question is, can we handle it and scientifically benefit from it to improve measurement practices?

REFERENCES

Anderson, J. R. (1983). *Cognitive psychology and its implications* (2nd ed.). New York: Freeman.

Andrich, D. (1978). A rating formulation for ordered response categories. *Psychometrika, 43,* 561–573.

Bejar, I. I. (1991). A methodology for scoring open-ended architectural design problems. *Journal of Applied Psychology, 76,* 522–532.

Bejar, I. I. (1995). From adaptive testing to automated scoring of architectural simulations. In E. L. Mancall & P. G. Bashook (Eds.), *Assessing clinical reasoning: The oral examination and alternative methods* (pp. 115–130). Evanston, IL: American Board of Medical Specialities.

Bennett, R. E., Gong, B., Hershaw, R. C., Rock, D. A., Soloway, E., & Macalalad, A. (1990). Assessment of an expert systems ability to automatically grade and diagnose students' constructed-responses to computer science problems. In R. O. Freedle (Ed.), *Artificial intelligence and the future of testing* (pp. 293–320). Hillsdale, NJ: Lawrence Erlbaum Associates.

Bennett, R. E., Morley, M., & Quardt, D. (1998). *Three response types for broadening the conception of mathematical problem solving in computer-adaptive tests* (ETS Research Report RR-98-45). Princeton, NJ: Educational Testing Service.

Bennett, R. E., & Sebrechts, M. M. (1997). A computerized task for measuring the representational component of quantitative proficiency. *Journal of Educational Measurement, 34*, 64–77.

Bennett, R. E., Steffen, M., Singley, M. K., Morley, M., & Jacquemin, D. (1997). Evaluating an automatically scorable, open-ended response type for measuring mathematical reasoning in computer-adaptive testing. *Journal of Educational Measurement, 34*, 162–176.

Bergan, J. R. (1983). Latent class models in educational research. In E. W. Gordon (Ed.), *Review of Research in Education* (Vol. 10, pp. 305–360). Washington, DC: American Educational Research Association.

Birnbaum, A. (1968). Some latent trait models and their use in inferring an examinee's ability. In F. M. Lord & M. R. Novick (Eds.), *Statistical theories of mental test scores* (pp. 397–479). Reading, MA: Addison-Wesley.

Bock, R. D., Gibbons, R., & Muraki, E. (1988). Full-information factor analysis. *Applied Psychological Measurement, 12*, 261–280.

Braun, H. I., Bennett, R. E., Frye, D., & Soloway, E. (1990). Scoring constructed responses using expert systems. *Journal of Educational Measurement, 27*, 93–108.

Breland, H. M., & Lytle, E. G. (1990, April). *Computer-assisted writing skill assessment using WordMap™*. Paper presented at the annual meeting of the American Educational Research Association, Boston.

Burstein, J., Kaplan, R., Wolff, S., & Lu, C. (1997, December). *Automatic scoring of advanced placement biology essays* (ETS Research Report RR-97-22). Princeton, NJ: Educational Testing Service.

Burstein, J., Kukich, K., Wolff, S., & Lu, C. (1998, April). *Computer analysis of essay content for automated score prediction*. Paper presented at the meeting of the National Council on Measurement in Education, San Diego.

Chalifour, C., & Powers, D. E. (1988). *Content characteristics of GRE analytical reasoning items* (GRE Board Professional Report No. 84-14P; ETS Research Report RR-88-7). Princeton, NJ: Educational Testing Service.

Clauser, B. E., Margolis, M. J., Clyman, S. G., & Ross, L. P. (1997). Development of automated scoring algorithms for complex performance assessments: A comparison of two approaches. *Journal of Educational Measurement, 34*, 141–161.

Clogg, C. C., & Goodman, L. A. (1985). Simultaneous latent structure analysis in several groups. In N. B. Tuma (Ed.), *Sociological methodology, 1985* (pp. 81–110). San Francisco: Jossey-Bass.

Clyman, S. G., Melnick, D. E., & Clauser, B. E. (1995). Computer-based case simulations. In E. L. Mancall & P. G. Bashook (Eds.), *Assessing clinical reasoning: The oral examination and alternative methods* (pp. 139–149). Evanston, IL: American Board of Medical Specialties.

Cronbach, L. J., & Gleser, G. C. (1957). *Psychological tests and personnel decisions*. Urbana, IL: University of Illinois Press.

Davey, T., Goodwin, J., & Mettelholtz, D. (1997). Developing and scoring an innovative computerized writing assessment. *Journal of Educational Measurement, 34*, 21–41.

Dayton, C. M., & Macready, G. B. (1976). A probabilistic model for validation of behavioral hierarchies. *Psychometrika, 41*, 189–204.

Dayton, C. M., & Macready, G. B. (1980). A scaling model with response errors and intrinsically unscalable respondents, *Psychometrika, 45*, 345–356.

Drum, P. A., Calfee, R. C., & Cook, L. K. (1981). The effects of surface structure variables on performance in reading comprehension tests. *Reading Research Quarterly, 16*, 486–514.

Embretson, S. E. (1984). A general latent trait model for response processes. *Psychometrika, 49*, 175–186.

Embretson, S. E. (1993). Psychometric models for learning and cognitive processes. In N. Frederiksen, R. J. Mislevy, & I. I. Bejar (Eds.), *Test theory for a new generation of tests* (pp. 125–150). Hillsdale, NJ: Lawrence Erlbaum Associates.

Fischer, G. H. (1983). Logistic latent trait models with linear constraints. *Psychometrika, 48*, 3–26.

Fischer, G. H. (1993). The linear logistic test model. In G. H. Fischer & I. W. Molenaar (Eds.), *Rasch models: Foundations, recent developments and applications* (pp. 131–155). New York: Springer-Verlag.

Fischer, K. W., & Pipp, S. L. (1984). Processes of cognitive development: Optimal level and skill acquisition. In R. J. Sternberg (Ed.), *Mechanisms of cognitive development* (pp. 45–80). New York: Freeman.

Flavell, J. H. (1984). Discussion. In R. J. Sternberg (Ed.), *Mechanisms of cognitive development* (pp. 187–210). New York: Freeman.

Glas, C. A. W. (1992). A Rasch model with a multivariate distribution of ability. In M. Wilson (Ed.), *Objective measurement: Theory into practice* (pp. 236–258). Norwood, NJ: Ablex.

Glaser, R. (1963). Instructional technology and the measurement of learning outcomes: Some questions. *American Psychologist, 18*, 519–521.

Glaser, R. (1973). Educational psychology and education. *American Psychologist, 28*, 557–566.

Goldstein, H., & Wood, R. (1989). Five decades of item response modeling. *British Journal Mathematical Statistical Psychology, 42*, 139–167.

Goodman, L. A. (1974). Exploratory latent structure analysis using both identifiable and unidentifiable models. *Biometrika, 61*, 215–231.

Goodman, L. A. (1975). A new model for scaling response patterns: An application of the quasi-independence concept. *Journal of the American Statistical Association, 70*, 755–768.

Hambleton, R. K., & Swaminathan, H. (1985). *Item response theory: Principles and applications*. Boston: Kluwer-Nijhoff.

Hanson, B. A. (1998, April). *Bayes modal estimates of a discrete latent variable distribution in item response models using the EM algorithm*. Paper presented at the annual meeting of the American Educational Research Association, San Diego, CA.

Horst, P. (1933). The difficulty of a multiple-choice test item. *Journal of Educational Psychology, 24*, 229–232.

Kaplan, R. M., & Bennett, R. E. (1994). *Using a free-response scoring tool to automatically score the formulating-hypotheses item* (ETS Research Report RR-94-08). Princeton, NJ: Educational Testing Service.

Kirsch, I. S., & Mosenthal, P. (1988). *Understanding document literacy: Variables underlying the performance of young adults* (ETS Research Report RR-88-62). Princeton, NJ: Educational Testing Service.

Lehmann, E. L. (1983). *Theory of point estimation*. New York: Wiley.

Lord, F. M. (1980). *Applications of item response theory to practical testing problems*. Hillsdale, NJ: Lawrence Erlbaum Associates.

Lord, F. M., & Novick, M. R. (1968). *Statistical Theories of Mental Test Scores*. Reading, MA: Addison-Wesley.

Luecht, R. M. (1996). Multidimensional computerized adaptive testing in a certification or licensure context. *Applied Psychological Measurement, 20*, 389–404.

Luecht, R. M., & DeChamplain, A. (1998, April). *Applications of latent class analysis to mastery decisions using complex performance assessments*. Paper presented at the annual meeting of the American Educational Research Association, San Diego, CA.

Luecht, R. M., & Miller, T. R. (1992). Unidimensional calibrations and interpretations of composite traits for multidimensional tests. *Applied Psychological Measurement, 16,* 279–293.

Masters, G. (1982). A Rasch model for partial credit scoring. *Psychometrika, 17,* 149–171.

McDonald, R. P. (1982). Linear versus nonlinear models in item response theory. *Applied Psychological Measurement, 6,* 41–63.

McDonald, R. P. (1997). Normal-Ogive multidimensional model. In W. J. van der Linden & R. K. Hambleton (Eds.), *Handbook of modern item response theory* (pp. 258–269). New York. Springer.

Miller, T. R. (1991). *Empirical estimation of standard errors of compensatory MIRT model parameters obtained from the NOHARM estimation program* (ACT Research Report Series 91-2). Iowa City, IA: ACT.

Mislevy, R. J. (1987). Exploiting auxiliary information about examinees in the estimation of item parameters. *Applied Psychological Measurement, 11,* 81–91.

Mislevy, R. J. (1989). *Foundations of a new test theory*. (ETS Research Report RR-89-52-ONR). Princeton, NJ: Educational Testing Service.

Mislevy, R. J. (1993). Foundations of a new test theory. In N. Frederiksen, R. J. Mislevy, & I. I. Bejar (Eds.), *Test theory for a new generation of tests* (pp. 19–40). Hillsdale, NJ: Lawrence Erlbaum Associates.

Muraki, E. (1992). A generalized partial credit model: Application of an EM algorithm. *Applied Psychological Measurement, 16,* 159–176.

Muraki, E., & Ankenmann, R. D. (1993, April). *Applying the generalized partial credit model to missing responses: Implementing the scoring function and a lower asymptote parameter*. Paper presented at the annual meeting of the American Research Association, Atlanta, GA.

Page, E. B., & Petersen, N. S. (1995). The computer moves into essay grading. *Phi Delta Kappan, 76,* 561–565.

Ragosa, D. (1991). A longitudinal approach to ATI research: Models for individual growth and models for individual differences in response to instruction. In R. E. Snow & D. E. Wiley (Eds.), *Improving inquiry in social science: A volume in honor of Lee J. Cronbach* (pp. 221–248). Hillsdale, NJ: Lawrence Erlbaum Associates.

Reckase, M. R. (1985). The difficulty of test items that measure more than one ability. *Applied Psychological Measurement, 9,* 401–412.

Samejima, F. (1969). Estimation of latent trait ability using a response pattern for graded data. *Psychometrika Monograph, 17.*

Samejima, F. (1972). A general model for free-response data. *Psychometrika Monograph, 18.*

Samejima, F. (1995). Acceleration model in the heterogeneous case of the general graded response model. *Psychometrika, 60,* 549–572.

Scheuneman, J., Gerritz, K., & Embretson, S. (1989, March). *Effects of prose complexity on achievement test item difficulty*. Paper presented at the annual meeting of the American Educational Research Association, San Francisco.

Schnipke, D. L., & Scrams, D. J. (1997). Modeling item response times with a two-state mixture model: A new method of measuring speededness. *Journal of Educational Measurement, 34,* 213–232.

Segall, D. O. (1996). Multidimensional adaptive testing. *Psychometrika, 61,* 331–354.

Siegler, R. S. (1986). *Children's thinking*. Englewood Cliffs, NJ: Prentice-Hall.

Snow, R. E. (1989). Toward assessment of cognitive and conative structures in learning. *Educational Researcher, 18,* 8–14.

Snow, R. E., & Lohman, D. F. (1993). Cognitive psychology, new test design and new test theory: An introduction. In N. Frederiksen, R. J. Mislevy, & I. I. Bejar (Eds.), *Test theory for a new generation of tests* (pp. 1–18). Hillsdale, NJ: Lawrence Erlbaum Associates.

Sternberg, R. J. (1984). Mechanisms of cognitive growth: A componential approach. In R. J. Sternberg (Ed.), *Mechanisms of cognitive development* (pp. 163–186). New York: Freeman.

Tang, K. L., & Eignor, D. R. (1997, August). *Concurrent calibration of dichotomously and polytomously scored TOEFL items using IRT models*. (TOEFL Technical Report TR-13; ETS Research Report RR-97-6). Princeton, NJ: Educational Testing Service.

Thissen, D. (1983). Timed testing: An approach using item response theory. In D. J. Weiss (Ed.), *New horizons in testing: Latent trait theory and computerized adaptive testing* (pp. 179–203). New York: Academic Press.

Thissen, D., & Steinberg, L. (1986). A taxonomy of item response models. *Psychometrika, 51*, 567–577.

van der Linden, W. J. (1998). A decision theory model for course placement. *Journal of Educational and Behavioral Statistics, 23*, 18–34.

van der Linden, W. J., & Hambleton, R. K. (1997). *Handbook of modern item response theory*. New York: Springer.

Weiss, D. J., & Kingsbury, G. G. (1984). Application of computerized adaptive testing to educational problems. *Journal of Educational Measurement, 21*, 361–375.

Wilson, M. R. (1989). Saltus: A psychometric model of discontinuity in cognitive development. *Psychological Bulletin, 105*, 276–289.

Yamamoto, K., & Gitomer, D. H. (1993). Application of a HYBRID model to a test of cognitive skill representation. In N. Frederiksen, R. J. Mislevy, & I. I. Bejar (Eds.), *Test theory for a new generation of tests* (pp. 275–295). Hillsdale, NJ: Lawrence Erlbaum Associates.

On Complexity in CBT

Wim J. van der Linden
University of Twente, The Netherlands

In hindsight, the early days of research on CBT were characterized by one-sided expectations. The main motive for the interest in using computers rather than paper and pencil for testing was the wish to make tests adaptive. Because the first computers were too slow to estimate ability online, most efforts were directed at finding testing formats that approximated the idea of adaptive testing in a conventional environment. These formats were seen only as temporary substitutes. One day, it was expected, the computer industry would offer plentiful cheap computational power and all testing would become fully adaptive.

The actual advent of computers in the practice of testing has made the idea of adaptive testing practically feasible indeed. At the same time, however, it has led to an unforeseen revolution in many aspects of testing. Luecht and Clauser (chap. 3, this volume) discuss how the enormous power of the current generation of personal computers, along with their ability to control multiple presentation media, has been an effective stimulus to developing new, realistic test item formats. It is no longer necessary to restrict test items to questions formulated in a few lines of text. We now can build testing environments with graphics, pictures, video, and sound. Examinees can respond by maneuvering cursors on the screen, clicking and dragging objects, talking back to the computer, working with application programs, or manipulating devices with built-in sensors. In addition, testing can be made more realistic by imposing time limits on test items or forcing examinees to coordinate multiple tasks simultaneously.

Also, the first experiences with adaptive testing showed that test assembly based solely on the principle of adapting the difficulty of the items to the ability estimates of the examinee would have led to unacceptable results. Test content could easily become unbalanced across examinees, who might feel treated unfairly because of over- or underrepresentation of some topics. In addition to the statistical principle of maximum information on the ability estimator, item selection should realize the typical content specifications paper-and-pencil tests have had to meet. Folk and Smith (chap. 2, this volume) discuss a range of testing formats that have been proposed to deal both with the statistical and the content aspects of CBT. Some of these formats are new; others, ironically, date back to the early days of adaptive testing research but have been rediscovered because of their easy control of test content.

Finally, the design of CBT systems has become a much more complicated process than anticipated. The old idea of just storing a pool of calibrated items in the computer and having an algorithm select the items for administration has turned out to be much too simple. For example, it quickly became obvious that item pools had to be designed well to guarantee the promise of high measurement efficiency. Also, because of the vulnerability of item pools to security breaches in high-stakes testing, item selection had to be controlled for the exposure rates of the items and item pools had to be replaced more often than expected. As a consequence, and because items now had to be calibrated online, the costs of item calibration were higher than anticipated. In addition, the demand for more realistic item types has necessitated more complicated, multi-parameter response models that require larger amounts of data for item calibration.

In this chapter I discuss these three sources of complexity in CBT further. First, I dwell on one of the points made by Luecht and Clauser, who observe that it is easy to get carried away with the new computerized technology of constructing more realistic test items but that creating complexity should not be a goal in itself. My main message is that it is easy to confuse the notion of a realistic item with the one of test score validity, but that the ultimate proof of the effectiveness of the new computer technology lies in the latter. Second, I consider the several forms of CBT discussed by Folk and Smith, evaluate them from the point of view of the severity of the set of constraints they impose on the item-selection process, and indicate the consequences of these sets of constraints for their measurement quality. Third, I address the problem of designing a CBT system, review some of the unexpected interactions that exist in such systems, and make a case for a more systematic approach to CBT design. However, my main conclusion is that we do not know enough yet to guarantee optimal results.

COMPLEX ITEM TYPES FOR COMPUTERIZED TESTING

Luecht and Clauser (chap. 3, this volume) analyze the methodological assumptions and implications involved in the new technology of computerized test items. On the one hand, they welcome the many new opportunities made possible by this technology, which they have contributed to through their research and developmental work at the NBME (e.g., Clauser, Margolis, Clyman, & Ross, 1997; Luecht & Nungester, 1998). On the other hand, they demonstrate vigilance for the pitfalls involved in it. They emphasize that test developers can only benefit from this technology if they remain focused on their test purposes and needs for test scores. Complexity of test items is fruitful only if it helps to meet these purposes and needs. In addition, they emphasize these new test items should lead to precise scores scaled to be comparable across examinees.

I concur with this position. Elsewhere (van der Linden & Hambleton, 1997), I have defended the notion of a test as a series of small experiments. In these experiments, the independent variables are the test items offered as treatments designed to elicit the knowledge or skill the test is intended to measure. The dependent variables are the responses resulting from the interaction between the examinee and the treatment. Test scores are estimates of the true scores of the examinee on the variable the test measures inferred from these responses.

As in any other experiment, variables other than the intended independent variable may affect the dependent variables. The effects of these error or nuisance variables, existing, for example, in the physical environment of the test or in additional personality or perceptual factors evoked by it, should be controlled to guarantee the validity of the experiments. The notion of measurement validity is thus much the same as the notion of internal validity developed in the literature on experimental design.

A graphical representation of the causal relations among the independent, dependent, and error variables in a series of test items is given in Fig. 4.1. In this example, $U_1, \ldots, U_n$ are the dependent or response variables, θ is the independent variable measured by the test, and $\varepsilon_1, \varepsilon_2, \ldots,$ are the error variables to which $U_1, \ldots, U_n$ are sensitive. For a more complete introduction to graphical modeling of response behavior on test items, see Almond and Mislevy (1999).

The methodological literature offers three basic techniques to control for the effects of the error variables $\varepsilon_1, \varepsilon_2, \ldots,$ on the response variables,

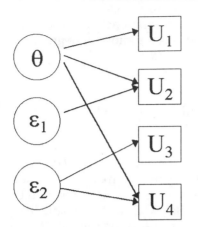

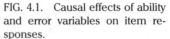

FIG. 4.1. Causal effects of ability and error variables on item responses.

$U_1, \ldots, U_n$: (a) standardization or matching, (b) randomization, and (c) statistical adjustment.

Classical test theory has been developed for tests with experimental control through standardization and randomization. The effects of all error variables are assumed to be matched across examinees by rigorous standardization or to be purely random across replications. As a result, the only systematic differences among examinees are in their scores on the variable measured by the test (true scores); all remaining variation among the observed scores is random (measurement error).

The quintessence of statistical adjustment in test theory is IRT. The first IRT models were developed to adjust for the effects of such test item properties as their difficulty, discriminating power, and susceptibility to guessing. From a measurement point of view, these effects are systematic errors interfering with the variable to be measured. Because IRT models have explicit parameters for these item properties, estimates of the examinees' abilities are automatically adjusted for their effects, and, as a consequence, these abilities are measured on a common scale.

The same principle of statistical adjustment is followed in multidimensional IRT to allow for nuisance abilities to which the items are sensitive in addition to the ability they are supposed to measure. This case can be used to illustrate one of the critical differences between the classical and modern approaches to maintaining the validity of a test. The classical approach is to prevent such abilities from operating in the test items. For example, if the items in a test of numerical intelligence appear to be sensitive to verbal ability, the natural reaction would be to develop a test with nonverbal items. The modern approach, however, is to build a model with explicit parameters for both the numerical and verbal abilities but to have interest only in the parameter estimates for the numerical ability. An example of this approach is Segall's (2001) attempt to measure the g-factor in the Armed Services Vocational Aptitude Battery (ASVAB) tests independently of the factors operating in the individual tests by modeling all factors as a hierarchical structure from which the g-factor is estimated.

Note the difference in where the demands are placed in the two approaches to controlling for test validity. In the classical approach, high demands are placed on the test item writer, who is required to produce items not sensitive to possible nuisance abilities or matched carefully on their effects. In the modern approach, high demands are placed on the skills of the psychometrican, who is required to model the interactions among all variables with effects on the item responses and to develop the statistical techniques needed to make efficient, unbiased inferences with respect to the variables of interest.

A deeply rooted belief among many modern consumers of test scores is that the validity of test scores is positively related to the complexity of the test items. This belief seems to follow from the observation that reality is complex; therefore, useful information never can be extracted from test items that simplify the conditions and stimuli in daily life. This belief is often expressed as protest against the unrealistic, standardized test items produced by the classical approach. The same consumers seem to embrace CBT as a natural outlet for their discontent with unrealistic test items. They expect computers to bring realism, "standardized out of the test" in classical paper-and-pencil testing, back to it.

Though I am much in favor of CBT and am convinced it offers many new avenues to solving old problems in educational and psychological testing, adding more realism to test items does not automatically lead to valid measurements. In fact, as follows from the preceding discussion of experimental control in testing, the concepts of realism and validity involve contradictory requirements. Maximizing the degree of realism of test items means adding to them as many of the factors operating in real life as possible. Maximizing the validity of the test scores means removing from them the effects of each factor that has nothing in common with the variable intended to be measured by the test. The confusion between the two concepts arises when (potentially positive) properties of items are uncritically ascribed to test scores.

The distinction between the validity of test scores and the degree of item realism is illustrated using the hypothetical case of a test of social skills that offers examinees a sample of social interactions and then scores their judgments. In a paper-and-pencil version of the test, these interactions would be described verbally in a highly controlled language. A computerized test, on the other hand, could use video recording to display actual social interactions among real people. In addition to listening to their verbal communications, the examinees could watch the facial expressions and gestures of the participants. This higher degree of real-

ism may help them to get better insights into the dynamics in the recorded social processes and make more valid evaluation. At the same
time, however, the recordings may reveal the social background of the
participants, capitalize on the high verbal skills of some of them, show
them arguing over an issue with a specific content, make some of the
participants more salient than others because of the angle of the camera,
and so on. Each of these conditions could also affect the interpretation of
the social process by the examinees. Conceivably, some examinees may
operate better under one set of conditions than another. If so, the scores
on the video test do not automatically generalize to realistic cases outside the test, and the test scores are not valid.

To sum up, CBT offers many new opportunities to improve testing. At
the same time, each of these opportunities forms a new challenge to the
validity of the test scores. Any new feature added to a test that is not essential to the variable the test is intended to measure is a potential threat
to validity. The effects of such features must either be standardized in a
way more sensitive than ever before or be adjusted for using more refined response models. No doubt we will become more skilled in both
forms of experimental control. If not, ironically, attempts to make test
items more realistic may decrease test score validity because they may
place unrealistic demands on test constructors and psychometricians.

COMPLEXITY OF SET OF CONTENT CONSTRAINTS ON CBTS

It would be shortsighted to focus a discussion of the complexity in CBT
entirely on the nature of the individual test items. Test scores are the result of the full set of test items, and the question of how to assemble a
CBT is another source of complexity. This point can be illustrated using
some of the forms of CBT reviewed in the chapter by Folk and Smith
(chap. 2, this volume). These authors distinguish among the following
forms, each differing in the way they deal with the content specifications
the test has to meet:

1. CAT,
2. constrained adaptive testing,
3. testlet-based adaptive testing,
4. multistage testing, and
5. LOFT.

The point of view I adopt to evaluate these forms of CBT is that the
process of selecting the items in each form should be considered an ap-

plication of an algorithm for solving an optimization problem. The objective of the optimization problem is to select the test items so that the statistical information in the test on the ability of the examinee is maximized. At the same time, the selection of the items has to meet a usually large number of constraints to guarantee that the test realizes the same set of content specifications across examinees. In a more conventional parlance, the goal of the test is to maximize its reliability; constraints are necessary to maintain its content validity. Optimization problems of this type are instances of constrained sequential optimization.

A combination of items from the pool that meets all constraints for a given set of test specifications is called a *feasible* test. The best test is thus a feasible test with an optimal value for the objective function. Generally, a trade-off exists between the optimal value possible for the objective function and the number of constraints imposed on the test. If more constraints are imposed, the set of feasible tests tends to become smaller, and the best test in this set typically has a lower value for the objective function. Hence, it is important to impose the smallest set of constraints needed to represent the content specifications. If the set chosen is too large, the problem becomes overconstrained and the result is less favorable than necessary.

The preceding five forms of CBT are ordered by the complexity of the sets of constraints imposed on the item-selection process. In the early days of research on CAT (e.g., Lord, 1970; Owen, 1975; Weiss, 1983), content specifications were ignored. The motive was to maximize the statistical efficiency of the ability estimator. This objective was realized by selecting the items best matching the current ability estimates of the examinee during testing. No interest in the realization of possible nonstatistical specifications for the test existed. These early CAT algorithms can therefore be viewed as algorithms that realize the objective of maximum information at the true ability value of the examinee in a nearly unconstrained fashion. The only formal constraint is the one on the length of the test imposed either directly by fixing its number of items or indirectly by choosing a predetermined degree of precision of the ability estimator.

The first practical experiences with CAT caused a quick change of interest from the statistical to the nonstatistical aspects of adaptive testing. It was immediately realized that to make adaptive tests acceptable to examinees, they had to be controlled for their content. Also, early concerns about test item security led to the need to control the test for the exposure rates of the items in the pool.

Three types of adaptive testing with content constraints have been proposed. Kingsbury and Zara (1991) suggested partitioning the item pool according to the content attributes addressed in the test specifications and selecting the items from the classes in the partition such that the class most behind receives the highest priority. Stocking and Swanson's (1993) WDM also assumes partitioning of the item pool and formulates upper or lower bounds, or both, on the number of items to be selected from each class. In addition, upper and lower bounds are specified on the values of the test information function for a selected number of θ values. The items are selected to minimize a weighted sum of deviations from these bounds. A third method of optimal constrained adaptive testing was proposed in van der Linden and Reese (1998). The key feature of their method is a full test (*shadow test*) reassembled each time an item has been selected for administration in the adaptive test. The test is assembled online solving a 0–1 linear programming model that has all content specifications formulated as constraints and maximization of the test information at the current ability estimate as its objective function. The item actually administered is the most informative one at the ability estimate. The method has been generalized in van der Linden (2000) and is now known as constrained adaptive testing with shadow tests.

Adaptive testing with constraints on the item-exposure rates was proposed by Sympson and Hetter (1985). Their algorithm imposes upper bounds on the exposure rates of the items for a population of examinees and realizes these bounds by imposing stochastic constraints on the selection of the items at the level of the individual examinees in the population.

All these forms of constrained adaptive testing differ in the way the constraints are realized. In both the Kingsbury–Zara (1991) and the Stocking–Swanson (1993) approaches, the constraints are realized sequentially in an order determined by the weighing of the bounds. As a result, each previously selected item places an additional constraint on the selection of the next item. The effect of these additional constraints is lower statistical information. Also, because of the same overconstraining, some of the original content constraints might have to be violated to finish the test. In the van der Linden and Reese (1998) approach, the critical feature is the formulation of the 0–1 linear programming model for the shadow test. If the model is formulated efficiently, a minimum number of constraints is imposed. Thomasson (1995) demonstrated the tradeoff between the number of constraints and the optimal value for the Sympson and Hetter method of item-exposure control in a simulation study for subtests from the ASVAB. Generally, the loss of information due to the constraints on the exposure rates was estimated to be in the range of 25% to 35%.

In testlet-based adaptive testing (Wainer & Kiely, 1987), small subsets of items in the pool are preassembled to meet sets of content specifications. Testlets are always selected as intact units. They may have internal or external branching schemes, or both. Every possible route results in a test that meets the full-set specifications. However, from the point of view of constrained optimization, preassembly of testlets imposes logical constraints on sets of items in the pool, constraints that enforce the selection of a conjunction of a set of items if any of the individual items is selected. Again, the effect of these additional constraints is a lower value for the objective function, that is, lower information on the ability level of the examinees.

Multistage testing is one of the oldest known formats in CBT. It was proposed by Lord (1970) as an implementation of adaptive testing when online ability estimation was not yet practical. Multistage testing can be viewed as a more rigid precursor of testlet-based adaptive testing. In multistage testing, the subtests are generally longer than the testlets proposed by Wainer and Kiely (1987), the first subtest is common to all examinees, and the subtests do not have internal branching. Consequently, multistage testing is a more severely constrained form of adaptive testing than testlet-based adaptive testing.

The final form of CBT discussed by Folk and Smith (chap. 2, this volume) is LOFT, developed by ETS to guarantee item security in a CBT environment. As in any of the other forms of CBT, this form assumes the availability of a pool of calibrated items. Each examinee is administered a unique linear test from the pool assembled to meet all specifications. In fact, LOFT is the mirror image of classical adaptive testing. The latter was only concerned with maximum information in the test at the ability level of the examinee; the former is concerned only with its content specifications. However, if background information on the examinees is available, the efficiency of LOFT could be improved by assembling each test to be optimal at prior ability estimates for the examinees (van der Linden, 1999).

Other criteria for the evaluation of these five forms of CBT can be formulated. For example, these forms differ in the degree of adaptation to ability estimation possible during the test, the extent of item coding necessary to assemble the test or the subtests, and the possibility of expert review of intact testing material before the test administration. For a comparison among these CBT forms based on these criteria, see van der Linden (2000).

COMPLEXITY OF CBT SYSTEM DESIGN

Most research on CBT has been focused only on the relations among a few aspects of computerized testing. Examples are studies that explore the relation between the size of the calibration sample and the distribution of error in a specific ability estimator or the effects of a method of item-exposure control on the actual exposure rates of the items. However, the relations found in such studies do not necessarily hold for an actual CBT system. Such systems may display interactions among parameters with effects not anticipated when the system was assembled. The final section of this discussion addresses the complexity in CBT at the system level. In particular, I describe CBT system design as an optimization process that has to deal with complex interactions and trade-offs among its parameters and with various constraints on the values of these parameters. I do not pretend to give a complete description of the process. For example, several of the practical issues met when designing a large-scale CAT program that have been discussed in Mills and Stocking (1996) are not addressed here.

A natural objective for CBT system design is to minimize the length of the test. The costs of CBT are directly related to the length of the tests. The shorter the test, the smaller the size of the item pool and the time slots needed for the examinees. The former affects the costs of writing, reviewing, and calibrating the items; the latter affects the operational costs of running the system.

The independent variables the testing agency can use to control the length of the test include a choice of the following:

1. distribution of the item parameter values in the pool,
2. distribution of content attributes of the items in the pool,
3. ability estimator,
4. item-selection criterion,
5. design of calibration sample,
6. estimator of item parameter values,
7. method of balancing test content across examinees,
8. method of controlling the item exposure rates, and
9. method of controlling the speededness of the test.

The first two parameters summarize the design of the item pool. Various relations between these parameters have been studied in the chapter by Way, Steffen, and Anderson (chap. 7, this volume) and in Veldkamp and van der Linden (2000). Several ability estimators are available (e.g., MLE, weighted MLE, Bayesian method; for a review, see van der Linden & Pashley, 2000). Also, different choices can be made for the initial estimator, the interim estimator used to adapt the item selection to the examinee's ability during the test, and the final estimator used to produce the examinee's score. Well-known choices for the item-selection criterion include the maximum-information criterion and Bayesian methods. A more complete review of possible choices of ability estimators and item-selection criteria is given in the chapter by Folk and Smith (chap. 2, this volume). The design of the calibration sample controls which examinees respond to which items in the pool. The design may also determine what kind of background information on the examinees is collected if this information plays a role in the estimation procedure chosen to calibrate the items. Various methods of controlling item exposure are discussed in the chapter by Davey and Nering (chap. 8, this volume).

Minimization of test length only makes sense if some of the other dependent variables are constrained to have values between desired bounds. Variables with values most likely to be constrained are the following:

1. mean-squared error and bias of the final ability estimator,
2. distributions of content attributes of the items in the test,
3. exposure rates of the items, and
4. distributions of total response times on the test.

For the most part, the constraints on the values of these variables are required to hold at the level of the individual examinees or for a series of well-chosen ability levels. Generally, a flat mean-squared error function is considered desirable, as is a bias function uniformly close to zero. The desired distribution of the content attributes in the test follows directly from the test specifications. Typically, the item-exposure rates are constrained away not only from one but from zero. The right-hand tails of the distributions of the examinees' total response times on the test should not be too far above the time limit.

As already mentioned, some parameters may show interactions with effects that were not anticipated when the system was assembled. Three of my recent findings are used to demonstrate this point. One finding involves a positive effect; two involve a negative effect. The positive effect was found in a study in which prior empirical information on the examinees was used to improve the statistical properties of the ability estimator in adaptive testing (van der Linden, 1999). The idea was to regress the initial ability estimator or prior for the ability parameter on a well-chosen set of background variables. The predicted positive effect was initialization of ability estimation much closer to the true ability of the examinees, and hence earlier convergence of the estimator compared with a fixed initial estimate somewhere in the middle of the ability scale. However, regression of the initial ability estimator on background information also resulted in much improved exposure rates of the items in the pool. (This effect is not documented in the reference.) With a fixed initial ability estimate, every examinee starts with the same item and the items in the pool close to it typically have high exposure rates. If ability estimation starts from a prior regressed on background variables, a more variable choice of initial item occurs and a tendency toward more uniform item usage is introduced. When the correlation between the background variables and the ability variable are stronger, tendency is also stronger.

An unanticipated negative effect was observed in a study by van der Linden, Scrams, and Schnipke (1999), which addressed the problem of differential speededness in adaptive testing. Because each examinee gets an individual selection of items and items generally differ in the amount of time needed to solve them, adaptive testing without response-time constraints on the item selection may result in tests that are differentially speeded across examinees. A simulation study based on an empirical data set revealed that differential speededness can have serious effects for some of the examinees. However, unexpectedly, the students who ran out of time were the more able students! This result appeared to be the effect of the interaction between two well-known empirical facts and the adaptive nature of item selection. The first fact was that ability and speed were uncorrelated. Thus, among the more able examinees there were as many examinees working slowly as among the less able examinees. The second fact was a strong positive correlation between the difficulty of the items and the time needed to solve them. Because item selection was adaptive, the more able examinees got the more difficult items and needed more time per item. As a result, a large proportion of them ran out of time during the test.

The third example is from a study conducted to assess the effects of capitalization on chance on ability estimation in adaptive testing for various item-selection criteria (van der Linden & Glas, 2000). Because each item-selection criterion in adaptive testing involves optimization of a quantity based on item parameter values with estimation error, capitalization on these errors is likely to occur. An empirical item pool was used to demonstrate the phenomenon. The phenomenon was found to be strongest for the examinees on the area of the ability scale where most of the items were located. For this area, the mean absolute error in the ability estimates was roughly twice as large as for the areas with less densely distributed items. This result seemed counterintuitive because having more items in the neighborhood of the examinee's ability entails the possibility of selecting items from a set with larger variation of the parameter values. However, more items available also means a lower selection ratio, which is known to be one of the key factors inducing capitalization on estimation error. Thus, unless the calibration sample is large, increasing the size of the item pool may result in larger rather than smaller measurement errors.

Many of the relations among the various system parameters listed previously are still unknown. For example, we simply cannot predict the effects of the interaction between the ability estimator and item-selection criterion on the response-time distribution for a given choice of values for all other system parameters. We also cannot predict how these effects would be modified if the choice for some of these other parameters, for example, the distribution of item-content attributes in the pool, were changed. Nevertheless, such relations need to be known to make optimal decisions.

It seems we have a long way to go before we can predict the behavior of CBT systems for any configuration of parameter values with enough precision and design CBT systems to have guaranteed optimality. Until then, a practical approach seems to be to make a few intuitive proposals and simulate their behavior on the computer. This approach has been practiced, for example, by Eignor, Stocking, Way, and Steffen (1993). Though practical, the approach is not ideal. The phrase "more research needs to be done" seems to hold more strongly for CBT system design than for any other topic in educational testing.

REFERENCES

Almond, R. G., & Mislevy, R. J. (1999). Graphical models and computerized adaptive testing. *Applied Psychological Measurement, 23,* 223–238.

Clauser, B. E., Margolis, M. J., Clyman, S. G., & Ross, L. P. (1997). Development of automated scoring algorithms for complex performance assessments: A comparison of two approaches. *Journal of Educational Measurement, 34,* 141–161.

Eignor, D. R., Stocking, M. L., Way, W. D., & Steffen, M. (1993). *Case studies in computerized adaptive test design through computer simulation* (ETS Research Report RR-93-56). Princeton, NJ: Educational Testing Service.

Kingsbury, G. G., & Zara, A. R. (1991). Procedures for selecting items for computerized adaptive tests. *Applied Measurement in Education, 2,* 359–375.

Lord, F. M. (1970). Some test theory for tailored testing. In W. H. Holtzman (Ed.), *Computer-assisted instruction, testing and guidance* (pp. 139–183). New York: Harper & Row.

Luecht, R. M., & Nungester R. J. (1998). Some practical examples of computer-adaptive sequential testing. *Journal of Educational Measurement, 35,* 229–249.

Mills, C. N., & Stocking, M. L. (1996). Practical issues in large-scale computerized testing. *Applied Measurement in Education, 9,* 287–304.

Owen, R. J. (1975). A Bayesian sequential procedure for quantal response in the context of adaptive mental testing. *Journal of the American Statistical Association, 70,* 351–356.

Segall, D. O. (2001). General ability measurement: An application of multidimensional item response theory. *Psychometrika, 66,* 79–97.

Stocking, M. L., & Swanson, L. (1993). A method for severely constrained item selection in adaptive testing. *Applied Psychological Measurement, 17,* 277–292.

Sympson, J. B., & Hetter, R. D. (1985, October). Controlling item-exposure rates in computerized adaptive testing. *Proceedings of the 27th annual meeting of the Military Testing Association* (pp. 973–977). San Diego, CA: Navy Personnel Research and Development Center.

Thomasson, G. L. (1995, June). *New item exposure control algorithms for adaptive testing*. Paper presented at the annual meeting of the Psychometric Society, Minneapolis, MN.

van der Linden, W. J. (1999). Empirical initialization of the trait estimator in adaptive testing. *Applied Psychological Measurement*, *23*, 21–29. [Error correction in *23*, 248].

van der Linden, W. J. (2000). Constrained adaptive testing with shadow tests. In W. J. van der Linden & C. A. W. Glas (Eds.), *Computer-adaptive testing: Theory and practice* (pp. 27–52). Boston: Kluwer.

van der Linden, W. J., & Glas, C. A. W. (2000). Capitalization on item calibration error in adaptive testing. *Applied Measurement in Education*, *13*, 35–53.

van der Linden, W. J., & Hambleton, R. K. (1997). Item response theory: Brief history, common models and extensions. In W. J. van der Linden & R. K. Hambleton (Eds.), *Handbook of modern item response theory* (pp. 1–28). New York: Springer-Verlag.

van der Linden, W. J., & Pashley, P. J. (2000). Item selection and ability estimation in adaptive testing. In W. J. van der Linden & C. A. W. Glas (Eds.), *Computerized adaptive testing: Theory and practice* (pp. 1–25). Boston: Kluwer.

van der Linden, W. J., & Reese, L. M. (1998). A model for optimal constrained adaptive testing. *Applied Psychological Measurement*, *22*, 259–270.

van der Linden, W. J., Scrams, D. J., & Schnipke, D. L. (1999). Using response-time constraints to control for differential speededness in computerized adaptive testing. *Applied Psychological Measurement*, *23*, 195–211.

Veldkamp, B. P., & van der Linden, W. J. (2000). Designing item pools for computerized adaptive tests. In W. J. van der Linden & C. A. W. Glas (Eds.), *Computer-adaptive testing: Theory and practice* (pp. 149–162). Boston: Kluwer.

Wainer, H., & Kiely, G. L. (1987). Item clusters in computerized adaptive testing: A case for testlets. *Journal of Educational Measurement*, *24*, 185–201.

Weiss, D. J. (Ed.). (1983). *New horizons in testing*. New York: Academic Press.

Test Models for Traditional and Complex CBTs

William Stout
University of Illinois at Urbana-Champaign

INTRODUCTION

The economic challenge of CBT is particularly sobering. The basic products manufactured by testing companies are tests that are in turn collections of test items. CBTs, if adaptive, often used to increase measurement efficiency, require many more operational items to be available than do paper-and-pencil tests, especially because of test security. Therefore, there are intrinsic problems in converting a paper-and-pencil test to a CBT. Initially, at least, the production costs for each administered computerized item considerably exceeds the cost for an analogous paper-and-pencil item. Moreover, the initial administration costs for a CBT are also higher. Additionally, if the test is adaptive, each more expensive computerized item is "sold" to fewer examinees because a larger operational item pool is needed although the number of tests sold remains constant.

The solution to this economic problem would seem to be to raise the prices for these new (and better) CBTs. This is potentially workable when it is clear to the user that the CBT is sufficiently superior to its paper-and-pencil version. But, in many cases, the price of a CBT cannot be raised enough to compensate for the shifted financial reality of CBT because of political, economic, or ethical considerations. The financial burden of CBTs can occasionally be compensated for indirectly. For example, the

103

computerization of the military ASVAB test has been cost effective because the test is scored immediately. The military no longer has to pay the cost of lodging and a physical exam for failed recruits in contrast to the paper-and-pencil setting where the results of the paper-and-pencil test were not available for several days. Unfortunately, such ancillary financial benefits are rare.

An alternative and attractive solution to the problem would be to capitalize on the power and flexibility of the CBT environment to produce tests that are substantially superior to their paper-and-pencil counterparts, from both the reliability and the validity viewpoints. A testing company exploring the use of a CBT of the same length as their paper-and-pencil test anticipates a substantial increase in reliability because of item-delivery CAT algorithms that tailor the difficulties of items to be administered to the currently estimated examinee ability.

Also, the CBT environment can be used to redesign existing paper-and-pencil tests to assess new and cognitively complex components of the targeted construct by introducing new item types made possible by the enormous flexibility of computer-based item delivery and scoring, moving standardized testing closer to having genuine cognitive diagnostic capacity. This has the potential to transform existing tests into more psychometrically valid tests that can assess cognitive components of the targeted construct that would be beyond the reach of paper-and-pencil testing. As one example, the TOEFL 2000 under development, though still measuring English proficiency, will now assess certain fundamental cognitive components in English language proficiency, in principle producing a more valid test of English proficiency.

Finally, the CBT environment can facilitate the development of tests with new targeted constructs and new item types, in particular designed to accomplish cognitive diagnostic goals not possible without CBT. To illustrate this shift, one can envision a CBT designed to reliably (and likely adaptively) assess understanding and mastery of each of a core set of algebra competencies (quadratic formula, factoring, exponents, etc). We should view such a change in focus as sharpening the validity and usefulness of algebra competency measurement. Moreover, if such a test is adaptively targeted to each examinee, it will be more reliable than a fixed-length, paper-and-pencil test having the same cognitive diagnostic purpose. Note that the CBT roles in this and the previous paragraph are distinguished by whether the CBT is an outgrowth of an existing paper-and-pencil test such as the TOEFL or whether it addresses a new construct such as the cognitive components of algebra mastery that are viewed as beyond the reach of conventional paper-and-pencil testing.

Ideally, the move to CBT can become worth its high initial investment costs by meeting the increasing demand for tests that are psychometrically both more reliable and more valid, especially by addressing cognitive competencies not traditionally addressed by paper-and-pencil testing. If CBT produces these improvements, it will provide an invaluable service to educational organizations, students, government, and society. Then, the increased demand created by this new generation of tests will help the testing companies recover their research and development costs. The issue remains of how we can accomplish the two lofty goals of increased reliability and increased validity for CBT.

I discuss two chapters from this book that focus on test modeling issues oriented toward increasing CBT reliability and validity. Luecht and Clauser (chap. 3, this volume) focus on IRT modeling of complex CBT items that are especially appropriate for measuring new and more cognitively based constructs instead of merely scaling examinees on single, broad, content-based constructs (a worthy role of testing that will always be useful). That is, complex items become useful when designing a CBT that targets the simultaneous assessment of multiple cognitively defined abilities and attributes instead of a single, broad-based, content-defined ability. Folk and Smith (chap. 2, this volume) focus on IRT-model-based algorithms for the delivery (to the examinee sitting at the computer terminal) of CATs from a large item bank (perhaps consisting of complex and cognitively oriented items from the Luecht and Clauser viewpoint) to maximize reliability. Both Luecht and Clauser and Folk and Smith persuasively argue (implicitly and explicitly) that stochastic IRT modeling is essential if we are to succeed at making CBT a societally useful and economically feasible enterprise.

REVIEWER COMMENTARY ON LUECHT AND CLAUSER

Luecht and Clauser's chapter (chap. 3, this volume) amounts to a clarion call for maximizing the potential of CBT through complex item usage. Although it provides no detailed answers on how to achieve this, it is valuable in the time-honored way of posing the right questions, questions that are necessary to solve so that complex items can become part of the CBT repertoire. Essentially, Luecht and Clauser argue that the real pay-off in CBT will come by designing tests that assess complex cognitive processing, which is much more difficult to achieve using paper-and-pencil testing. Such cognitive processing assessment requires complex items. An item is *complex* if it provides more usable information about an examinee than can be easily encoded by the currently widely used right–wrong or even partial credit scoring of items (the reviewer's definition, not necessarily what the authors would say).

One interesting format for a complex item occurs when the examinee's solution path varies because of the software-driven adapting of the item to the examinee's intermediate computer-recorded responses to the item. An example of such an internally adaptive complex item is an item that consists of the examinee's interacting with a simulated symptom-presenting medical patient (could be computer generated or live) to produce a medical diagnosis. The scoring of such an item should reflect both the assessed wisdom of the examinee's clinical decisions and the correctness of the final diagnosis; such scoring must be rich and complex to be useful.

Although complex items have the potential to measure more cognitive complexity, such a complex item will not be any more informative psychometrically than a right–wrong scored multiple-choice item unless we can record and measure the relevant richness and complexity of the examinee's response. To do so, we must model item complexity using sophisticated stochastic IRT modeling. For instance, 3PL modeling is not sufficiently sophisticated to model such richly informative complex items. Moreover, even using polytomous scoring or multidimensional compensatory IRT modeling (denoted MIRT) seems to help only moderately. Unfortunately, producing statistical (i.e., stochastic) models that are sufficiently detailed to model cognitively complex examinee responses to complex items and using model-driven data analysis techniques that are statistically and computationally tractable is a difficult intellectual challenge. But, as Luecht and Clauser suggest, it is an essential one. Such detailed cognitively oriented models will need to explicitly address which cognitive attributes are required for solving each item correctly.

The computer is a natural medium for administering and scoring (recording relevant information in a numerically codified way) complex and possibly interactive examinee responses. Of course, we human "experts" need to determine how to algorithmetically instruct the computer to do these things. In the construction of CBTs, tests must be designed, modeled, and their examinee data collected while keeping the cognitive complex purpose of the test firmly targeted. In particular, the IRT modeling of cognitively diagnostic items should both draw on cognitive psychology and educational psychology and use complex statistical modeling (e.g., see DiBello, Stout, & Roussos, 1995, and Mislevy, 1995, for two such attempts).

The elementary psychometric concept of item information has to be broadened: The information provided by right–wrong scoring of unidimensionally IRT-modeled items no longer suffices. The creation of valid complex-item-focused IRT models, as called for by Luecht and Clauser, will lessen the inferential burden placed on data. Numbers (i.e., item scores) should not be asked to speak for themselves; they should be helped to speak more reliably and validly by being partnered with complex IRT models of complex item types scored in a complex manner. Indeed, abstracting the issue, effective model-based statistics consist of combining sufficiently deep (that is, authentically describing the substantive reality being modeled) statistical models with sophisticated and appropriate model-driven statistical data-analysis procedures.

A statistician's caution here is that models of complex items cannot have the number of their parameters outstrip the information in the data. As the number of parameters in a model increases (which often happens when a model attempts to attend to complex detailed features of the data), the model can be made to fit the data closely, even if it is a wrong model and hence useless for both future prediction and scientific explanation. Thus, a model fitting the data closely does not guarantee the model is useful either for scientific explanation or for prediction. As a simple example, six (x, y) data points can always be perfectly fit by a fifth-degree polynomial and well fit by a fourth-degree polynomial, when in fact the data were produced by (and hence should be fit by) a linear regression with error model. Thus, both the fourth- and fifth-degree polynomial models are wrong! A second example of such "overfitting" of the data, occurred when a statistician I know challenged an artificial-intelligence-oriented modeler to fit a set of data. After the modeler fit the data well with a highly complex model, this (mildly devious) statistician said to the modeler, "Oh, by the way, I made a mistake and randomly omitted half the data. Please confirm the correctness of your calibrated model by calibrating it again on the entire data set." The reader can guess the unfortunate result.

Additionally, Luecht and Clauser point out that separating signal (this being what we want to detect, such as the underlying cognitive state of an examinee) from noise can be difficult. There are two errors possible in statistically attempting to extract signal from noise. The usual error we are all familiar with and too often experience is failing to extract the signal from what appears to be only noise (i.e., lacking statistical power and reliability). But the overfitting erroneously discussed in the preceding paragraph is becoming more common, namely taking mere noise and, assisted by reductive complex statistical models, declaring it to be signal. With the complex models Luecht and Clauser call for, if we are not careful we risk making this second error, as occurs in the examples given earlier. This was a major concern the development of the Unified Model (see DiBello et al., 1995) in that its authors sought a deep but not over-parameterized stochastic model for cognitive diagnostics of multiple-item test data.

I was inspired and reoriented by reading the Luecht and Clauser chapter. Consider the following setting to explain the reorientation. Ask any professor the best way of accurately testing detailed knowledge and cognitive processing abilities for a particular substantive area, and he or she is likely to propose an oral exam (assuming testing must be secure and time constrained, thus ruling out a take-home exam). The reason for this is the examiner can administer relatively few complex items *interactively* (that is, the examiner can frequently interrupt the examinee with comments, suggestions, and redirections) that combine to produce a test that assesses competence accurately. As mentioned, the professor can and likely will intervene during the student's solving of each such complex item. The point is that we should be able to emulate this highly reliable and valid oral-exam-based interactive complex item-administration process using CBT with complex interactive items.

Keeping in mind there are many settings, current and contemplated, where a primary goal is to provide a detailed assessment of complex cognitive behavior, Luecht and Clauser drive home the importance of using complex items as test companies embrace CBT. But, the much maligned standardized multiple-choice test can do well in assessing educational achievement and skills in part because solving memory-recall problems and solving admittedly inauthentic, overly simple problems correlates well with the problem-solving skills we really want to measure. Essentially, we are not replacing bad with good by introducing complex item types; we are replacing decent with better. CBT means we can at least deemphasize correlationally valid useful memory and simple problem items used in paper-and-pencil testing and come much closer to testing authentic cognitive processing by emphasizing complex interactive items. Luecht and Clauser correctly emphasize that for a test to measure a particular cognitively complex domain well, the measurement goals of the test to be designed must guide item construction, IRT modeling, data collection, CBT item delivery algorithms, and item scoring. Several psychometrically and stochastic modeling oriented researchers interested in cognitive diagnosis are researching cognitive diagnosis, although they need to consider how to model and score complex examinee responses to new, interactive CBT item types.

Primarily, as already discussed, there is more authenticity possible with complex items in that solving such items more closely emulates the constructs they are intended to measure. There is one additional advantage to using complex and possibly interactive items for CBTs. Such complex items, and interactive items in particular, should be more resistant to compromise. That is, contamination by coaching for the test should be less of an issue for complex and interactive items. For example, suppose the three items of a test are to play chess, poker, and backgammon against the computer. These three items are so complex and interactive (and presumably authentic relative to the measurement goal) that it is highly unlikely any other test-training strategy than teaching students how to play these games well will be effective. Because of this latter advantage, fewer of such complex items would need to be manufactured.

A hidden challenge in using complex items is that it may be hard to manufacture time-efficient, cognitively complex items that are relatively free of serious extraneous distractions (construct irrelevant) and that do not require the examinee to spend time producing irrelevant data (from the perspective of the measurement goal) or doing irrelevant mental processing. For example, suppose a complex item in a writing skills test consists of examinees watching a 5-minute video clip and then being given 5 minutes to write a short, creative essay about it. Here the 10 minutes required might be excessive when compared with the amount of reliable and valid information gained about the examinee. In particular, the essay may not contain enough information about examinee writing ability to have justified the total 10-minute administration time of the item.

REVIEWER COMMENTARY ON FOLK AND SMITH

Whereas Luecht and Clauser focus on modeling of complex items, Folk and Smith (chap. 2, this volume) concentrate on modeling CBT item-delivery algorithms. Thus, they focus on maximizing the psychometric estimation power for a fixed, already-created item pool (consisting, perhaps, of complex items from the Luecht and Clauser perspective). Because we need good items that are wisely administered (delivered) for an effective CBT, the two chapters complement each other well. Folk and Smith stress the importance and richness of various CBT-delivery methods and imply that the careful stochastic IRT modeling of such delivery methods is crucial.

Essentially, Folk and Smith focus on two test types. The first type, CAT, sequentially selects items for each examinee based on ongoing inferences about each examinee's ability. The second type, computerized mastery testing (CMT), assigns each examinee to a mastery or non-mastery state based on results from a content-appropropriate and often adaptive test. Folk and Smith survey various models and approaches, including item-information maximizing and Bayes ability-posterior-distribution minimizing with constraints such as content balancing and time limits. They refer to an interesting idea (discovered independently by Wim van der Linden and Doug Jones, I believe) to do whole test optimization at each item-choosing stage rather than the one-item-at-a-time optimization that could violate content and other test level constraints. For mastery testing, sequential probability ratio testing (SPRT) and Bayes confidence interval approaches are described.

The issue of test construction by combining testlets (items administered together, such as the items following a reading passage) versus test construction by combining individual items separately is well presented and important. One advantage of testlets not discussed by Folk and Smith is that it facilitates subjective human inspection of all possible tests, thus eliminating poorly designed tests that do not actually violate the explicit test specifications. For example, a single test could have a science passage and a humanities passage (as called for by the specifications) that are both about dinosaurs, an undesirable situation unlikely to be flagged by formal test construction constraints but easily spotted by human inspection. Constructing a test using testlets facilitates this impressionistic human task, which is nearly combinatorially impossible to carry out at the item level. An additional advantage of testlets is that they can more easily be balanced for difficulty than can individual items. They can also be statistically useful when testlet-based stages are used in the CAT delivery algorithm. All examinees that have passed through the same set of stages or even through a single stage can have their raw scores compared to estimate their IRT latent ability for that stage or the common stages because the examinees have all taken the same items (e.g., see the Bayes EAP approach of Thissen, 1999).

Certain CBT delivery modeling issues should be addressed in light of Folk and Smith. In particular, a mathematically beautiful paper by Bickel, Buyske, Chang, and Ying (2001) on the sensitivity of the information-maximizing item-selection strategy to the assumed item response function modeling family is recommended. To establish this sensitivity, the authors show that two item response functional families that are similar in shape can in fact have different information optimizing strategies. If the IRT model uses one type of functional family, one obtains the usual optimal item-selection rule of choosing an item with difficulty close to current estimated examinee ability. But if the IRT model uses the other type of functional family, one obtains the counterintuitive optimal item-selection rule of choosing an item with difficulty as far away from the estimated ability as possible. Although we do not understand this study from a practical perspective, yet, it suggests possible overreliance on the standard item-delivery approach of matching item difficulty to estimated examinee ability.

There are some important issues in CBT that extend beyond model development. On a carefully designed paper-and-pencil test, items at the pretest stage are usually delivered at the same general location in the test (such as near the beginning) as they will be when they are operational. But we cannot do this for CBT. Hence, if location matters for an item, the item may be miscalibrated for most examinees. The issue is really how much location in the test affects the stability of item parameter estimates.

A second potential problem is item-parameter drift over time, noting that a CBT item in an item bank may be a live operational item for a fairly long time. For example, a passage about home run hitting in baseball would have drifted in item difficulty from before to after the McGwire–Sosa home run competition became a hot media topic.

Differential item functioning (DIF) seems more difficult to assess in CBT environments than in paper-and-pencil environments: Because more items must be pretested, there will be fewer examinees per pretest item (especially for low percentage minorities). This may be partially resolved by altering delivery strategies of pretest items to increase DIF estimation accuracy per examinee taking the item. Additionally, CBT introduces issues of examinee time allocation, computer usage skills, new item types, and so on, that require more careful DIF analysis. This equity issue is serious for CBT and requires careful attention.

The time a CAT exam takes to administer could be problematic. In particular, if examinees take longer on average per CAT item (because overly easy and overly difficult, and hence skippable, items are largely eliminated), the increased reliability for a CAT test per item does not translate into increased reliability per testing time unit.

ETS-sponsored research has examined certain information-maximizing strategies for CAT assembly that take into account the initial unreliability of ability estimates. In particular, Chang and Ying (1999) have a proposed multistage CAT algorithm that reserves the use of high discrimination items until they can be maximally effective in their narrow range of high information. This is useful because true examinee ability will be closer to its ongoing estimated ability after many CAT items have been administered. This is another example of how delivery models really matter, the topic of Folk and Smith's chapter.

CONCLUDING REMARKS

The chapters by Luecht and Clauser and Folk and Smith are stimulating and focus on issues important to the future of CBT. Luecht and Clauser offer a vision of the great benefits (and financial value) that CBT with complex items can offer to the testing companies and to society, especially for cognitive diagnosis purposes. Folk and Smith appropriately point us toward the challenging IRT modeling issues that arise when we attempt to design model-based test delivery systems for a CBT environment.

REFERENCES

Bickel, P., Buyske, S., Chang, H., & Ying, Z. (1998). On maximizing item information and matching difficulty with ability. *Psychometrika, 66*, 69–78.

Chang, H., & Ying, Z. (1999). α-stratified multistage computerized adaptive testing. *Applied Psychological Measurement, 23*, 211–222.

DiBello, L., Stout, W., & Roussos, L. (1995). Unified cognitive/psychometric diagnostic assessment likelihood-based classification techniques. In P. Nichols, S. Chapman, & R. Brennan (Eds.), *Cognitively diagnostic assessment* (pp. 361–390). Hillsdale, NJ: Lawrence Erlbaum Associates.

Mislevy, R. (1995). Probability-based inference in cognitive diagnosis. In P. Nichols, S. Chapman, & R. Brennan (Eds.), *Cognitively diagnostic assessment* (pp. 73–102). Hillsdale, NJ: Lawrence Erlbaum Associates.

Thissen, D. (1999). *Preliminary results obtained using various methods for scoring adaptive tests using (patterns of testlet) summed scores*. Unpublished manuscript.

TEST ADMINISTRATION

Maria T. Potenza
Microsoft Corporation

As was suggested in the previous part opener, the advent of computer-based testing (CBT) has provided the means for the development and practical implementation of a vast range of innovations with the potential to touch all aspects of the traditional, paper-based assessment process. The proliferation of the microprocessor and the explosion of other technological advances have finally provided the ability to incorporate long-standing psychometric theory into large-scale, standardized testing programs. But as is often the case when the bold and dramatic step is taken to move theory into practice, many unforeseen practical issues and formidable challenges come to light. Indeed, as many of the potential new testing models outlined in the previous section have begun to be implemented in the CBT environment, an entirely new array of issues surrounding test administration have emerged.

In traditional paper-based practice, the high-stakes testing industry has relied on a well-established and orchestrated set of standardized test administration procedures that have served the dual function of facilitating the psychometric integrity of the test development process (e.g., administration of pretest sections to thousands of examinees at the same time) and of upholding standards of fairness and equity (e.g., retirement of test forms after a single administration). The implementation and delivery of CBTs, however, have significantly impacted our ability to continue to rely on many of these long-standing administrative procedures. Enhancements made possible by CBT, such as targeted proficiency estimation, adaptive test designs, innovative item formats, continuous on-demand testing, and immediate score reporting have all introduced new and difficult issues for the administration of high-stakes, high-volume standardized tests. This section will focus on the impact that the operational implementation and delivery models employed for CBT administration have had in three key areas: (1) the item development process, (2) the maintenance of test and item bank security, and (3) the determination and application of policy decisions that must be made by testing programs.

A major difference between paper-based and computer-based tests revolves around the policies that govern how they are administered. Taken together, these chapters illustrate the fact that good psychometric practice alone is not sufficient to uphold the traditional standards of test development and security. As discussed by the authors of this section, the administration and delivery of CBTs also require good business and strategic modeling; for example, factors such as volume forecasting must now be considered when test design and associated policy decisions are being implemented. In addition, various features supported by CBT administration, such as the shorter test lengths of adaptive tests and the ability to provide more frequent test administrations, have also impacted test development and security in a number of ways. For example, while the provision of on-demand testing is perceived to be one of the major advantages of CBT, its implementation has also been shown to be a primary source of vulnerability to test security. Thus, this interplay between psychometric and practical policy considerations has forced testing organizations to find new means to support the development and implementation of CBTs using the current administrative model. The three chapters that comprise this section do a remarkable job of both providing a high level overview of many of these new challenges and a review of the research that has attempted to address many of these issues.

In chapter 6, Parshall highlights the issues introduced by the interaction between CBT administration and test development, specifically as this relates to obtaining the response data necessary for the pretesting and calibration of test items.

Parshall begins by providing an overview of the factors that influence pretesting needs and the importance of obtaining good pretest statistics in the exam development process. She then provides an overview of the practical constraints imposed on each of these by the current CBT test administration environment. Factors discussed include the test purpose, frequency of test administration, test delivery and measurement models employed, and item formats utilized. After an exploration of the process of pool development and the potential concerns regarding pretest data collection methods for each model, Parshall suggests future research directions to address CBT item development and pretesting needs. Some of the areas that she highlights include (1) causes of item changes across test modes, (2) use of response data from volunteer examinees, (3) methods for reducing the number of responses required for item calibration, (4) seeding pretest items and test delivery methods, (5) calibration and pretesting issues for adaptive tests, and (6) development of computer generated items.

In chapter 7, Way, Steffen, and Anderson present a model that can be used as a tool for determining and implementing a strategic approach to item and pool management. The authors present a hypothetical scenario to illustrate its use and application in the high-stakes, high-volume testing arena at one testing organization. While they admit the approach is that of "a single testing organization in response to a single set of circumstances," their presentation highlights the complex interaction of policy and psychometric considerations in planning, implementing, and maintaining adaptive testing given the administrative and delivery models in use today.

In this chapter, the authors present and describe the concept of an item VAT and the factors that impact its maintenance. Then the authors describe how the technique of System Dynamics Modeling (SDM) can be used as a tool for forecasting item development needs and for testing scenarios that can impact the partitioning of the item vat. Following this presentation, the authors provide an illustration of how SDM can be applied, and discuss policy considerations associated with maintaining an item inventory for high-stakes adaptive tests.

The authors of chapter 7 also point to the fact that many of the formidable challenges to the mechanics of CBT revolve around the provision of a continuous testing environment, and note that the successful use of any pool management strategy will partly be a function of the set of assumptions or policy decisions that are made. Policy issues that must be considered in formulating any pool management strategy include criteria for item retirement and item bank refreshment. However, as noted by the authors, these decisions are currently somewhat arbitrary because we do not have a foundation of empirical study to confirm assumptions regarding change in performance over time. We currently use the number of exposures as the primary criteria for item retirement; the authors point to the need to test assumptions associated with this policy approach. Other policy considerations the authors discuss include the reuse of disclosed items and response to legislative actions.

In the next chapter, Davey and Nering use a recent incident in admissions testing as the context for a high level overview of the factors impacting test and item pool security. The authors present an engaging comparative discussion of several factors that differentially impact test security in the traditional paper-based and CBT administration environments: (1) public relations, (2) logistics, (3) economics, and (4) pretesting. This discussion helps to underscore the practical issues and business considerations that the administrative aspects of CBT have introduced to the high-stakes testing industry. Davey and Nering point out that because "CAT is here to stay," the critical challenge before measurement professionals today is to develop and implement approaches that deal with continuous test administration effectively and efficiently, and in a manner that supports secure testing practices. The authors make the assertion that one way to achieve this goal is to improve the psychometrics underlying existing adaptive testing models.

Davey and Nering continue by discussing three approaches for maintaining security standards: (1) item exposure control, (2) managing item pools strategically, and (3) enhancing the self-correcting nature of adaptive tests. Two approaches are discussed for exposure control. In the first, intentional limits to the frequency any particular test item can be administered are enforced. In the second approach, the item selection algorithm incorporates exposure control with the goal of creating a more balanced use of the entire item pool. The authors then present a taxonomy of item exposure control approaches that delineates the classes of procedures and methods developed for each approach.

This chapter concludes with the seemingly simple and indisputable observation that *items will be exposed*. Davey and Nering make the important observation that techniques used to control item exposure in isolation are not sufficient to maintain security. They claim that the critical factor to upholding security in the current CBT delivery paradigm will be the application of a strategy that can simultaneously manage the economic, logistic, and development techniques needed to combat item exposure, in such a way that corrective action can be taken before any practical difference in test performance can be made. Chapter 7 provides a concrete example of one approach for strategically managing some of these factors.

This section concludes with two sets of discussants' comments on the preceding three chapters. In "New CBT Technical Issues: Developing Items, Pretesting, Test Security, and Item Exposure," Hambleton provides a review of the changes in research emphases that have been made in CBT since 1990. This overview underscores the point that the critical issues surrounding item development methods, item pool replenishment and item bank maintenance, and item and test security are a direct result of our ability to make CBT an operational reality. Hambleton goes on to observe that testing organizations employing CBT in high-stakes testing environments must now simultaneously address the "inextricable link" between the psychometric work and the practical or policy decisions that undergird each of these topics.

In the area of item development, Hambleton discusses factors associated with pretesting, sample size issues, and item quality. To help reduce pretesting sample size needs, he proposes that obtaining estimates of item statistics from item writers can help make useful gains. He then provides examples of current research in this arena and presents a summary of the techniques that can be used to support this approach. He also indicates that the development of procedures to help employ optimal sampling techniques of examinees holds great promise.

Hambleton outlines a series of research directions that can help inform the need to create large numbers of test items. The areas he predicts will be most fruitful for future research include (1) new methodologies for creating and developing items, specifically cloning methods, algorithmic item writing, and improved training for item writers, and (2) new methods for obtaining estimates of item statistics from item writers. He predicts that it will be the combination of item judgments and estimation procedures that will best help alleviate the pretesting sample issues reviewed by Parshall.

To help address issues of test security, Hambleton suggests that ascertaining acceptable item exposure rates should be addressed by increasing our efforts to identify items that have been exposed by monitoring changes in item statistics over time. In addition, he calls for the study and introduction of new item formats, and proposes that we revisit alternative test designs such as multi-stage testing, in an attempt to address some of these challenges. Finally, Hambleton calls for the need to expand simulation research to better inform policy decisions that are impacted by the complex interaction of statistical and administrative factors.

This section of the volume concludes with "Issues in CBT Administration" by Crocker. In her review, Crocker discusses each chapter from the perspective of traditional psychometric principles, namely content sampling, score equivalence, and fairness. Crocker observes that taken together, these chapters make explicit the fact that the introduction of operational CBT has resulted in the formulation of concepts and issues in the field of item and test administration that were not integral to the traditional administration methods of large-scale testing. She points out that the emergence of these new topics has resulted in the derivation of new terminology for the field of measurement. She underscores how important it is that measurement professionals and students-in-training become familiar with both this new measurement vernacular, and the substantive issues which it reflects.

Crocker makes the assertion that in addition to psychometric issues, each of the test administration issues and concomitant policy determinations raised across this set of chapters must also be viewed and evaluated from the perspective of the end-user (i.e., examinee and admissions officers). For example, Crocker introduces the practical concern of the college-level administrator who must use test scores produced in the CBT environment to make critical admissions decisions. She points to the fact that while CBT now affords us the convenience of on-demand testing, traditional admissions programs have yet to modify their admissions practices in response to the continuous availability of test scores.

Finally, it is Crocker's concluding point and its associated implication that is perhaps the most pivotal message of this section: If the complexities introduced by CBT administration practices should come to be viewed as threats to the validity and psychometric quality of standardized tests, the value of these tools in the high-stakes admissions arena could be diminished.

Item Development and Pretesting in a CBT Environment

Cynthia G. Parshall
Institute for Instructional Research and Practice
University of South Florida

INTRODUCTION

The test development process typically requires that many more items be written then will be used, even across multiple forms. Once items have been written, they must be evaluated for conformance to certain format and style considerations. More critically, they are evaluated in terms of testing program requirements for levels of content, difficulty, and fairness. Items that satisfy initial reviews are pretested, or administered to program examinees. Results of the pretesting are used to inform decisions about these items. Poorly performing items are removed from further consideration; items that demonstrate less serious problems are modified (followed by another round of pretesting); items that demonstrate still better performance are incorporated into the test program bank or pool. Classical item statistics may be used to ensure items in the bank satisfy certain criteria for difficulty, discrimination, and distractor performance. IRT criteria for the item statistics may specify acceptable ranges or values for the b, a, and c item parameters.

There is a need for good item pretest data for any test development. For standardized paper-and-pencil tests, pretest data aid in the assembly of parallel forms. For computerized tests, good pretest data are also necessary, whether the test will be delivered in an adaptive or nonadaptive method, and whether classical test form construction or IRT methods will be used. And, some form of examinee response data (i.e., pretest or operational data) are necessary whether the testing program will be converted from an existing paper-and-pencil test program or developed new for initial delivery on computer.

Item pretest data are used in computerized tests, just as they are in paper-and-pencil tests, as part of the test-assembly process. For nonadaptive test delivery methods, such as computerized fixed tests (CFT) and computerized exams assembled using automated test assembly (ATA) methods, the item statistics may be either classical or IRT based, and are used to help ensure statistical comparability across test forms. For adaptive test delivery models, such as CAT, computerized classification tests (CCT), and CMT, the item statistics are almost always IRT based and are used even more directly. When the 1P IRT model is used, the b parameter, or item difficulty, is used to select appropriate items for administration to individual examinees. When the 3P model is used for an adaptive test, the item information function is typically used to select items for administration. The information function is derived from all three item parameters: the b parameter; the a parameter, or item discrimination; and the c parameter, or lower asymptote of the item.

SEVERITY OF NEED FOR PRETEST ITEMS AND EXAMINEES

Although good item pretest data are important for CBT, they may be difficult to obtain for several reasons. Obtaining pretest data can be more difficult and more expensive when the items are administered on computer. The greater frequency of test administration dates for computerized exam programs may pose additional challenges; relatively few examinees test at any single time across these multiple exam dates, resulting in a slower process for accumulating examinee response data.

To further complicate matters, most CBTs actually need an increased number of items compared with their paper-and-pencil test counterparts. Adaptive test models in particular require many more items in the available pool, and they require many more examinees per item to obtain good item parameter estimates. Furthermore, highly efficient or short adaptive tests can less easily support the same number of item pretestings, because the proportion of pretest to operational items taken by a given examinee should be low. The demands for pretesting depend on aspects of the testing program, including the test purpose, the frequency of test administration dates, the test delivery model, the measurement model, and the types of items in the pool.

A fundamental aspect of the testing program that affects the need for items is the *test purpose*. A high-stakes exam, for example, will have greater demands for a large item pool than will a low-stakes test. When the test score is used to make critical decisions, there is more potential for examinee cheating and thus a greater need to limit item exposure and test overlap. A high-stakes test will usually require a large initial item pool as well as frequent pool additions or replacements. Testing programs with less critical score outcomes may only need to maintain an item pool large enough to provide good measurement; security is not a major concern.

A related issue is the *increased number of test dates* that are typically made available for computerized exams. When the number of test dates is increased, items are more exposed over time, even though the same number of examinees are testing. This may also create a need for more items, particularly in high-stakes tests.

Another factor affecting the amount of pretest data needed is the *test delivery method*. The test delivery method directly affects the number of items needed for the pool, with nonadaptive delivery methods requiring fewer items than adaptive methods. Fixed CBTs intended to support a limited number of test forms may not require any more items than a paper-and-pencil test. Test delivery methods such as the ATA might come next in order of item requirements (Parshall, Spray, Kalohn, & Davey, 2002; Spray, 1999). These computer-generated parallel test forms are assembled based on test specification requirements for content classifications and item statistics. They may put more demand on the item pool than fixed-form CBT delivery, but they will still be less demanding than statistically optimal adaptive test delivery methods. Adaptive testing may take one of several approaches. Classification tests such as the CCT delivery method typically draw heavily on the items that are most informative around the cut score (Spray & Reckase, 1994). CMTs are another type of classification test in which testlets are used; the testlets themselves are often constructed to emphasize measurement at the cut score (Way, 1994). Both of these test delivery methods place greater demands on the item pool than do nonadaptive methods, particularly in the vicinity of the cut score. Finally, the "standard" CAT places very heavy demands on the item pool, often needing to support extensive use throughout the range of examinee proficiency.

The severity of the need for examinee response data also depends on the *measurement model* used for the testing program. The measurement model affects the number of examinee responses needed for each item, rather than the number of items. CBTs can be nonadaptively administered using classical statistics; this model requires the fewest pretest examinees per item. For any of the adaptive test delivery models, IRT parameters are usually needed. The two IRT models used most often in practice are the 1P and the 3P models. As in any application of statistical estimation, more examinees are needed when more parameters are estimated. The number of examinees needed to obtain good calibration data is far greater for the 3P model than for the 1P model. Whereas 200 examinees may be sufficient for calibration in the 1P model (Wright & Stone, 1979), up to 1,000 examinees may be more suitable for the 3P model (Hulin, Lissak, & Drasgow, 1982; Mislevy & Stocking, 1989).

Finally, the number and kind of *item types* included in the pool have implications for pretesting. Traditionally, standardized tests have been constructed primarily of discrete, multiple-choice items. Pretest data for these items may be obtained from either paper-and-pencil tests or CBTs. Some of the new item types, developed specifically for computerized testing, cannot be administered in paper-and-pencil form. Thus, some pretest data-collection efforts may be restricted to computer administrations, even for minimally innovative items. Item formats that are more extensively innovative require more consideration. These item types typically involve far greater developmental effort and expense, require more examinee testing (or pretesting) time, and are more memorable, resulting in a need for a larger number to ensure item and test security. Finally, an additional problem may arise when a test uses several innovative item types (O'Neill & Folk, 1996). When there are multiple types, but relatively few items of some types, it may be difficult to pretest each of the types without presenting examinees with too many item formats.

In summary, item-development and pretesting needs vary across types of testing programs. A high-stakes CAT program using the 3P model and including innovative items has demanding item-development and pretest needs. This type of program is also likely to use exposure control to guard test and item security, as well as techniques such as vats or rotating pools. (See Davey & Nering, chap. 8, and Way, Steffen, & Anderson, chap. 7, this volume, for further discussion of these issues.) A low-stakes CBT program, using classical item statistics or the 1P IRT model and consisting entirely of traditional, multiple-choice items, would have much lower item-development demands, although it may still be more complex and demanding than would be typical for a paper-and-pencil exam program.

The need for large numbers of items in many CBT programs is often coupled with a need for large numbers of appropriate examinees on which to pretest those items. If the item parameters are obtained without an adequate examinee sample size, they are likely to be poorly estimated (Hambleton, & Jones, 1994). Poor item parameter estimates will affect examinee scores and test score decisions under any test delivery model. Under adaptive testing models, they will also have a more direct effect on examinees, given that item selection, as well as scoring, is typically based on those item parameter estimates. The process of item development and pretesting are of critical concern to the development of good tests and accurate, meaningful scores.

TYPICAL PROCESS OF POOL DEVELOPMENT

There are three typical pool development stages under which examinee response data are needed for the purposes discussed earlier. The first is the *initial start-up* of a testing program. If the testing program was previously administered in paper-and-pencil mode, a common solution is to start the CBT using operational examinee response data from paper-and-pencil administrations of the exam. If it is a new testing program, and no operational examinee response data are available, volunteers may be solicited to take the items (either in paper-and-pencil or computer mode). The volunteers' responses to the items are used to estimate how the items will function with actual examinees during operational testing.

Next, after some period of operational administration of the exam, examinee response data are needed to recalibrate the items in a pool (Haynie & Way, 1995; Stocking, 1988; Sykes & Fitzpatrick, 1992). *Recalibration* may be desirable because the initial item calibrations were obtained from paper-and-pencil administrations, because the examinees used in the initial calibration were volunteers, or because sufficient time has passed and the functioning of some of the items may have changed because of changes in the underlying content or construct or because of parameter drift.

As the CBT is used operationally, it will also be necessary to maintain a process of adding items to the pool. This ongoing maintenance need, or *pool replenishing* (Stocking, 1994) task, requires examinee response data to pretest the additional items. If the testing program is continuing to be offered in dual modes, the pretest statistics could be obtained from paper-and-pencil administrations. It may be more efficient and less expensive to pretest in paper-and-pencil mode, although there might be some fairness concerns about the two modes if all the pretesting was conducted in only one mode. On the other hand, for testing programs that are only offered on computer, and for most innovative items, pretesting can only be conducted on the computer.

Although CBTs require sufficient pretest data, as discussed earlier, problems may be associated with pretesting and item calibration at each of these test development stages. Some of these pitfalls can be avoided if care is taken; others are more problematic.

Potential Problems With the Data

One potential problem for test development and pretesting is that the item statistics obtained from examinee responses under paper-and-pencil testing may be inappropriate for CBTs. Factors that may contribute to a mode effect include aspects of the paper-and-pencil mode such as item ordering, context, local item dependency (Reese, 1998; Spray, Parshall, & Huang, 1997), and flexibility differences (e.g., item review) between paper-and-pencil and computer modes. Additionally, there may be a cognitive difference maximized by the two modes. Different optimal test-taking strategies for each mode may be applied by some examinees, but not by others. Given that paper-and-pencil item parameters may be inappropriate for CBT, a related concern is the potential effect of concurrently using item statistics obtained under both modes.

Another concern for either method of pretesting items relates to the use of volunteer subjects. Volunteers are likely to be nonrepresentative of the examinee population as a whole. Furthermore, when operational test examinees are asked to voluntarily take additional items, they are aware their performance on those items will not affect their scores. Although it may be reasonable for these examinees not to try as hard on these items, this change in motivation clearly has implications for the accuracy and quality of the resultant item statistics. However, in many cases it may be difficult, not to say unethical, to keep hidden from examinees the fact of pretest items. A different type of concern regarding volunteer examinees is the cost associated with these means of obtaining pretest data. Few individuals will volunteer to take a test without some incentive; often, that incentive is payment for participation.

Difficulties with recalibrating CBT items may also occur. Problems with recalibrating data are particularly likely under adaptive administrations. Adaptive tests result in sparse data matrices, which may affect calibration precision. Some few items may have been seen by many of the examinees, but a larger proportion of the items will have been seen by relatively few examinees. In addition, there may be little overlap of test items across examinees. Adaptive tests often result in examinee responses from a limited range of proficiency for the items in the pool, especially for highly informative items. For example, an item that is relatively difficult for the pool will only have been presented to high-ability examinees. This restricted ability range may distort the accuracy of the calibration.

Replenishing the item pool may also be problematic. If the items are pretested in paper-and-pencil mode, the potential problems mentioned earlier apply. If the items are pretested on volunteers, both motivation and representativeness are concerns. Pretesting during operational testing may yield the best data, but short, adaptive tests cannot always support the quantity of pretest items needed. Finally, there is the question of how the pretest items will be administered. They may be randomly seeded to examinees or they may be targeted to examinees at specific levels of proficiency. In an adaptive test, random seeding of pretest items may result in examinees' encountering items that are highly inappropriate for them (e.g., not at all matched to the examinees' abilities). Furthermore, it is natural to expect that some pretest items will be of lesser quality than the operational items in the pool. The presence of these inappropriate or poor quality items may negatively affect examinees' performance on the operational items.

Courses of Action Available

Several immediate, administrative actions may be taken to address some of these item development, pretesting, and calibration problems across the stages of test development and maintenance. A few of these actions are satisfactory, whereas others actually limit the value and utility of the CBT program. For example, reducing the number of dates available for examinees to take the CBT would probably help reduce the demand for pretest items, but it would also lessen one of examinees' favorite aspects of CBTs. Other actions may be even less feasible. It may not be possible for a high-stakes testing program to lessen the stakes without changing the utility of the test.

A more satisfactory immediate course of action for a testing program is to administer a fixed CBT, automatically constructed linear test, or other nonadaptive test. For adaptive tests, choice of measurement model can also reduce the need for examinee response data. Tests that use item types with a minimal guessing factor (e.g., a math item type that calls for the examinee to type a response) might be able to fit the data satisfactorily to a 2P IRT model. This would reduce the sample size needed for 3P IRT calibrations. Of course, many testing programs, particularly in the certification and licensure areas, have chosen to use the 1P model to great effect. Use of this model lessens the number of examinee responses needed per item and may lessen the number of items needed in the pools. This model also appears to be less subject than the 3P model to overexposure of the more "informative" items (Way, 1997).

Although some existing operational CBT programs have addressed these problems, a great need remains for improving certain aspects of the item-development and pretesting process for CBT administration.

SUMMARY OF SOME RESEARCH DIRECTIONS

A wide range of research and developmental topics have implications for CBT item-development and pretesting needs. Pertinent topics include: the appropriateness of using paper-and-pencil exam item calibrations in CBTs, the effect of obtaining pretest data from volunteer examinees, methods to reduce the number of examinees needed for item calibrations, considerations for seeding pretest items, problems for adaptively administered tests, alternative test delivery methods, and the development of computer-generated items.

Paper-and-Pencil Item Calibrations

Some test items do not display an effect for mode of administration, and others display only a minor effect. Nevertheless, the mode effect has important implications and should be further researched. If the causes of item changes across test mode can be identified, perhaps they can also be controlled. This might take the form of controlling aspects of either the paper-and-pencil or the computer mode administration. It might also take the form of statistically adjusting item parameters obtained in the paper-and-pencil mode to use them appropriately in the computer mode.

Several studies have been conducted on the comparability of paper-and-pencil tests and CBTs. In general, these studies found that total test scores were often affected by test mode, although usually minimally. However, a larger effect was found for some individual items that performed differently in the two modes. Several studies found some items to be easier in the computer mode and other items to be more difficult (see Bugbee & Bernt, 1990, Mazzeo & Harvey, 1988, and Mead & Drasgow, 1993, for summaries of some of this literature). In CATs, where proportionally fewer items are administered to examinees, the effect of any single item's performance could be exacerbated.

Potential causes of the mode effect include attributes of the examinees, the items, the computer interface, and the test-taking experience as a whole. One of the earliest mode effects to be identified was for speeded tests (Greaud & Green, 1986; Mead & Drasgow, 1993). Mead and Drasgow (1993) suggested that a likely explanation for this effect is the difference in motor skills between responding in the two modes. Parshall and Kromrey (1993) isolated subsets of examinees who displayed substantial mode effect: one group of examinees performed better than expected in the paper-and-pencil mode and another group performed better than expected in the computer mode. Several examinee characteristics (including demographic, attitudinal, and test-taking strategy variables) were investigated as potential contributors to this mode effect, but only weak relationships were found.

Some of the earlier comparability studies, discussed by Mazzeo and Harvey (1988), found mode differences for tests that used graphics and multiple-screen items. As screen resolutions get closer to print quality this type of effect is likely to be mitigated or even disappear. However, other aspects of the computer interface may have a more insidious influence on performance differences across the two modes. Booth (1991) stated, "CBT item presentation involves a complex fusion of cognitive, psychological, and perceptual dynamics. As such, we should not, and cannot expect to merely transform on a one-to-one basis . . . paper-and-pencil test items to [computer] format and expect such test items to be equivalent to their printed counterparts" (p. 282). Vicino and Moreno (1997) confirmed this, indicating that "reactions to computer tasks are largely dependent on the software interface" (p. 158).

Bugbee and Bernt (1990) more directly addressed the concept of task constraints by noting that "computer technology imposes unique factors that may affect testing" (p. 97). Bennett and Bejar (1998) pointed out that any testing situation imposes constraints on the problem-solving and response behaviors of an examinee. They suggest that "the challenge . . . is to fashion an interface that balances the need for easily scored input against remaining true to the nature of problem solving in the domain" (p. 11).

Thus, differences in examinee performance across paper-and-pencil and computer modes may be caused by differences in the nature and extent of task constraints, as reflected in *either* paper-and-pencil format requirements or the computer user interface. Research that identifies facets of task constraints that contribute to a mode effect should lead to better control over the effect. Improved measurement, as well as greater comparability across modes, may result from changes in the task constraints for either mode.

Finally, more extensive research into content and cognitive features of test items might reveal critical causes of item performance shifts across test modes. Mislevy, Sheehan, and Wingersky (1993) summarized some promising research into item parameter variance accounted for by item characteristics, including content specifications and cognitive processing requirements. Further work in this area could be addressed toward finding the item characteristics associated with changes in item parameters across test mode. For cognitive attributes of the items, this might have particular implications for user interface issues, as discussed earlier.

Further research is needed into the causes of differences in item parameter estimates across paper-and-pencil and computer test modes, and into the means for isolating or controlling the undesired effects. A greater understanding of a predictable mode effect may enable research-ers to identify a useful statistical adjustment for paper-and-pencil test item parameters that will be used in CBTs. Alternatively, changes in the task or response constraints, or in the cognitive processing demands of the items, may remove the effect. Depending on the response constraints and the cognitive demands of the item, either the paper-and-pencil or the computer mode administration may need to be changed. These changes may improve measurement and increase the match between item pa-rameters obtained in the two modes, in the process making the use of item calibrations obtained from paper-and-pencil administrations in CBTs less problematic.

Response Data From Volunteer Examinees

Items are routinely pretested in paper-and-pencil exams. Sometimes this pretesting is evident to the examinees (as in a specially marked test sec-tion); sometimes it is hidden from the examinees. In a CBT, the pretest items may also be presented in a separate test section, perhaps after op-erational testing is complete, or they may be embedded throughout the actual exam. There are several concerns about the accuracy of pretest data based on the examinees who provide the item responses.

When possible, the best item parameter estimates are probably ob-tained by having examinees respond to items during an operational but nonadaptive, CBT, without any cue as to which items are the unscored, or pretest, items. Examinees who are aware they are responding to un-scored items, either during operational testing or in nonoperational, vol-untary pretesting, may not respond in a motivated fashion. However, in several situations legal and ethical considerations limit pretesting items without examinees' knowledge and consent. Unfortunately, volunteer examinees may not be representative of the test population as a whole in terms of demographic characteristics, knowledge of the content area, or computer skill.

Research in the area of paper-and-pencil pretesting may provide hy-potheses to investigate for computer pretesting. For example, research could be used to determine the most effective administrative techniques (e.g., paying for high scores, offering students the option of using their scores) for increasing examinee motivation, and thus improving the ac-curacy of pretest data obtained from volunteers. Research could also be conducted on optimal volunteer groups and on weighting responses for different subgroups, where their representation differs from the test-taking population as a whole. If the effect of using volunteers in a testing program is sufficiently reliable or predictable, research might identify a useful statistical adjustment for modifying the item parameters before us-ing them in operational CBT.

Reducing the Number of Examinees Needed for Item Calibrations

The development of methods to estimate item parameters using fewer examinees would be valuable for many applications, including but not limited to CBT. Several researchers have investigated ways to limit the need for calibration examinees. Various approaches have been considered, including using additional information or adding statistical constraints during the item-calibration process.

Several modifications to calibration models have been investigated in terms of their utility with small samples of examinees. Modifications to parameter estimation models include using a fixed, nonzero c (Barnes & Wise, 1991; Sireci, 1992); constraining the prior variance of the a parameter (Harwell & Janosky, 1991; Parshall, Kromrey, Chason, & Yi, 1997); and using a mixed-model approach, that is, a combination of IRT models within a single pool (Patsula & Pashley, 1996; Sireci, 1992).

Barnes and Wise (1991) conducted a simulation in which the item parameter estimates obtained under small sample conditions for typical 1P and 3P models were compared with modified models, which incorporated a fixed, nonzero c parameter. They found that model modifications yielded more accurate parameter estimates than the standard 1P and 3P models. Harwell and Janosky (1991) conducted a simulation study on 2P models in which estimation of the a parameter was affected by imposing different variances on the prior distribution of the as. Under the conditions in this study, item parameter estimates for small samples were recovered more accurately when a more informative (i.e., narrower) prior variance was used. Parshall et al. (1997) also conducted a simulation investigation into modified models. In this study, a common c parameter was estimated and a more informative prior variance was imposed on the a parameter. The item parameter estimates in this study were also evaluated in terms of their performance with cross-validation data. The study findings indicated that in some cases the modified models yielded less accuracy in the calibration samples, but greater accuracy (and less variability in accuracy) in the cross-validation samples. Although the results of these studies are not conclusive, there appear to be grounds for additional research.

Another calibration approach has attempted to reduce the need for examinee response data by capitalizing on additional information about the items themselves. This collateral information may take several forms, such as expert judgments, test specifications, or cognitive processing features of the items (Billeaud & Steffen, 1996; Mislevy et al., 1993).

Mislevy et al. provided a model for incorporating collateral information about items to augment response data available on a small sample of examinees. An initial data set, including both examinee responses to the items and the associated collateral information, is needed to apply this model. Furthermore, Mislevy et al. indicated the data must be fit by an IRT model, and the collateral information must be correlated with their IRT parameters. The data are then used to build predictive distributions for the item parameters. These distributions are used as informative priors and combined with examinee responses to the items to obtain item parameter estimates. Mislevy et al. illustrated this method by equating operational test data. They calibrated item parameters, using predictive distributions from collateral data in conjunction with responses from 250 new examinees. The results were very similar to baseline data obtained on a minimum of 5,000 examinee responses per item.

Billeaud and Steffan (1996) attempted to apply similar methods to predict item parameters for some categories of GRE Analytical and Verbal items. Their investigation was less successful, with most of the predictive models functioning poorly in cross-validation samples. However, they attributed their difficulties to problems with inadequate sample sizes and a high number of dichotomous item characteristics in the model. Item characteristics that had more variance and that were shared across more of the item types would have more power in the multiple regression analysis. Billeaud and Steffen also suggested research into collateral information models that include cognitive processing and psycholinguistic information about the items.

One other research direction regarding calibration models is only applicable to pretest applications. In this line of research, the number of pretest examinees may be reduced by capitalizing on information available in the concomitant operational data (Hsu, Thompson, & Chen, 1998; Patsula & Pashley, 1996). Patsula and Pashley (1996) investigated the use of polynomial logistic regression techniques for modeling pretest data. This method uses a standard statistical program, such as SAS or SPSS, to conduct the regression. Patsula and Pashley found the 3P IRT model to be fit by a cubic logistic model. Estimates of examinees' ability, computed from their responses to operational items, were used to fit polynomial logistic functions to the pretest items. Stepwise elimination analysis enabled Patsula and Pashley to identify items that could be adequately fit with lower parameterized models, such as the 2P model. These reduced models were found for a substantial number of items. Patsula and Pashley suggested this approach could be used to obtain preliminary, less demanding pretest data. Any items found to perform poorly could be removed from further consideration without requiring additional examinee responses. Additional advantages of the method included the ability to model item distractors and to fit poorly performing pretest items (e.g., items that do not satisfy the IRT assumption of being nonmonotonically increasing).

Another approach that uses operational data to assist in the calibration and scaling of pretest data was used in Hsu et al. (1998). In this approach, the operational test items are not recalibrated; rather, they are used to define the trait measured by the test and to set the scale. Pretest items are calibrated with the operational data, one item at a time. The Pretest Item Calibration (PIC) program (Davey, 1990) computes the full posterior distribution for each examinee over the set of operational items to define the composite trait measured by the test. Each pretest item is then calibrated, one at a time, in sequence. This method may reduce the need for pretest examinees, given that the operational item parameters are held constant and so very few parameters are estimated in each calibration run.

Research into item parameter recovery with small samples could be conducted to evaluate the accuracy and efficiency of these approaches, across generalizable data sets and CBT program conditions. As indicated previously, numerous testing applications would benefit from methods for calibrating data that require fewer examinee responses, including most CBT programs.

Considerations in Seeding Pretest Items

Several issues regarding methods for distributing pretest items to examinees need to be considered. First, pretest items may be embedded within the operational items, or they may be administered as a unit at the end of the test. Under administrations where time is a factor, pretest items appended to the end of an operational test may display an effect due to testing time or examinee fatigue. For paper-and-pencil testing, Vale (1986) has demonstrated that an interlaced (or embedded) design is best for efficient placement of items onto the same scale. However, further research on these considerations is warranted for both non-adaptive and adaptive CBTs.

Pretest items may also be administered to examinees either randomly or with a systematic attempt to match an item to an examinee's proficiency. In an adaptive test, potential problems arise with random seeding of pretest items to examinees. Under random seeding, examinees may be presented with items inappropriate for their ability level. On the one hand, this may provide a cue to the examinee that the item is a pretest item and thus not scorable. If examinees then respond to the item in a nonmotivated manner, this may result in inaccurate pretest item statistics. On the other hand, encountering these inappropriately hard or easy items may affect an examinee's emotional state during testing; potentially affecting the examinee's performance on the operational items, and thus his or her test score. A similar concern stems from the fact that some pretest items are of lesser quality than the operational items. There may be an effect on examinees' performance on operational items when an exam includes pretest items of relatively poor quality. Research could be conducted on this effect, related to the length of the adaptive test, the proportion of bad or inappropriate items encountered by the examinee, and the distance between the pretest items and the examinee's true ability. (Targeted seeding of items, including pretest items, is discussed later.)

For IRT-based tests, especially CATs, issues regarding the calibration and *scaling* of pretest items need to be addressed. If a set of pretest items were to be calibrated independently of operational data, a scaling problem might arise. Although the items would be scaled relative to one another, they would not necessarily be on the same scale as the operational pool. In fact, if the pretest items are not fully representative of the item pool, they might be scaled in reference to a different composite trait.

The PIC method (Davey, 1990) discussed previously is one approach to rescaling pretest items. In this method the operational items are held to their previous values; the pretest items are then automatically placed on the operational scale as they are calibrated. Because a single pretest item is calibrated with the operational data at a time, no pretest item can contaminate any other. Additionally, even if the set of pretest items should constitute a different composite trait from the set of operational items, no shifting of the scale should occur. Additional research is needed to confirm the functionality and utility of this approach.

Another method for scaling pretest items in IRT-based exams is to present examinees with anchor items along with the pretest items (Folk & Golub-Smith, 1996; Haynie & Way, 1995, 1996; Stocking, 1988). Stocking (1988) investigated two methods for online calibration, over multiple cycles of pool recalibration and replenishment. She investigated a method in which the scale is set, in the calibration program LOGIST, by estimating examinee ability on the operational items alone; the further calibration of pretest items was then referenced to that scale. To compensate for error inherent in the ability estimates, Stocking investigated a method in which anchor items were seeded along with pretest items. In this method, the calibration run was followed by rescaling the pretest items through the anchor items (Stocking & Lord, 1983). Scale drift tended to accumulate under both methods, across the four cycles of recalibration investigated. The anchor item method was more demanding in terms of numbers of pretest items (or examinee responses); however, it mitigated scale drift to some extent.

Folk and Golub-Smith (1996) used both anchor items and item priors to calibrate and scale pretest items. They calibrated the operational items concurrently with the anchor and pretest items, using an option in Bilog to place strong priors on the operational items to constrain them to values close to the original parameter estimates. After the calibration run, the pretest items were scaled through the anchor items onto the operational scale, using the Stocking and Lord (1983) procedures. The results indicated that using specific priors on the operational items enabled good recovery of the pretest item parameters, but results for using anchor items was more ambiguous.

Further research on methods for calibrating pretest items is needed, and more information is needed about the use of operational data or anchor items to fix the scale. Confirmed methods for enhancing the accuracy and precision of pretest item parameter estimation, while using as few examinees as possible, would be very useful.

Specific Problems for Adaptive Tests

For CATs several specific issues arise, pertaining to both recalibration and pretesting of items in the pool. These issues include the effects that use of different examinee groups as calibration samples may have on the resultant item parameter estimates and the problems that may arise from sparse data.

Haynie and Way (1995) stated several critical issues for adaptive exams, "The problem in recalibrating operational CAT items is that although the item pool may consist of many items, data on any given item are typically both sparse and based on a restricted range of ability. The problem faced in the pretest calibrations is that the adaptive CAT data must somehow be utilized in the calibration and scaling of the pretest data" (p. 1). The nature of the examinee response data available from CATs is not optimal for item parameter estimation, and Haynie and Way pointed out two of the most critical issues: sparseness and restricted range. Sparseness is addressed a little later in this discussion; examinee ability range is addressed here.

Simulations conducted by Ito and Sykes (1994) illustrate a problem with recalibrating data based on a restricted range of examinee ability. This study of a 1P CAT simulated a statistically efficient exam, in which proficient examinees responded only to difficult items and less able examinees responded only to easy items. The recalibrated b values obtained under these restrictions were not sufficiently accurate under most of the conditions investigated.

More generally, several researchers have considered optimal distributions of examinee ability for IRT item parameter estimation (Berger, 1994; Berger & van der Linden, 1992; Jones & Jin, 1994; Stocking, 1990;

Vale, 1986). Stocking (1990) identified optimum distributions of ability for item parameter estimation under the 1P, 2P, and 3P IRT models under the assumption that examinee ability and some item parameters are known. In brief, Stocking found that information about the c parameter is only obtained from low ability examinees, the optimal ability level for information about the b parameter is close to the value of b, and the most informative points for estimating a are above and below b (points that are too close to b, or too far above and below it, are uninformative). Taken together, these results suggest that a broad distribution of abilities, possibly rectangular, is optimal for calibrating a set of items.

Although in general this is not the distribution of examinee ability likely to arise by chance or under adaptive test administrations, it may provide guidance for selecting examinees for calibration or recalibration purposes. More specifically, if some preliminary information is known about a given item, consideration of optimal ability distributions may provide guidance for the targeted examinee abilities needed to calibrate that item. In fact, a *sequential* process could be followed for estimating both the item parameters and the optimal examinee distributions (Berger, 1994; Jones & Jin, 1994). A set of examinee responses could be used to provide initial information about an item. That information could then be used to estimate the optimal distribution of ability for calibrating the item. This updated distribution could be used for targeting examinees from given ability levels to provide additional responses to the item.

Berger (1994) presented a multistage procedure for estimating item parameters under optimal sampling designs. His results suggested that a two- or three-stage design might be adequate for efficient estimation of item parameters. In a two-stage design, for example, a small number of examinees might be used for initial pretesting; the parameter estimates obtained on these examinees would then enable determination of optimal ability levels for remaining pretest data collection. Berger's simulation results suggested that item parameter estimation using examinee responses from a normal distribution would have required approximately one fourth more examinees than the optimal approach used. Jones and Jin (1994) also developed a sequential process for online calibration of a pretest item on an optimal distribution of examinee ability. The results of their simulation study found this method to be more efficient than random seeding of the items. Jones and Jin discussed the simultaneous calibration of a set of items and an approach to allocating examinees to items.

Additional research is needed into approaches for identifying and using optimal examinees to efficiently estimate item parameters. This has implications for accurately recalibrating a pool, as well as for seeding pretest items to examinees. For example, in variable-length classification tests, examinees near the cut score may receive far more operational items than examinees at the extremes of proficiency. In such a model, it might be appropriate to administer proportionally more pretest items to those extreme examinees. This approach might help hold the total test to more similar lengths across examinee proficiency, while also approaching a uniform distribution of ability for calibration purposes.

As mentioned previously, another issue for data collected under adaptive administration is the effect of sparse data on item parameter estimation. The sparseness of the data matrix resulting from adaptive testing may limit the precision or accuracy of recalibrated item parameters. Hsu et al. (1998) simulated CAT administration of a 600-item pool to 100,000 examinees. In this simulation, a subset of the items was administered to at least 1,000 examinees; these 336 items were selected for recalibration. The resultant 100,000 by 336 matrix was highly sparse, because of the large numbers of "not-presented" items in the matrix for every simulated examinee. Hsu et al. compared the precision of item parameter estimates obtained under this sparse matrix with estimates obtained under nonadaptive conditions. This comparative data set had a full matrix, with responses from 1,000 examinees to the same 336 items identified previously and with no omitted or not-presented data. Results of this study suggested that the sparse, CAT data matrix required approximately 10 times as many examinees to yield item parameter estimates with the same level of precision as that obtained in the full, nonadaptive data matrix. Further research is needed to confirm this effect and to identify more efficient methods to address recalibration of sparse data from adaptively administered exams.

Test Delivery Methods

Several studies have been conducted on alternative approaches to CBT delivery. Some of these methods may be useful for item development and pretesting.

Developmental work on the ATA approach to CBT suggests it may be a promising method (Parshall, Spray, Kalohn, & Davey, 2002; Spray, 1999). This test delivery method has some features and benefits in common with the LOFT method, discussed in Folk and Smith (chap. 2, this volume). In the ATA, items are sampled from a pool according to rigorous content and statistical criteria; either classical or IRT item parameters may be used. The result is a set of test forms that satisfy test content specifications as well as first and second moment parallelism, while still offering some degree of exposure control and randomness across forms. An ATA exam may be constructed interactively during the administration of each examinee's CBT. Alternatively, a full set of ATAs may be constructed before any operational testing; each examinee is then randomly administered one of the parallel test forms. If well conducted, this method of test construction may eliminate the need for equating, for standard setting studies, and for scaled scores (scores can be reported as percent correct). Because this test delivery method is not adaptive, it should require fewer items for operational use. Promising work on the development of this and other alternative test delivery methods should be followed up by rigorous evaluation of their effectiveness and their potential for reducing pretest demands.

Another recommendation that warrants further research was proposed by Hsu et al. (1998). They suggested an approach to administering CBTs in which items are used operationally when only minimal, preliminary pretest data are available. These data may be obtained under any quick, low-examinee sample methods. The critical point in this method is that the items are weighted based on the quality of their parameter estimates. Items with limited information about their parameter estimates would be weighted to contribute only a minimal amount toward the examinees' scores. Over time, sufficient additional information about the items would be collected to enable recalibration. The items would then be weighted more heavily for future operational use and score computation. Further investigation of this approach is needed to determine its utility for operational testing.

One problem in item parameter estimation for the 2P or 3P IRT models is that the a parameter may be overestimated. This leads to inflated estimation of the test information function (Hambleton & Jones, 1994) and to bias in examinee scores and scale drift (Stocking, 1988). One possible approach to the problem is to reduce the item-selection algorithm's dependence on the a parameter. For example, Chang and Ying (1997) have recommended a stratified CAT design in which the item pool is stratified into several levels based on the values of the a parameter. Early in the adaptive test, when information about the examinee's score is low, item selection is constrained to the lowest levels of the stratified a values. As the test progresses, and estimation of the examinee's proficiency becomes more accurate, items with higher a values (and narrow information functions) are administered. Problems resulting from poor estimation of the a parameter may be lessened under this approach.

Chang and Ying have also discussed the exposure control benefits of this design. Like other exposure control methods (Parshall, Davey, & Nering, 1998; Stocking & Lewis, 1998; Sympson & Hetter, 1985), it should both limit the overexposure of some items and increase overall pool usage. There is a conflict between efficient testing and full pool usage; however, one relevant advantage of improved pool usage is a reduction in the sparseness of the response data matrix, thus aiding online calibration. Further research into methods for selecting items that provide an ideal compromise in this conflict would be of value.

Research may also be needed into appropriate methods for controlling the item pool scale when using mixed models. There are sample size advantages to fitting some items with a 1P or 2P IRT model even when other items in the pool require a full 3P model. However, the scales obtained when calibrating across IRT models with different numbers of parameters may not be comparable. Another scaling issue that warrants further investigation arises when a test includes both dichotomous and partial-credit items. Optimal methods are needed for administering these types of items adaptively and computing total scores.

Computer-Generated Items

Another avenue of research includes work on developing item templates precise enough to enable the computer to generate parallel items that do not need to be individually calibrated (Bejar, 1996; Meisner, Luecht, & Reckase, 1993). Some content areas may be sufficiently clearly defined so that item templates can be developed that can capture those elements of the item reflected in the item parameters. If this approach is effective, both item-development and pretest needs will be addressed.

Meisner et al. (1993) stated, "It seems reasonable to assume that items requiring the same knowledge and skills for their solution would be likely to exhibit parallel statistical characteristics. . . . The ability to reliably predict item statistics would have obvious implications for efficient parallel forms construction and computerized adaptive testing" (p. 6). These researchers used the Math Item Creator (MIC) software (Meisner, 1993) and 16 mathematics item-generation algorithms to develop a set of 128 items. Results of paper-and-pencil pretest analyses indicated most of the item-generation algorithms produced items with highly similar statistical characteristics. Additional work was planned on the remaining algorithms to determine whether they could be refined and made useful.

Bejar (1996) has developed what he terms *generative response modeling*. In this approach to CBT, a content area is analyzed to such an extent that the underlying knowledge and psychological processes could be programmed. The computer program would then be capable of generating items, and their associated statistics, *during* a computerized exam. "In a generative approach, instead of collecting item response data to estimate item statistics or parameters, items and parameters are produced algorithmically, or at least according to a set of principles" (Bejar, 1996, p. 14). In this method, pretesting might be limited to an initial stage during which the algorithms are validated; later item develop-

ment would include the assignment of item parameters so that no pretesting would be needed. This system has been investigated on a test of
writing skills. Simulation results suggest the item parameter estimates
showed promising levels of precision.

This line of research may be in the initial stages, but it holds promise
for addressing several problems at a substantive level. Work in this area
will need content and cognitive knowledge, along with measurement
skills.

SUMMARY

The topics presented here include paper-and-pencil item calibrations, response data from volunteer examinees, calibration methods that may reduce the need for examinee responses, methods for seeding pretest
items, optimal ability distributions for calibration, problems with sparseness and restricted ability ranges, alternative test delivery models, and
computer-generated items.

These research areas are not meant to be a comprehensive summary
of either the issues that should be investigated or of the valuable studies
that have been conducted. There are undoubtedly other studies and
other issues that could also be considered in light of item development
and pretesting. However, I hope this will serve as a springboard for further discussion and research.

REFERENCES

Barnes, L. B., & Wise, S. L. (1991). The utility of a modified one-parameter IRT model with
    small samples. *Applied Measurement in Education, 4*, 143–157.
Bejar, I. I. (1996). *Generative response modeling: Leveraging the computer as a test delivery
    medium* (ETS Research Report ETS-RR-96-13). Princeton, NJ: Educational Testing Ser-
    vice.
Bennett, R. E., & Bejar, I. I. (1998). Validity and automated scoring: It's not only the scoring.
    Educational Measurement: Issues & Practices, 17, 9–17.
Berger, M. P. F. (1994). D-optimal sequential sampling designs for item response theory
    models. *Journal of Educational Statistics, 19*, 43–56.
Berger, M. P. F., & van der Linden, W. J. (1992). Optimality of sampling designs in item re-
    sponse theory models. In M. Wilson (Ed.), *Objective measurement: Theory into practice*
    (Vol. 1, pp. 274–288). Norwood, NJ: Ablex.
Billeaud, K., & Steffen, M. (1996, April). *Predicting GRE item parameters from collateral in-
    formation.* Paper presented at the annual meeting of the National Council on Measure-
    ment in Education, New York.
Booth, J. (1991). The key to valid computer-based testing: The user interface. *Revue
    europeene de Psychologie Applique, 41*, 281–293.

Bugbee, A. C., & Bernt, F. M. (1990). Testing by computer: Findings in six years of use 1982–1988. *Journal of Research on Computing in Education, 23*, 87–100.

Chang, H. H., & Ying, Z. (1997, June). *Multi-stage CAT with stratification design*. Paper presented at the annual meeting of Psychometric Society, Gatlinburg, TN.

Davey, T. (1990). *Pretest item calibration (PIC)*. Software.

Folk, V. G., & Golub-Smith, M. (1996, April). *Calibration of on-line pretest data using BILOG*. Paper presented at the annual meeting of the National Council of Measurement in Education, New York.

Greaud, V. A., & Green, B. F. (1986). Equivalence of conventional and computer presentation of speed tests. *Applied Psychological Measurement, 10*, 23–34.

Hambleton, R. K., & Jones, R. W. (1994). Item parameter estimation errors and their influence on test information functions. *Applied Measurement in Education, 7*, 171–186.

Harwell, M. R., & Janosky, J. E. (1991). An empirical study of the effects of small datasets and varying prior variances on item parameter estimation in BILOG. *Applied Psychological Measurement, 15*, 279–291.

Haynie, K. A., & Way, W. D. (1995, April). *An investigation of item calibration procedures for a computerized licensure examination*. Paper presented at symposium entitled Computer Adaptive Testing at the annual meeting of the National Council on Measurement in Education, San Francisco.

Haynie, K. A., & Way, W. D. (1996, March). *Stability of item calibrations for the NCLEX-RN and NCLEX-PN using computerized adaptive testing*. Paper presented at the annual meeting of the American Educational Research Association, New York.

Hsu, Y., Thompson, T. D., & Chen, W. (1998, April). *CAT item calibration*. Paper presented at the annual meeting of the National Council on Measurement in Education, San Diego, CA.

Hulin, C. L., Lissak, R. I., & Drasgow, F. (1982). Recovery of two and three-parameter logistic item characteristic curves: A Monte Carlo study. *Applied Psychological Measurement, 6*, 249–260.

Ito, K., & Sykes, R. C. (1994, April). *The effect of restricting ability distributions in the estimation of item difficulties: Implications for a CAT implementation*. Paper presented at the annual meeting of the National Council on Measurement in Education, New Orleans, LA.

Jones, D. H., & Jin, Z. (1994). Optimal sequential designs for on-line item estimation. *Psychometrika, 59*, 59–75.

Mazzeo, J., & Harvey, A. L. (1988). *The equivalence of scores from automated and conventional educational and psychological tests* (Report No. 88-8). New York: College Entrance Examination Board.

Mead, A. D., & Drasgow, F. (1993). Equivalence of computerized and paper-and-pencil cognitive ability tests: A meta-analysis. *Psychological Bulletin, 114*, 449–458.

Meisner, R. (1993). *Math Item Creator (MIC)*. Software.

Meisner, R., Luecht, R., & Reckase, M. (1993). *The comparability of the statistical characteristics of test items generated by computer algorithm* (ACT Research Report No. 93-9). Iowa City, IA: ACT.

Mislevy, R. J., Sheehan, K. M., & Wingersky, M. (1993). How to equate tests with little or no data. *Journal of Educational Measurement, 30*, 55–78.

Mislevy, R. J., & Stocking, M. L. (1989). A consumer's guide to LOGIST and BILOG. *Applied Psychological Measurement, 13*, 57–75.

O'Neill, K., & Folk, V. (1996, April). *Innovative CBT item formats in a teacher licensing program*. Paper presented at the annual meeting of the National Council on Measurement in Education, New York.

Parshall, C. G., Davey, T., & Nering, M. L. (1998, April). *Test development exposure control for adaptive testing*. Paper presented at the annual meeting of the National Council on Measurement in Education, San Diego, CA.

Parshall, C. G., & Kromrey, J. D. (1993, April). *Computer testing versus paper-and-pencil testing: An analysis of examinee characteristics associated with mode effect*. Paper presented at the annual meeting of the American Educational Research Association, Atlanta, GA.

Parshall, C. G., Kromrey, J. D., Chason, W. D., & Yi, Q. (1997, June). *Small samples and modified models: An investigation of IRT parameter recovery*. Paper presented at the annual meeting of the Psychometric Society, Gatlinburg, TN.

Parshall, C. G., Spray, J., Kalohn, J., & Davey, T. (2002). *Practical considerations in computer-based testing*. New York: Springer-Verlag.

Patsula, L. N., & Pashley, P. J. (1996, April). *Pretest item analyzes using polynomial logistic regression: An approach to small sample calibration problems associated with computerized adaptive testing*. Paper presented at the annual meeting of the National Council on Measurement in Education, New York.

Reese, L. M. (1998, April). *Impact of local item dependence on item response theory scoring in CAT*. Paper presented at the annual meeting of the National Council on Measurement in Education, San Diego, CA.

Sireci, S. G. (1992, August). *The utility of IRT in small-sample testing applications*. Paper presented at the annual meeting of the American Psychological Association, Washington, DC.

Spray, J. (1999, April). *Automated test construction for online delivery*. Paper presented as part of the NCME Training Session, "Computerized Testing: Issues and Applications," at the annual meeting of the National Council on Measurement in Education, Montreal, Canada.

Spray, J., Parshall, C. G., & Huang, C. (1997, June). *Calibration of CAT items administered online for classification: Assumptions of local independence*. Paper presented at the annual meeting of the Psychometric Society, Gatlinburg, TN.

Spray, J. A., & Reckase, M. D. (1994, April). *The selection of test items for decision making with a computer adaptive test*. Paper presented at the annual meeting of the National Council on Measurement in Education, New Orleans, LA.

Stocking, M. L. (1988). *Scale drift in on-line calibration* (ETS Research Report 88-28-ONR). Princeton, NJ: Educational Testing Service.

Stocking, M. L. (1990). Specifying optimum examinees for item parameter estimation in item response theory. *Psychometrika, 55*, 461–475.

Stocking, M. L. (1994). *Three practical issues for modern adaptive testing item pools* (ETS Research Report ETS-RR-94-5). Princeton, NJ: Educational Testing Service.

Stocking, M. L., & Lewis, C. (1998). Controlling item exposure conditional on ability in computerized adaptive testing. *Journal of Educational and Behavioral Statistics, 23*, 57–75.

Stocking, M. L., & Lord, F. M. (1983). Developing a common metric in item response theory. *Applied Psychological Measurement, 7*, 201–210.

Sympson, J. B., & Hetter, R. D. (1985). Controlling item-exposure rates in computerized adaptive testing. *Proceedings of the 27th annual meeting of the Military Testing Association* (pp. 973–977). San Diego, CA: Navy Personnel Research and Development Center.

Sykes, R. C., & Fitzpatrick, A. R. (1992). The stability of IRT *b* values. *Journal of Educational Measurement, 29*, 201–211.

Vale, C. D. (1986). Linking item parameters onto a common scale. *Applied Psychological Measurement, 10*, 333–344.

Vicino, F. L., & Moreno, K. E. (1997). Human factors in the CAT system: A pilot study. In W. A. Sands, B. K Waters, & J. R. McBride (Eds.), *Computerized adaptive testing: From inquiry to operation* (pp. 157–160). Washington, DC: American Psychological Association.

Way, W. D. (1994, September). *Psychometric models for computer-based licensure testing*. Paper presented at the annual meeting of CLEAR, Boston.

Way, W. D. (1997, April). *Protecting the integrity of computerized testing item pools*. Paper presented at the annual meeting of the National Council on Measurement in Education, Chicago.

Wright, B. D., & Stone, M. H. (1979). *Best test design*. Chicago: Mesa Press.

Developing, Maintaining, and Renewing the Item Inventory to Support CBT

Walter D. Way
Manfred Steffen
Gordon Stephen Anderson
Educational Testing Service

INTRODUCTION

The attention given to CBT by the measurement community has steadily increased in the past 10 years as several major testing programs have transitioned to the computer and several more are preparing to do so. The popularity of CBT is obvious from reviewing programs from annual meetings of the National Council on Measurement in Education, in which paper sessions devoted to CBT have steadily increased in recent years. This emphasis is natural given the exponential growth of computers and related technology. However, the attentiveness of the measurement community belies the fact that we are still struggling with the mechanics of bringing up and sustaining CBT.

　　Among the more formidable challenges for CBT, especially for high-volume, high-stakes examinations, is providing examinees a continuous opportunity to test. Continuous testing is a major perceived benefit of CBT because it provides greater convenience to examinees. On the other hand, continuous testing requires exposing the same items to test takers over an extended period; therefore, CBT is vulnerable to the threat of organized efforts that could compromise item security.

The CBT literature includes a substantial body of work on the problem of limiting item exposure, particularly in the context of a single CAT item pool (cf. Davey & Parshall, 1995; Kingsbury & Zara, 1989; Stocking, 1987; Stocking, 1993; Stocking & Lewis, 1995a, 1995b; Sympson & Hetter, 1985). However, to sustain any high-stakes CBT program over years of continuous testing, it is necessary to put an ongoing system in place for effectively using existing items and introducing new items. Such a system is concerned with maintaining and renewing an inventory of items in ways that can limit item exposure not only within a discrete pool of items used for a particular period, but also across multiple pools that are used across multiple periods.

In this chapter we discuss and illustrate systems that can be deployed to develop and maintain an inventory of items for CBT. The context for this paper is high-volume, high-stakes CAT programs that are developed and administered by ETS (cf. Eignor, Stocking, Way, & Steffen, 1993; Stocking, 1994). For these exams, the costs of computerized delivery depend on testing time limits, and a primary advantage of CAT is that it can achieve a similar level of measurement precision to conventional paper-and-pencil tests with significantly shorter tests. However, CAT also represents the most complex situation for maintaining an item inventory because selection and delivery occurs at the item level.

Compared with CAT, other computerized test delivery models such as *computerized mastery testing* (Lewis & Sheehan, 1990) and *computer adaptive sequential testing* (Luecht & Nungester, 1998) simplify item inventory management by chunking together items into larger groups and focusing selection strategies at these more macro levels (e.g., *testlets* as referred to by Wainer & Kiely, 1987). The issues associated with maintaining an inventory of items with such models is not considered here, although issues discussed and illustrated in this chapter within the context of CAT are relevant for other models as well.

This chapter consists of four major parts. In the first part, the concept of the *item vat* as the representation of the CBT item inventory is introduced and some of the factors that affect the maintenance of the vat are described. In the second part, a technique called *system dynamics modeling* (SDM) is introduced as a tool for forecasting item-development needs and for testing scenarios that could affect the item vat. In the third part, an illustration of how SDM can be used to model the inventory of a vat is provided. Finally, in the fourth part, we discuss some of the considerations associated with maintaining an item inventory for high-stakes CBT that are likely to evolve further in the future.

THE CONCEPT OF THE ITEM VAT

With continuous CBT, item pools that are employed during any given interval represent only a subset of the full universe of available items. This universe of items is referred to here as the item vat. The item vat is constantly changing both in quantity and quality as new item pools are formed and newly pretested items are added. The activities that change the item vat are dynamic and cyclical, and the management of the vat becomes a delicate exercise of balancing adequate item pool quality with maintaining an acceptable level of item security.

Sampling From the Vat With Replacement

Frequent rotation of item pools is a necessary precaution with high-stakes CAT programs. In an ideal world, a sufficiently large item vat would make it possible to form some large number of item pools and simply rotate these pools over time. However, in reality the vat of items is not infinitely large and it is constantly changing as newly pretested items become available and other items are taken out of use. By sampling from the vat with replacement to build pools, new items can be seeded into use with existing items in ways that spread out item exposure and help preserve item security.

A second reason for sampling pools from the vat on an ongoing basis is that the exposure rate for an individual item depends in part on the other items in the pool. Thus, an item that is exposed relatively frequently in one pool may be used less frequently in another pool. Figure 7.1 presents correlations between exposure rates for items across 10 pairs of Analytical pools, 13 pairs of Quantitative pools, and 8 pairs of Verbal pools from the GRE General Test (only pair-wise pool comparisons based on 20 or more common items are included). These correlations range from 0.05 to 0.95 across the three measures. Figure 7.2 presents a scatterplot of pairwise exposure rates for all items in the GRE Verbal vat that appeared in multiple pools. Figure 7.2 indicates that although the pairwise item exposure rates have a strong positive relationship, some items that were used seldom or not at all in one pool were among the most frequently used items in another pool. The variability of individual item exposure

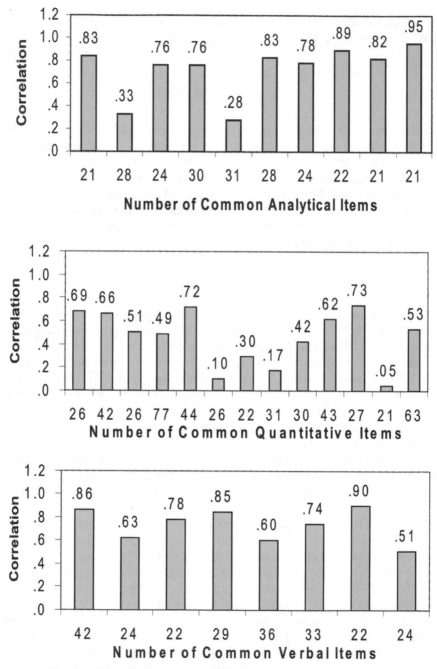

FIG. 7.1. Correlations of exposure rates for the same items in two different CAT pools for GRE analytical quantitative and verbal measures.

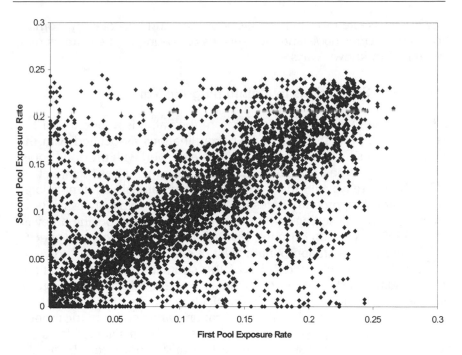

FIG. 7.2.   Pairwise exposure rates for GRE verbal items ($r_{XY} = 0.67$).

rates across pools supports a scheme of pool reformation as a way to spread out exposure for individual items, at least in the context of the GRE General Test.

Sampling the Vat Using Automated Item-Selection Techniques

The continuous process of sampling from a vat to form CAT item pools requires automated item-selection procedures (e.g., Swanson & Stocking, 1993; van der Linden & Boekkooi-Timminga, 1989). These procedures implement optimization algorithms and related heuristics to minimize or maximize an objective function subject to various constraints. The advantage of automated item selection is in providing an efficient method for ensuring that the collections of items sampled for each pool are reasonably similar. Furthermore, such algorithms allow the user to define constraints that can be used to control the ongoing pool formation process. These constraints include not only statistical and content characteristics but also characteristics related to how items have been used in the past. For example, previously accumulated item exposure can be used as a constraint in sampling a new pool. Although it is typically necessary to reuse items from previous pools, the numbers of items coming from the previous pools and the previous exposures of these items may be limited in known ways.

The Role of Simulations in Maintaining the Vat

When new item pools are selected from the vat, it is important for the psychometric properties of the CAT examinations associated with the pools to be as similar as possible to those observed with previous pools. This evaluation is best done through simulation procedures (Eignor et al., 1993). There are typically three purposes to operational CAT simulations: (a) to establish appropriate rates of item exposure, typically using iterative procedures for setting item exposure rate control (Stocking & Lewis, 1995a, 1995b; Sympson & Hetter, 1985); (b) to verify that content specifications are met to an appropriate level of satisfaction; and (c) to verify that psychometric characteristics of the simulated CAT examinations (e.g., conditional standard errors of measurement, reliabilities) are comparable to those of previous pools. Satisfactory simulation results with respect to item exposure, content specifications, and psychometric properties verify that an appropriate pool of items has been selected from the vat. When the results of simulations are unsatisfactory, it may be necessary to resample the pool of items from the vat. Thus, a major challenge in maintaining the vat is to ensure that the items available at any point are sufficient to support an item pool that will achieve the targeted psychometric characteristics.

Factors Affecting the Maintenance of the Vat

The concept of the item vat has little effect on the item-development needs of a testing program apart from the manner in which item or test security is imposed. The concept of security that we have adopted assumes it is imperative that an operational item pool never be left in place for long periods. By giving examinees daily access to testing, simple word of mouth and, more formidably, organized raids by external agencies can compromise a single pool quickly.

Rules for Constraining Item Use.   To preserve item security under CAT where item pools are continuously deployed, testing programs must struggle with rules governing item use over time. For example, we might want to minimize the probability that two examinees testing at different times will encounter the same item collection. It might be thought that after some time (or after some number of administrations), the mere repeated use of an item will cause the security of the item to be compromised. In the absence of the ability to produce novel tests for every test session, judicious management of item-usage density, pairwise overlap of pools, and total number of administrations per item can improve the ability to produce reasonably secure testing sessions.

An example of a collection of rules that could be used is as follows:

1. No more than 10% of a pool can overlap with any previous pool.
2. No item exposed to more than 500 examinees within the last 2 months may be used.
3. No item exposed to more than 1,000 examinees within the last 4 months may be used.
4. Any item exposed to more than 15,000 examinees must be retired.
5. At least 10%, and no more than 20%, of the items in a pool can have been used previously.

The second, third, and fourth rules are sometimes referred to as docking rules because they essentially result in the removal of items from the vat for some period. These rules present only one primary source of item retirement. Once an item has been exposed to 15,000 examinees, it is removed from the vat. Thus, this is a relatively closed system. The major challenge for the testing program is to create new items in such a way that they replace the items being retired. Although this may be relatively straightforward with respect to content, the ability to replace the psychometric quality of retired items is more difficult. Initially, the retired items tend to have psychometric characteristics that are in short supply in the vat. The major reason certain items are in short supply is because they are difficult to create.

Interactions of Item Characteristics and Docking Rules. Adaptive testing algorithms have been shown to be relatively inefficient in the use of item resources. That is, all things being equal, adaptive algorithms gravitate toward selecting the most informative items for each examinee. Additionally, the imposition of content constraints further complicates the picture. Unless the content space is well crossed with item difficulty and item information, the tension between these factors makes the management of item resources even more difficult. If some item types are inherently more difficult than others and the content specifications call for every examinee to be administered equal numbers of each, the algorithm will tend to choose the most difficult items from the easy content areas for the high-ability examinees. When rules are imposed to constrain the reuse of items over time, the content specific issues may result in overuse of items in certain difficulty strata even if items are successfully constrained at an overall level.

Other Sources of Item Loss.   Although the only self-imposed leak in the system comes about because of overall item exposure, several other leaks must be anticipated. First, all items do not work equally well for the duration of the usable life. Items can become dated, an item's operating characteristics can unexpectedly change, or a previously undetected flaw can be discovered. For aptitude tests (e.g., GRE General Tests, SAT, ACT), these sources would be expected to have minimal effect on the collection of available items. For more subject-matter-based tests, item datedness can cause nontrivial losses. To the degree that these losses do not interact with item difficulty, they are a factor that can be managed by simply adding items to the vat at a higher rate. However, should the losses accumulate in selected difficulty areas, it may prove especially difficult to meet all of the conditions imposed earlier and still construct adequate pools.

Test Disclosure Requirements.   Another potential area of item loss results from the need to disclose items or to provide examinees an opportunity to review their test sessions. Disclosure legislation first enacted in the state of New York has been updated to consider CBT as well as paper-and-pencil testing (Lissitz, 1997), although the specific ways this legislation will be applied is still being negotiated. Assuming the legislation will be operationalized in ways that will require specific tests to be disclosed, another source of item loss must be considered. If disclosure means making available to the public specific CATs or item pools, such items would have to be considered lost to further use. However, if legislation unfolds in such a way that merely requires affording examinees the opportunity to review their test sessions (in a controlled environment), the implications for item loss may be less dire. In fact, such sessions could be viewed by the testing agency merely as additional acquisition of item exposure volume not qualitatively different from an operational administration.

MODELING THE VAT USING SDM

The interactions of the various inflows and outflows to the vat result in a complex system that is all but impossible to manage without resorting to tools suited to such a task. In particular, the changes that occur to the vat over time are important to track because the effect of revised inflows and outflows may not become obvious until a much later time. For example, if the rate of item development must be increased to overcome a particular source of item loss, it may take several years to put the extra resources in place, write and pretest the new items, evaluate the resulting data, and add the items into the vat. SDM is a methodology that is well suited to studying the effect of changes on a system over time.

Description of SDM

System dynamics is a field that was originally pioneered and developed by Forrester and his colleagues at MIT in the 1960s (Forrester, 1961, 1968). SDM is a mapping of the causal relationships that represent a mental construct of an actual system. SDM is most useful when applied to complex systems that have multiple inputs, many of which may be nonlinear. The strength and direction of those system inputs may be both time and state dependent. The system response to stimuli depends on its initial state, the strength of the inputs, and the sequence of those input applications. System interdependency or feedback arises when the system's response causes a change to the system's state functions that in turn causes further system response. This ability to capture the feedback effects of the system's causal relationships is the real power of SDM. SDM provides a tool to represent graphically and functionally the causal relationships that make up a system. It then calculates the system's state functions and applies the new state functions for the next iteration of system state calculations. In this way it is possible not only to see a snapshot of the system's states but also to trace paths and causes of these states through time.

Advantages of SDM for Modeling the CAT Item Inventory

To project item-development needs for CAT, a systematic way of representing the flow of items into and out of a vat of available items requires a system memory of the history of exposure to the various items or at least a surrogate for the systemwide exposure profile. SDM satisfies this requirement. SDM also facilitates scenario testing of system levels such as the initial states and exogenous inputs, the functional relationships of item flows, and the structure and interdependencies of item subvats or holding bins (item docks). With SDM a system can be modified to examine quickly both the cause and effect of changing parts of the system. Immediate analysis can be performed tracing the results and the relative contributions of the changes made.

Although some of the modeling done in SDM can also be carried out with commonly used spreadsheet tools, the mathematical complexities associated with model testing are best handled using specialized software. Various software products on the market implement SDM. We use a software program called Vensim (1998) for modeling vat requirements at ETS, and the example carried out in the next section is based on simulations carried out in Vensim.

MODELING THE VAT INVENTORY: AN ILLUSTRATIVE EXAMPLE

An example is presented to illustrate the usefulness of SDM in planning item-development resources and assessing the potential effect of changes in requirements for item use. The example presented here is fictitious and simplified, but the variables modeled and the scenarios illustrated are similar to those faced with the large-scale, high-stakes CAT programs administered by ETS.

Base Testing Program Assumptions

Initial Assumptions.   We begin by assuming a single exam is transitioned to CAT in July 1998. The exam is used for admissions purposes and is administered to 250,000 candidates annually. To keep things simple, we assume the exam consists entirely of discrete items; that is, the CAT administration is not complicated by the administration of set-based items. We assume an extensive simulation process has informed CAT item pool development, and we further assume the simulations have demonstrated that the 60-item paper-and-pencil exam can be reduced to a (fixed) test length of 30 items using CAT. Following Stocking's (1994) recommendations, the testing program has assumed eight final forms of the exam (480 items) are needed to form a single item pool. Through the CAT simulations research, the program has determined final pools consisting of 360 items make the most efficient use of the available items (i.e., only 360 of the 480 items are needed in a pool to support CAT). The program has approximately 1,440 items available for the initial implementation of CAT.

Item Development.   The program considers the initial vat size of 1,440 items to be only minimally adequate for sustaining CAT and is committed to expanding the vat size in the early years of CAT administration. Specifically, the program plans to add the numbers of items needed to support two new pools per year for each of the first 3 years of CAT (i.e., it is assumed 960 items must be added to the vat per year to develop two 360-item CAT pools). Assuming a 20% loss of pretested items, 1,200 items would have to be developed and added to pretest pools per year. After 3 years, the program would like to steadily decrease item development to a maintenance level so that only 300 items are developed and 240 items

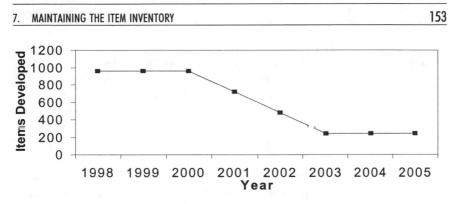

FIG. 7.3. Initial annual item-development plans.

are added to the pool each year. Figure 7.3 presents a summary plot of the initial item-development plans (i.e., items added to the vat) from 1998 through 2005.

Monthly Program Volumes.   Because the examination is used for admissions decisions, most of the annual volume of 250,000 examinees occurs between October and February. The program plans to calibrate, review, and add items to the vat approximately 2 months after they are pretested. Thus, as depicted in Fig. 7.4, most newly pretested items become available between December and April.

CAT Pool Rotation.   The continuous formation of new pools is seen as a key strategy in preserving item integrity and limiting vulnerability to organized attempts at memorizing questions. To better use existing items and to immediately deploy new items that are added to the vat, the program expects to build item pools on an ongoing basis. However, research has shown that as the numbers of pools in a given period are increased, the quality of the pools decreases (Patsula & Steffen, 1997). In addition,

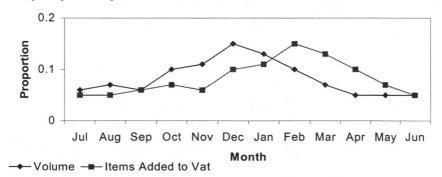

FIG. 7.4. Monthly proportion of annual testing volumes and monthly proportion of annual items added to the vat.

forming many pools is accompanied by increased costs associated with pool preparation, quality assurance testing, and pool distribution. Thus, the program decides to vary pool formation based on projected testing volume. For April through July, where volumes are relatively low, two pools per month will be formed and rotated into use. For the higher volume months of August through March, three pools per month will be developed.

Item Loss.   For general knowledge tests such as those used for academic admission, relatively few items are removed for reasons such as datedness or changes in practice associated with the content being measured. Nevertheless, for this example we assume approximately 5% of the items created at any one time will be removed from the pool for miscellaneous reasons.

Base Forecast of the Number of Available Items

As a baseline, it is straightforward to estimate the number of items in the vat available for use across time under the base testing program assumptions described previously. Figure 7.5 displays a graph of this base forecast. Because the system of available items is relatively closed in the sense that items are flowing into the system at a high rate but flowing out only at 5% of those created, the numbers of available items increases steadily over time. The largest increase is between 1998 and 2000, when 960 items will be added to the vat annually. As item production tapers off between 2001 and 2003, the rate of increase for available items slows but the increase is still noticeable. In the base forecast, the size of the item

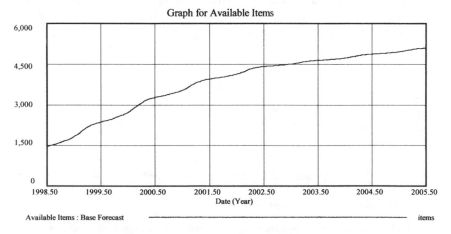

FIG. 7.5.   Base forecast for available items.

vat doubles from its initial size in a little more than a year and triples by the year 2003. However, the base forecast does not take into account the effect from several constraints that limit the numbers of available items in the vat.

Forecast of Available Items With Docking Rules Applied

As previously discussed, in a large-volume, high-stakes CAT, it is advisable to maintain docking rules that govern the extent to which items may be used and reused as pools are continuously assembled. We assume the testing program has established the following three docking rules to be followed as new pools are developed:

1. No item exposed to more than 500 examinees within the last 2 months may be used.
2. No item exposed to more than 1,000 examinees within the last 4 months may be used.
3. Any item exposed to more than 15,000 examinees must be retired (i.e., removed from use).

The effect of these rules on the number of available items in the vat is complex but may be modeled using SDM. This modeling must take into account the hierarchical nature of the different docks. For example, both Dock 2 and Dock 3 affect Dock 1 because items that are identified for these docks would not be put into Dock 1. Similarly, Dock 2 is affected by Dock 3 in the same way. Figure 7.6 presents a schematic causal tree for the three docking rules.

A contributing factor to each dock is the *max fraction* of items going into the dock. This fraction is estimated based on testing-program volume and an assumption that the proportion of items sent to the docks can be modeled using an exponential distribution (see the Appendix for a detailed description of this assumption).

The effect of introducing the docking rules on the forecast of available items is displayed in Fig. 7.7. Imposing the docking rules has an adverse effect on the number of available items. The interactions of Dock 1 and Dock 2 with the monthly testing volumes cause both the small jagged fluctuations and the larger sine wave fluctuations in the graph. The effect of Dock 3 is seen in the generally decreasing availability of items that begins halfway into 2002.

One concern readily apparent from Fig. 7.7 is that the initial months of testing will be accompanied by a shortage in the available items given the constraints imposed by the docking rules. In fact, the shortage ap-

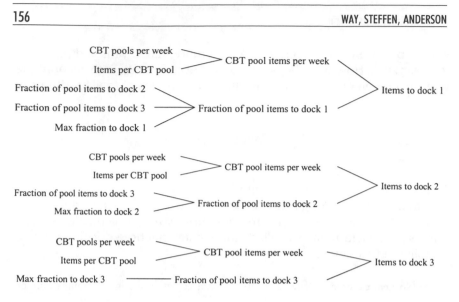

FIG. 7.6.   Schematic causal tree for items sent to the three item docks.

pears to be so severe that it probably will not be possible to both maintain the docking rules and meet the pool-assembly requirements. Thus, it is likely the docking rules will have to be violated for several months if the pool rotation schedule is to be maintained.

The more obvious and disturbing trend in Fig. 7.7 is the decreasing level of available items overall. Clearly, this trend is not tenable. To address the trend, the testing program considers two possible alternatives.

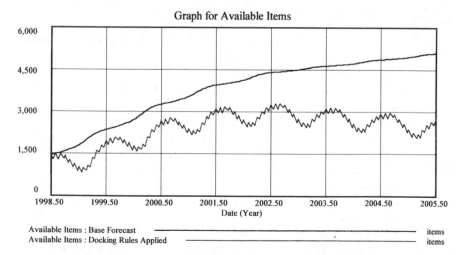

FIG. 7.7.   Effect of item docking rules on forecast of available items.

TABLE 7.1
Original and Proposed Revised Annual Item Development

Plan/Year	1998	1999	2000	2001	2002	2003	2004	2005	Totals
Original	960	960	960	720	480	240	240	240	4800
Revised	960	960	960	960	720	480	480	480	6000

One alternative is to increase item development. Table 7.1 summarizes the original and proposed revised item-development requirements.

The effect of the proposed increased item development on the vat of available items is presented in Fig. 7.8. As expected, the increased item development helps offset the items being retired so that the overall number of available items follows an increasing trend through 2005.

Because the increased item development will be associated with increased costs, the program decides to consider an alternative, which is to recycle 3% of the retired items back into use each month beginning in 2001. The estimated effect of this alternative is displayed in Fig. 7.9. It can be seen that by recycling retired items the program can reach the same level of available items that would be reached by increasing item production. Of course, this item development saving does not come free. The recycling of items increases the risk of item exposure, and the effect of this additional exposure must be weighed against the cost savings achieved by deferring the increased item development.

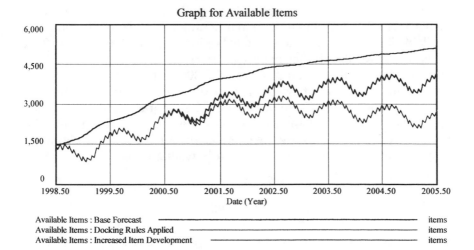

FIG. 7.8.   Effect of increased item production on available items given docking rules.

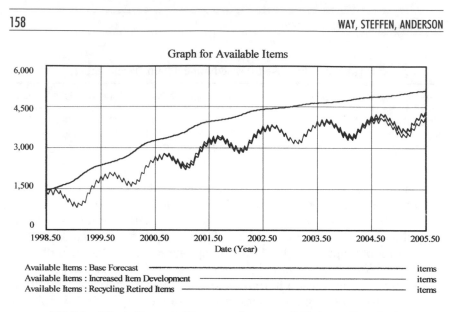

Graph for Available Items

FIG. 7.9.   Effect of increased item recycling on available items given docking rules.

Forecast of Available Items Given Required Test Disclosure

As previously discussed, the full effect of the New York state truth-in-
testing legislation on CAT programs for admissions is still unclear. However, for the sake of our example, we assume the testing program will
have to disclose the equivalent of six CAT examinations per year (or 180
items), beginning 1 year after CAT is implemented. The effect of comply-
ing with the disclosure requirements on the available items in the vat is
displayed in Fig. 7.10. It can be seen that under disclosure the number of
available items reaches a steady state beginning about halfway into 2002.
Given these results, the testing program will have to decide whether a
constant vat size that fluctuates around 2,800 items provides a sufficient
level of item security or whether item development must increase to
counteract the effect of item disclosure. The program could also liberal-
ize its rules for item retirement or increase the rate of recycling, but either
of these actions will increase the overall exposure of the item vat, which
may or may not be a risk the program is willing to take.

DISCUSSION

The SDM example presented in this chapter is only a sampling of the
ways this approach can be used in modeling the performance of an item
vat over time. As a tool for detailed prediction, SDM is not optimal be-

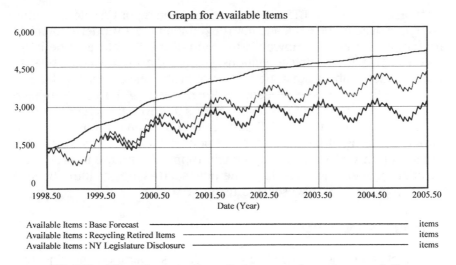

FIG. 7.10. Effect of meeting item disclosure requirements on available items.

cause many of the input assumptions (such as the maximum docking fraction described in the Appendix) are gross estimates at best. However, what becomes clear from using SDM is the parts of the system that have the most leverage on the vat inventory over time. This in itself justifies the use of the methodology.

As we learn from and improve our approach to CBT, we expect that the way we develop, maintain, and renew the item vat will also evolve. Much of what has been shared in this chapter reflects practices at ETS for managing the CAT item inventory that have been developed and applied only recently. Nevertheless, several of our current practices are being reconsidered and are likely to change in the near future.

Item Retirement

In the example provided in this chapter, the most significant source of item loss was item retirement, which was imposed on an item when it achieved 15,000 exposures. Such a docking rule assumes there is a point at which an item is exposed so much it will no longer function as intended. This is not an assumption that has basis in empirical data. Rather, the 15,000-exposures retirement dock represents a conservative precaution against security threats that are largely unknown. However, this precaution has significant costs associated with it.

As an alternative to retiring items based on total exposures, a potentially superior basis for retiring items is changes that are detected in item functioning. Currently, ETS screens the functioning of CAT items within each pool used in the field, and items exhibiting gross model–data misfit are removed from use. However, the kind of misfit that might be introduced from an item being continuously exposed over time could be subtle and undetectable from its performance in any single pool. For this reason, operationally viable procedures for monitoring item performance over time are important to establish. Efforts to develop such procedures are currently under way at ETS and once implemented may reduce or eliminate the need for an item retirement dock. In the meantime, as items used in CAT programs approach imposed retirement thresholds, the effect of alternative recycling schemes (such as the one introduced in the example) can be investigated using SDM.

Reusing Disclosed Items

The effect of reusing disclosed items in CAT was examined under a worst case scenario in a simulation study by Stocking, Ward, and Potenza (1998). Their study indicated that the use of up to 10% disclosed items with CAT produces increases in observed scores that are, from the standpoint of practical statistical significance, small compared with changes in test scores that occur from retesting. Although the possibility of reintroducing disclosed items into the item vat has appeal, it is something that must be approached cautiously and deliberately. We did not address this possibility in our example. However, the SDM we use with CAT programs at ETS does incorporate reusing disclosed items, and we expect to explore the potential effect of this possibility on the vat inventory in the near future.

Subtle Interactions of Item Characteristics

One of the drawbacks of using SDM to model the vat inventory is that it is difficult to model the subtle interactions between item characteristics and the selection of items by the CAT algorithm. The SDM model we use considers item exposure at a gross level, and the accumulation of item exposure is based on estimating mean exposure rate, which in turn is mostly influenced by testing volumes and the number of pools in use. A further limitation of the SDM is that it makes no qualitative distinctions in modeling the vat inventory. That is, no distinctions are made between items from different content areas or at different levels of difficulty and discrimination. In practice, we have addressed the content issues to some extent by applying the model separately to different content areas within a particular measure. For example, within the GRE Quantitative Reasoning measure, we apply SDM to model the vat inventory separately for quantitative comparison, problem solving, and data interpretation. However, we are still exploring the extent to which SDM can ignore these subtleties of item characteristics and still portray a reasonable representation of the system.

Variable Short-Term Docking Rules

In maintaining the vat, short-term docking rules (e.g., not using any item that has been seen more than 500 times within the past 2 months or more than 1,000 times within the past 4 months) are used to spread out the use of items across pools so that the same items are not overselected at the expense of other items that are rarely used. Depending on the testing program and measure, it may or may not be possible to impose the docking rules and still construct a CAT pool with the desired characteristics. When such conflicts occur, the docking rules are typically violated. In general, committing violations to docking rules is preferred to building pools with inferior psychometric characteristics because the docking rules are arbitrary and the effect of violations are unknown, whereas the test specifications are more firmly grounded and violations to the test specifications are likely to have detrimental effects on measurement.

Because it may consistently be the case that docking rules have to be violated, especially when a testing program is building up the item vat, one alternative is to impose variable docking rules that change depending on what is available in the vat at the time of pool assembly. In this way, the docking rules could be strict within content areas where the supply of items at the needed difficulty levels is abundant and relaxed within content areas where the supply of needed items is scarce. Such an approach would treat the docks as windows rather than rules, and a measure of pool adequacy could be based on how small a docking window the pool can consistently support.

CLOSING COMMENT

In this chapter, we have attempted to provide a taste of the kinds of issues faced in managing the item inventory for large-volume, high-stakes testing programs where CAT is employed. To a great extent, the concepts and approaches described here represent the current state of practices evolving within a single organization in response to a particular set of circumstances. But without question, the underlying issues generalize to all organizations considering CBT. Because test validity in a continuous testing environment hinges on our ability to preserve item security, the management of the CBT item inventory will continue to require the closest of attention from the measurement community.

REFERENCES

Davey, T., & Parshall, C. G. (1995, April). *New algorithms for item selection and exposure control with computerized adaptive testing*. Paper presented at the annual meeting of the American Educational Research Association, San Francisco.

Eignor, D. R., Stocking, M. L., Way, W. D., & Steffen, M. (1993). *Case studies in computer adaptive test design through simulation* (ETS Research Report RR-93-56). Princeton, NJ: Educational Testing Service.

Forrester, J. W. (1961). *Industrial dynamics*. Portland, OR: Productivity Press.

Forrester, J. W. (1968). *Principles of systems*. Portland, OR: Productivity Press.

Kingsbury, G. C., & Zara, A. R. (1989). Procedures for selecting items for computerized adaptive tests. *Applied Measurement in Education, 2*, 359–375.

Lewis, C., & Sheehan, K. (1990). Using Bayesian decision theory to design a computer mastery test. *Applied Psychological Measurement, 14*, 367–386.

Lissitz, R. (1997). The New York standardized testing legislation. *NCME Quarterly Newsletter, 5*(1), 2.

Luecht, R. M., & Nungester, R. J. (1998). Some practical examples of computer-adaptive sequential testing. *Journal of Educational Measurement, 35*, 229–249.

Patsula, L. N., & Steffen, M. (1997, April). *Maintaining item and test security in a CAT environment: A simulation study*. Paper presented at the National Council on Measurement in Education, Chicago.

Stocking, M. L. (1987). Two simulated feasibility studies in computerized adaptive testing. *Applied Psychology: An International Review, 36*, 263–277.

Stocking, M. L. (1993). *Controlling item exposure rates in a realistic adaptive testing paradigm* (ETS Research Report RR-93-2). Princeton, NJ: Educational Testing Service.

Stocking, M. L. (1994). *Three practical issues for modern adaptive testing item pools* (ETS Research Report RR-94-5). Princeton, NJ: Educational Testing Service.

Stocking, M. L., & Lewis, C. (1995a). *A new method of controlling item exposure in computerized adaptive testing* (ETS Research Report RR-95-25). Princeton, NJ: Educational Testing Service.

Stocking, M. L., & Lewis, C. (1995b). *Controlling item exposure conditional on ability in computerized adaptive testing* (ETS Research Report RR-95-24). Princeton, NJ: Educational Testing Service.

Stocking, M. L., & Swanson, L. (1993). A method for severely constrained item selection in adaptive testing. *Applied Psychological Measurement, 17*, 277–292.

Stocking, M. L., Ward, W. C., & Potenza, M. T. (1998). Simulating the use of disclosed items in computerized adaptive testing. *Journal of Educational Measurement, 35*, 48–68.

Swanson, L., & Stocking, M. L. (1993). A model and heuristic for solving very large item selection problems. *Applied Psychological Measurement, 17*, 151–166.

Sympson, J. B., & Hetter, R. D. (1985, October). Controlling item-exposure rates in computerized adaptive testing. *Proceedings of the 27th annual meeting of the Military Testing Association* (pp. 973–977). San Diego, CA: Navy Personnel Research and Development Center.

van der Linden, W. J., & Boekkooi-Timminga, E. (1989). A minimax model for test design with practical constraints. *Psychometrika, 54*, 237–247.

Vensim DSS32 Version 3.0C [Computer software]. (1998). Harvard, MA: Ventana Systems.

Wainer, H., & Kiely, G. L. (1987). Item clusters and computerized adaptive testing: A case for
    testlets. *Journal of Educational Measurement, 24*, 185–201.

APPENDIX

Estimating the Maximum Fraction of Docked Items

The maximum fraction of docked items refers to the proportion of items
in use during a particular period (e.g., month) that is estimated to have
exceeded the threshold of a particular docking rule. This is considered a
maximum fraction because of the hierarchical nature of the docks (i.e.,
the fraction of items in Dock 1 may be reduced from the maximum by the
items that also satisfy Dock 2 or Dock 3). The docking fraction is determined by calculating a docking ratio, which is the ratio of the docking
rule threshold divided by the total average item exposure for the month.
Total average item exposure is composed of two components: average
new exposures and average recent exposures. Average new exposures is
a straightforward calculation of the total number of item exposures per
month divided by the total number of items in use per month. These in
turn depend on testing volumes and number of pools in use. Average recent exposures is a rolling average composed of the level of recent exposures at the start of the period, plus the number of new exposures from
the last month, less items removed or disclosed, and less exposures that
expired. Because these quantities fluctuate over time, the maximum
fraction of docked items also changes over time.

It is assumed in the model that the maximum fraction of docked items
is a function of the docking ratio and that this relationship can be modeled by the exponential distribution:

$$\text{Max. Docking Fraction} = \exp^{(-\text{Docking ratio})}$$

Figure A7.1 displays the relationship between the docking ratio and
the maximum docking fraction based on the exponential distribution.
Given a docking ratio where the average exposures per month is equivalent to the docking rule (i.e., a docking ratio of 1.0), one would expect a
maximum docking fraction of 0.37.

The docking ratio is influenced by testing volume, the number of pools
in the field, and the magnitude of the docking rule threshold. For the examples in this chapter, the maximum docking fraction for Dock 1 (using
a threshold of 500 exposures) ranges over time from about 0.4 to 0.7. The
maximum docking fraction for Dock 2 (using a threshold of 1,000 exposures) ranges from about 0.2 to 0.5.

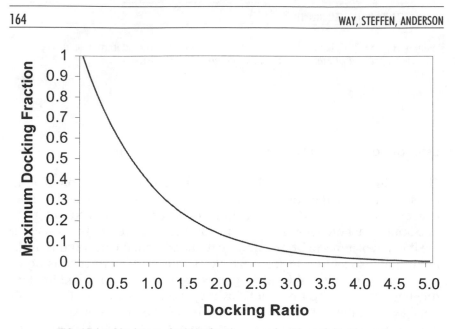

FIG. A7.1.   Maximum docking fraction as a function of docking ratio.

The assumption that the maximum fraction of docked items can be modeled using the exponential distribution was explored when the SDM was initially developed, and at that time the assumption appeared to be reasonable. As a broader empirical baseline of item docking and use is gathered, it will be possible to evaluate further the reasonableness of the original assumption.

Controlling Item Exposure
and Maintaining Item Security

Tim Davey
Educational Testing Service

Michael Nering
Measured Progress

INTRODUCTION

An old show business adage states that any publicity is good publicity. However, it is doubtful whether this claim applies to the testing business as well. It is certain that those involved with the GRE must have been less than delighted with the front-page headlines that greeted them the morning of December 16, 1994. "Computerized Test Hits Glitch" blared page 1 of the *USA Today*'s "Life" section. *The Washington Post* lead with "Computerized Graduate Exam Called Easy Mark." *The New York Times* headlined a similar story with "Computer Admissions Test Found to be Ripe for Abuse."

What had happened that prompted such attention from the press is by now well known. The GRE was one of the first operational CATs. CATs differ from conventional paper-and-pencil tests in many ways, but two differences are relevant to this story. The first is that different examinees testing at the same time are administered different tests. Each examinee's test is individually constructed by drawing questions from a large bank or pool. Although some questions are certain to be in common across examinees, the extent of overlap is, at least in theory, minimal. The second difference is a direct consequence of the first: Because different examinees are administered different tests, it is generally believed safe to use the same question pool repeatedly across multiple test dates.

But something went terribly wrong with the computerized GRE. Kaplan Educational Centers, a test-preparation company, had registered 20 employees to take the test and memorize the questions they were administered. Collecting the memorized questions across examinees allowed Kaplan to reconstruct a major portion of the question pool on which the GRE was based. Because the test was being continuously administered from this pool, there was clear opportunity for future examinees to take advantage of previous exposure to some or many of the questions they were likely to be administered.

The response by the GRE's publisher to Kaplan's report that the question pool had been seriously compromised was immediate. Test administration was entirely suspended for 1 week and severely curtailed over several months. Plans to switch the GRE entirely from pencil-and-paper to computerized administration were delayed by years. Lawsuits were filed and legal wrangling began in earnest.

Two lessons can be drawn from the GRE incident. The first is hardly news: Highly motivated and resourceful examinees facing a high-stakes test bear close watching. The second is that at least some of what has been learned over the years about securing conventional high-stakes tests must be updated to meet the new problems posed by CBT administration. It is to this matter that this chapter is directed.

SECURING CONVENTIONAL TESTS

Despite the widely held belief that the world was once a more innocent place, concern about test security is long standing. In 1599 members of the Jesuit order published methods of testing students for evaluation and placement. Several of their recommendations dealt with maintaining test security. For example:

> Care should be taken that no copying be done by bench mates; if two compositions are found to be exactly alike, both of them are to be suspected since it is impossible to discover which of the two did the copying. (cited in DuBois, 1970, p. 9)

As the Jesuits must have realized, the fundamental goal of test security is to protect the validity of a test by insuring that the scores assigned to examinees are genuine measures of their capabilities. There are at least three things to worry about here.

1. *Copying.* The testing environment should be such that examinees are forced to rely on their own efforts rather than on those of their "benchmates." This is done by physi-

cally separating examinees, carefully proctoring examinees at work, and, in some cases, distributing different test forms across examinees.

2. *Misrepresentation.* Precautions against copying are of no use if an examinee's identity has not been positively established. Many tests require examinees to present photograph identification cards to prevent imposters from testing in place of other examinees. Some tests photograph each examinee for future reference should questions arise, and a few high-stakes tests even require examinees to provide thumbprints or other biometric data.

3. *Question pre-exposure.* The concern here is that some or all examinees may have had access to some or all of the test questions before the test was administered. Regardless of whether examinees make an effort to memorize these questions, answers to familiar questions are different from answers to novel questions. The result is that the test measures different things in different ways in the exposed group, leading to less valid scores.

Questions are vulnerable to exposure at several points of their life cycle, the first being at birth, when the question is developed. Questions are frequently written by independent contractors who do not work directly for the test developers, introducing a few complications. Question writers are asked to work alone and are required to sign confidentiality agreements. The number of questions that a single writer can contribute to a test is also often restricted. Care is taken to see that all communications with writers remain private and that all materials are physically secured.

Security tightens further once the test developers take possession of the new questions for editing and test construction. Questions are kept in locked cabinets or protected computers. Extraneous paper copies are shredded. Test editors and developers have access to questions only on an as-needed basis. Test booklets are printed at facilities designed for handing sensitive documents and stored safely until the moment they are distributed to examinees.

These procedures reduce to nearly zero the chance of any examinee seeing a question before it is administered as part of a test. Whether question exposure during test administration becomes a problem depends on policies that govern when and how often a test is administered and when and whether test forms are reused. These policies have evolved over time.

It was not unusual in the early days of psychological measurement for test developers to produce only a single form and to administer that form whenever it was needed. For example, the Stanford version of the Binet–Simon Intelligence Scale stood alone for 21 years. It was not until 1937 that a pair of equivalent forms, labeled L and M, finally replaced the single initial form (Anastasi, 1976). At about this time, researchers working with the U.S. Army Testing Program determined that the important consequences attached to the tests they were developing made security a concern. They accordingly produced multiple forms of each test to discourage coaching (Dubois, 1970).

The approach taken by the Army tests was also being taken by various similarly moderate- and high-stakes programs. The Iowa Tests of Educational Development, precursors of the Iowa Tests of Basic Skills, were constructed as multiple, parallel forms in the early 1940s. The College Board and the ETS made the same decision and began producing multiple forms of the Scholastic Aptitude Test in 1941 (Donlon & Angoff, 1984). American College Testing, an offshoot of the original Iowa Tests, has created multiple forms of the ACT college admissions test since its inception in 1959 (Peterson, 1983).

An important policy introduced in turn by each of these academic programs was that each test form was administered on a single occasion to a large number of examinees and then discarded. Because of the time and expense required to develop forms, this rule effectively restricted testing to only a few days each year. However, using a test form just once rather than repeatedly eliminated one of the last possible sources of question preexposure.

The result of all of the policies and precautions is that high-stakes conventional testing programs are secure indeed. Although determined examinees will forever attempt to cheat through copying and misrepresentation, opportunities for doing so are limited, and suspected cases are vigorously pursued. Just as important, the possibility is minimal that examinees will have previously encountered, by chance or by design, any of the questions on the test they were administered.

SECURING ADAPTIVE TESTS

Most of the security concerns of conventional tests apply equally to adaptive tests. However, the two sorts of tests are not equally vulnerable to each security risk. The following comparison makes this point.

Copying

Adaptive tests are relatively immune to examinees copying from each other. CBTs are usually administered to examinees seated in individual carrels, restricting views of other examinee's screens. Even if examinees could see each other's screens, the fact that different examinees are administered different questions makes it unlikely that anything helpful would be visible. Furthermore, an examinee's responses are displayed on the screen only fleetingly. Once a question is answered, that question and its response are replaced by a new question. A copier would therefore have to be looking at just the right screen at just the right time to steal an answer. This is in contrast to conventional answer sheets where responses remain visible on each examinee's desk until the test is finished.

Even the worst possible case, one or more examinees acting in collusion, might not be serious. Because the process by which adaptive tests select questions usually includes a random component, examinees who attempt to answer the same questions in the same way will eventually have their tests diverge, frustrating further efforts at teamwork.

Misrepresentation

Adaptive tests are as vulnerable as conventional tests to examinees misrepresenting themselves so that one could test as another. The only effective way to combat misrepresentation is by having sound procedures in place at the testing site to check in examinees and confirm identification.

Question Preexposure

The questions produced for an adaptive test must be protected during development just as they are for conventional tests. Correspondence with question writers must be confidential, completed questions must be stored securely, and tests must be hidden from view except when being administered. It is on this last point that CBTs hold a slight advantage. Conventional tests have been compromised more than once by a test booklet being lost or stolen before it had a chance to be administered. Anyone finding or stealing a printed test booklet would recognize immediately what it is and be able to read and reproduce it. This is not the case with computerized tests, which are stored and transmitted electronically. Questions can and should be stored in an encrypted format that protects them not just from casual viewers but from determined hackers as well. The only way to see a CBT's questions should be as an examinee being administered the test.

As the Kaplan–GRE case so amply demonstrated, the major security weakness of adaptive tests lies with the policies under which they are administered. Unlike conventional test forms that are administered once and then discarded, adaptive tests are administered repeatedly from the same underlying question pool. As Kaplan discovered, the possibility of dangerous levels of question preexposure is real. Making matters worse, adaptive testing programs are commonly administered much more frequently and in a much more flexibly scheduled way than are conventional tests. For example, the computerized GRE is available on more than 100 days each year. By comparison, its conventional precursor was administered just three times per year.

CAT ADMINISTRATION POLICIES

There are good and defensible reasons for operating adaptive tests differently from conventional tests. These reasons fall into four categories: public relations, logistics, economics, and pretesting. Each is described, and defended, in turn.

Public Relations

Despite the promise of better, more efficient measurement, testing organizations can find adaptive testing a tough sell to examinees. CBTs are usually substantially more expensive, costing two to three times more than a comparable conventional test. CBTs are usually administered at a relatively small number of specialized sites, often requiring examinees to travel some distance. Finally, CBTs are just plain different, a fact many examinees understandably find disconcerting. Most examinees would rather read questions from paper than from a computer screen, and those with limited computer experience would rather stick with their tried-and-true #2 pencil.

One way that testing organizations respond to market resistance is by offering examinees something they do not usually get with conventional tests: flexible scheduling and fast score reporting. It is commonly found that examinees will pay extra for the right to procrastinate, and many tests charge successively higher registration fees as the date of an exam approaches. Adaptive tests take this to an extreme. If tests can be scheduled at any time and scores reported immediately, students could delay taking their college entrance test until just before college application deadlines. Professionals could defer taking a certification test until their training program ends and they are confident of passing. Examinees could test at their own convenience rather than consent to a schedule dictated by a testing company.

Logistics

Conventional tests are relatively cheap and easy to administer. No special equipment or dedicated facilities are needed; all an examinee needs is a place to sit and a pencil. Therefore, most high-volume tests are administered in rooms ordinarily used for other purposes. Classrooms, auditoriums, hotel meeting rooms, and the odd high school cafeteria are popular choices. This makes it possible and cost effective to test examinees in big batches, because the incremental cost of adding another examinee to a test site that currently accommodates 100 is minimal.

CBTs have different logistical requirements. It is and always will be more expensive and less convenient to supply examinees with computers rather than pencils. Suitable test sites are harder to come by and awkward to configure temporarily for test administration. Mass testing of thousands or hundreds of thousands of examinees at once is therefore not yet a viable option. There will come a day when tests can be routinely administered on established banks of computers usually used for other things but temporarily detailed to testing. Some academic placement testing is already handled in this way, with testing conducted occasionally in computer labs ordinarily used for teaching and training. However, such sites are not yet ready to meet the demands of high-volume, high-stakes tests.

The currently preferred alternative to periodic testing of large examinee groups is to continuously test smaller groups. By spreading test volume across the year rather than concentrating it on a small number of days, a relatively small number of test sites can handle the examinee flow. Because these sites operate continuously, it becomes possible to dedicate them to testing. Several networks of such sites have grown up in recent years, most notably the Sylvan Technology Centers, which operates more than 1,200 test centers.

Economics

Continuous rather than periodic testing does not in itself create question exposure problems of the sort that Kaplan exploited with the GRE. Continuous testing *from the same question pool* does. Unfortunately, fiscal realities prohibit daily retirement and replacement of question pools. For a CAT to be effective, the question pool should at minimum contain the equivalent of 5 to 10 conventional forms, potentially thousands of questions. This is roughly the number of forms that might be developed each year to support a typical high-volume, high-stakes conventional testing program. A program of this sort would therefore test anywhere from 100,000 to 2 million examinees with the questions that comprise a single CAT pool. Retiring an item pool after it has been administered to only the few thousand examinees likely to test on a single day is out of the question.

Pretesting

Even if a sufficient number of questions could be written to support frequent pool turnover, there remains the problem of pretesting. A CAT is efficient because it does not waste an examinee's time by asking questions that are inappropriately easy or difficult. Little is learned by asking questions that we know an examinee either can or cannot answer correctly. Instead, the CAT attempts to draw questions from the pool of a sort that an examinee is about equally likely to answer correctly as incorrectly. To do so, the CAT needs some way of predicting how a given examinee is likely to answer a given question. These predictions are formulated by pretesting, which entails administering every new question to at least several hundred examinees and checking how often it was answered correctly and by whom. Only after a question has been pretested is it allowed to become a member of an operational pool.

Because pretest questions generally do not contribute to an examinee's score, it is therefore hard to justify devoting much more than 15% or 20% of an examinee's total test to pretesting. This limits the extent to which a CAT can be self-supporting in the sense that today's examinees are used to pretest the questions that will constitute tomorrow's question pools.

Some rough calculations based on a few assumptions can be done to determine how many examinees are needed to pretest enough questions to fill a complete pool. Suppose 20% of each examinee's test is given to pretesting. Also, suppose because a CAT provides more efficient measurement, each examinee is administered a test about half as long as a comparable conventional form. This cuts each examinee's contribution to pretesting in half, to 10% of a conventional form. Finally, suppose each pretest question must be administered to at least 500 examinees. Then, 5,000 examinees are needed to pretest enough questions to replace a portion of the question pool equal to a single conventional form. To completely replace an average 5- or 10-form pool therefore requires pretesting on 25,000 to 50,000 examinees. Even this is a best-case estimate because many pretest questions will be found to be of inadequate quality to warrant a place in some future pool. It is not uncommon for half of the questions pretested to be discarded for one reason or another. The bottom line is that a question pool must be used to test a large number of examinees in order to generate sufficient pretest data to replace itself.

LIVING WITH CONTINUOUS TEST ADMINISTRATION

A charitable reading of the previous section leads to the conclusion that, for the time being at least, testing organizations have no real choice but to administer CATs continuously from the same question pool. It is therefore a matter of making the best of it. Various procedures have been developed to this end. These fall roughly into the three categories described briefly in the following and more extensively later.

Control Question Exposure Rates During Test Administration

When questions are selected during a CAT solely with regard to their measurement properties, certain items tend to be administered to nearly every examinee. Furthermore, in a classic example of Zipf's Law, a small proportion of the questions available in the pool will be administered very frequently while the vast majority of the pool goes all but unused. Because the frequently used questions are likely to become compromised quickly, this is a recipe for disaster. One solution is to intentionally limit the frequency with which each question can be administered. An ever-lengthening list of procedures for doing so has been developed, many of which are described here. A second approach, several versions of which are described, uses question-selection algorithms that make an inherently more balanced use of the entire question pool rather than draw continually from the same small subset of questions.

Manage Question Pools Strategically

Although pools can't reasonably be quickly retired, they can be given periodic vacations. Scheduling these vacations and arranging for alternate pools to fill in during absences is the job of strategic pool-management methods. These methods have confusion as their goal, shuffling question pools unpredictably into and out of use so that examinees (and test preparation schools) are unsure which pool will be in use on any particular day. This substantially increases the number of exposed items that an examinee would have to memorize to gain an advantage. Pool management is generally used as an adjunct to, rather than as a replacement of, exposure-rate control procedures.

Enhance the Self-Correcting Nature of Adaptive Testing

The last line of defense against question preexposure is to correct for it after it occurs. There is at least some evidence that adaptive tests are robust to the sort of unusual responses that might arise from question preexposure (Davey & Miller, 1992). Consider an examinee who is generally poorly skilled but has been exposed to some questions in the pool.

The CAT scoring procedures might be momentarily perturbed when a correct answer to an exposed question slips in alongside a string of otherwise wrong answers. But these perturbations would be short lived unless the examinee had gained access to a large percentage of the pool's questions and is able to repeat the feat. Several studies have explored the extent to which CATs are naturally robust to question preexposure. More important, various procedures have been developed to enhance this nature to some extent.

CONTROLLING QUESTION EXPOSURE RATES

Test questions differ from each other both in difficulty and in discrimination. The latter property measures the extent to which a question discriminates among examinees of similar proficiency. Low discrimination does not necessarily mark a question as badly written, although vagueness or ambiguities are potential causes. A question may fail to discriminate simply because it measures traits that are relatively untapped by the other questions on a test. In any case, highly discriminating items provide strong measurement, a fact that makes such items all but irresistible to CAT question-selection algorithms. Left unfettered, these algorithms tend to gravitate toward a small proportion of a pool's questions. These questions are administered, and exposed, with alarming frequency while the bulk of the pool languishes waiting for the call that never comes.[1]

Grossly unbalanced question usage rates present a clear security risk. Security is compromised to the extent that tests overlap across examinees. The extent of overlap is in large part a function of effective pool size, defined as the number of questions administered with substantial frequency. Because an unbalanced pool administers only a small number of items with nonnegligible frequency, it performs as though it were much smaller than it is. Size alone, therefore, is not enough to save a question pool from exposure problems. Only when coupled with a capable exposure-controlling procedure is a large pool of real value.

The goal of all exposure-controlling procedures is to more evenly balance question usage rates by limiting the frequency with which popular items can be administered. Several of these procedures are described in the following discussion, roughly in order of their year of discovery and their degree of effectiveness. A general theme underlying this description

---

[1]Unequal discrimination is recognized by some but not all of the response-prediction models that underlie CAT question-selection algorithms. Simpler models that assume equal discrimination avoid the problems of unbalanced pool use discussed here. But at what cost?

is conditionality, with more effective procedures making decisions that differ depending on the question being considered for administration, the examinee the question is being administered to, and the questions that have already been administered to that examinee. Less effective procedures tend to be less conditional and ignore some or all of this context.

Randomesque Control

One of the first and simplest methods to be proposed was the 4-3-2-1 procedure (McBride & Martin, 1983). This procedure has the selection algorithm identify not only the best (most informative) question for administration at a given point, but the second, third, and fourth best questions as well. Exposure rates are, at least in theory, limited by allowing the best question to be administered on only 40% of the cases in which it is selected. The second, third, and fourth best questions are presented 30%, 20%, and 10% of the time, respectively. The 4-3-2-1 is easy to implement, but in practice provides limited protection against overexposure of popular questions. This is largely because the method fails to distinguish between popular questions that are being selected constantly and unpopular questions whose numbers just happened to come up.

Question-Conditional Control

Sympson and Hetter (1985) recognized that the problem with randomesque control procedures was that all selected questions are administered or rejected with the same probabilities. A 40% administration rate is too high for popular questions that are frequently selected but too low for rarely selected questions. Their method therefore replaces the single, fixed administration rate with one that varies across questions. Each question is assigned an individual *exposure parameter*, a value between zero and one, which dictates how often the question is administered if selected. For example, a question with an exposure parameter of .25 is administered only 25% of the time it is selected. A question with an exposure parameter of 1.0 is administered every time it is selected. Properly set, exposure parameters can control not how often a question is selected, but rather how often it is exposed to examinees.

Exposure parameters are obtained through simulations conducted before operational testing. First, a maximum exposure rate is set. For example, it may have been decided that no question should be administered to more than 15% of all examinees. This target maximum rate is subjective and is a function of pool size, average test length, and desired security level.

Several thousand adaptive test administrations are then simulated, after which the number of times each question was administered is tallied. These observed exposure rates are compared with the target maximum rate. Exposure parameters for questions administered too often are adjusted downward. After all the exposure parameters are adjusted, the simulation is repeated. The cycle of adjusting and simulating continues until exposure parameters have stabilized and no questions exceed the maximum exposure rate.

Exposure parameters are used during operational test administration as follows. First, the CAT question-selection algorithm identifies the best question to be administered at any point in the test. A random number uniformly distributed between zero and one is then generated and compared with the selected question's exposure parameter. Only if the exposure parameter is greater than the random number is the question administered. Questions selected but not administered are handled in one of several ways, depending on the implementation. A revolving door, recidivist policy returns them immediately to the question pool where they are likely to be quickly selected again. A sterner, throw-away-the-key alternative sets them aside and bars their reselection unless the pool of freely eligible questions runs dry.

Question- and Examinee-Conditional Control

Although the Sympson and Hetter (1985) method is a considerable improvement on randomesque exposure control, it does not work well for very easy or very difficult questions. These questions are generally selected for administration only to equally extreme examinees. Because by definition such examinees are rare, extreme questions are unlikely to exceed the specified maximum exposure rate even if administered every time they are selected. Exposure parameters for these questions reflect this by allowing them to be administered every time selected. That this is a problem is illustrated by considering a group of very able examinees. Each of these examinees will receive questions drawn from the high and hard end of the question pool. Because these questions are administered whenever selected, tests presented to this group of examinees will overlap substantially.

The solution is to condition exposure control parameters not just on questions, but on the examinee being tested as well. Several procedures for doing so have been proposed (Stocking & Lewis, 1995a, 1995b; Thomasson, 1995). These procedures assign each question not a single exposure parameter, but a series of parameters that differ across proficiency or test score levels. A difficult question is rarely selected other than for able examinees, where it is an overwhelmingly popular choice.

We are therefore unconcerned about its being exposed too often to middling and low-proficiency examinees. The question's exposure parameters across this proficiency range can be then be left near unity, allowing it to be always administered as a welcome change of pace on those rare occasions when it is selected. However, we do want to protect hard questions against overexposure to high-scoring examinees. The exposure parameters in this proficiency range would then be set to restrict administration to only a small fraction of the many occasions the question is selected.

Question- and examinee-conditional exposure parameters are determined through simulations of the Sympson and Hetter (1985) sort. To start, the proficiency range is divided into several levels. Several thousand tests are then simulated and the frequencies of question administration are tallied, but these counts are kept separately for each of these levels. Observed frequencies are again compared with specified maximum rates (which may vary across proficiency levels) and exposure parameters are adjusted upward or downward accordingly. The only difference is that these comparisons and adjustments are made separately and independently at each of the proficiency levels. Questions will often have some of their exposure parameters adjusted upward and some downward in the same simulation cycle. As before, simulation cycles continue until some semblance of stability is reached.

The result is a list of m exposure parameters assigned to each question, where m is the number of proficiency levels on which things were tabulated. During testing, the examinee's current proficiency estimate is used to determine which of the m exposure parameters attached to a selected question is relevant. Things proceed identically to Sympson and Hetter from this point. A random number is generated and compared with the relevant exposure parameter. If the random number is less than the parameter, the question is administered. The question is otherwise either returned to the pool or set aside until the pool empties.

Question-, Examinee-, and Context-Conditional Control

Although conditioning on questions and examinees might seem sufficient, it is still sometimes not enough. To minimize test overlap across examinee it is necessary to combat *question clusters* as well. Question clusters are sets of questions that appear together with unwelcome frequency. For example, it might be found that when Question 16 appears, it is most often in the company of Questions 24, 98, and 155. Although clusters do not always drive up test-overlap rates on average, they do insure that the worst overlap cases are very bad indeed. The solution is to break up clusters by conditioning exposure parameters not just on questions and examinees, but also on questions that have been administered during the test so far. In the example earlier, the exposure parameter for Question 16 would drop sharply if one of its frequent companions has already been administered.

Davey and Parshall (1995) and Nering, Davey, and Thompson (1998) have proposed exposure-control procedures termed here as *fully conditional*. These procedures assign exposure parameters to questions much like other conditional control procedures. As usual, these parameters are obtained before operational testing through a series of simulations. The difference is that fully conditional procedures assign two lists of exposure parameters to each question. The first list contains m elements, $e_1, \ldots,$ e_m, where m is the number of proficiency levels or strata. Values in this list are identical both in interpretation and function to the question and examinee-conditional exposure parameters described earlier. They limit the frequency with which individual questions can be administered to examinees at each proficiency level. The second list contains $n - 1$ elements, where n is the number of questions in the pool. Each question is then assigned a parameter in conjunction with every other question in the pool. These parameters limit the frequency with which questions are allowed to co-occur.

The set of $n - 1$ lists that limit pair-wise question exposure can be collected into an $n \times n$ table with elements p_{ij}, like that shown in Table 8.1. This table is symmetric, with values above the diagonal equal to those below. The entries are the pair-wise exposure parameters used to prevent popular pairs or sets of items from co-occurring. These are on the same scale as other sorts of exposure parameters, with small values restricting and large values permitting administration. The Question 1–Question 3 combination is especially troublesome and will be strictly controlled by the assigned value of $p_{13} = p_{31} = .2$. However, Question 4 is apparently not closely associated with other questions and so can freely appear with any question.

During testing, both individual and pair-wise exposure parameters are used to control question administration by the following procedure. As

TABLE 8.1
Pair-wise Exposure Control Parameters

Item	1	2	3	4	5
1	—	0.8	0.2	1.0	0.4
2	0.8	—	1.0	1.0	1.0
3	0.2	1.0	—	0.8	0.6
4	1.0	1.0	0.8	—	1.0
5	0.4	1.0	0.6	1.0	—

usual, a question is chosen for administration based on the CAT selection procedure. The current proficiency of the examinee is used to determine which entry of the question's individual parameter list is relevant, just as with the examinee-conditional procedure. Denote this element as e_{ii}. The pair-wise parameters, from any table entries involving both the selected question and previously administered questions, are denoted by p_{ij} (where j ranges from 1 to the number of questions so far administered). Finally, the conditional probability of administering the selected question is computed by taking the mean of the set of p_{ij} values and multiplying the result by e_{ii}. The selected question is then administered with this probability using the usual random number draw.

As a concrete example, suppose Question 5 has been selected. Also, suppose Question 5 has an individual exposure parameter of .7 for the examinee being tested. Then, $e_{55} = .7$. Finally, suppose Questions 2 and 3 have already been administered. Because $e_{52} = 1$ and $e_{53} = 6$, the (conditional) probability of administering Question 5 given this examinee and given that Questions 2 and 3 have already appeared is .7 * (1 + .6)/2 = .56.

The simulation process used to assign individual and pair-wise exposure parameters is identical to that for other exposure-control procedures. One input to these simulations is the maximum exposure rate for individual questions at each proficiency level. Fully conditional procedures also require that a maximum co-occurrence rate for pairs of questions be specified. Following each simulation, the frequency with which each question is administered to examinees at each proficiency level is tallied as before. However, a second count is made of the frequency with which each question appears in conjunction with every other question in the pool. Both of these counts are compared with set maximum limits and the usual upward and downward adjustments are made. This process is repeated until things stabilize.

A Comparison Study

Nering et al. (1998) recently evaluated many of the procedures described above in a large-scale simulation study. Four observed properties of each procedure were of interest. The first was the extent to which the procedures minimized test overlap, or the degree with which similar tests are administered to different examinees. High overlap rates indicate different examinees were administered similar tests; low overlap rates indicate the opposite. The second property was the extent to which the overall or unconditional exposure rates of items were controlled. The third property, a corollary of the second, looked at the extent to which the control procedures forced a balanced use of the question pool. The final property of each procedure was the extent to which it hindered the efficiency of the testing process by barring access to the most informative questions in the pool. The goal was to identify the procedure that minimized overlap, controlled question-exposure rates, balanced pool use, and allowed efficient measurement across the score scale.

The results suggested, in general, things improve with increased conditionality. Conditioning on questions, examinees, and test context is better than conditioning only on questions and examinees, which is better than conditioning only on questions, which is better than conditioning on nothing. However, differences were not enormous, and there was a diminishing return as conditioning became more complex.

Question-Selection Procedures That Control Exposure Rates

A more recent approach to controlling pool exposure focuses on the way questions are selected rather than intervening once selection has been made. As such, these procedures do not fit conveniently into the taxonomy of increasing conditionality outlined earlier. These newer procedures recognize question selection algorithms that strive to maximize test efficiency do so at the cost of unbalanced pool use and question the wisdom of this economy. By slightly compromising measurement efficiency, these procedures yield a more inherently balanced use of the question pool. Two versions of these newer procedures are briefly described.

a-Stratified Pool Question Selection.   Chang and Ying (1997) suggested a method that controls exposure rates by first stratifying the question pool according to question discrimination. Less informative (less discriminating) questions go on the top layer whereas more informative questions go on the bottom. At each point of the test, questions are selected from only one of the strata. The active stratum changes as the test proceeds, with early questions drawn from the top, or least discriminating stratum. Selection is made from more discriminating strata toward the middle of the test and from the most discriminating stratum by the end. Within each stratum, questions are selected by finding the question whose difficulty level best matches the proficiency level of the examinee.

Chang and Ying's approach makes good sense from two perspectives. The first is that selecting questions strictly on the basis of difficulty leads to more balanced pool use. Ignoring discrimination fixes selection procedures that are otherwise drawn repeatedly to a small number of highly discriminating questions.

It also makes sense to begin a test with less discriminating questions and defer more discriminating questions until later. The goal of adaptive testing is to fit the questions to each examinee's skill level. But early in the test examiners have only a rough guess as to where that level might be. The problem with administering highly discriminating questions at this point is that such questions tend to discriminate well only over a narrow proficiency range. They are like a tightly focused spotlight that shines intensely but casts little light outside a narrow beam. Less discriminating questions are more like floodlights that illuminate a wide area but not too brightly. The idea is to use the floodlights early to search and locate the examinee, then switch to spotlights to inspect things more closely.

Specific-Information Question Selection. This method doles out discriminating questions not by chance or according to some fixed schedule, but by need (Davey & Fan, 1999). Simply put, discriminating questions are reserved for examinees who, because of circumstances, can make best use of them. To determine which examinees need discriminating questions and when they need them, it is first necessary to define what constitutes normal progress through the test. Progress, in this context, is the rate at which an ability estimate becomes precise, or, equivalently, the rate at which test information is accumulated as the test proceeds. Normal progress for a particular examinee is characterized by information accumulating at a rate typical of other examinees at the same performance level. This can be represented by a series of intermediate information values or targets that stipulate how much information should be accumulated after each question is administered. Each examinee's progress is monitored by continually comparing the amount of information accumulated with that required at each point throughout the test. Examinees who are making adequate progress receive moderately discriminating questions to maintain that pace. Examinees who are behind schedule are brought back in line by more highly discriminating items. Examinees ahead of pace are slowed by less discriminating questions. All of this is done subject to the usual content constraints and exposure-control mechanism.

When intermediate targets are properly defined, specific-information question selection can offer the same sort of naturally balanced pool use as the Chang and Ying (1997) approach. Highly discriminating questions would be used only occasionally to spur progress of examinees who have fallen behind. Relatively undiscriminating questions that might never be administered otherwise would play the important role of slowing the pace of examinees who have surged ahead. The bulk of the questions administered would be drawn from the broad, well-stocked middle of the pool.

In addition to balancing question use, specific-information selection allows each examinee to be measured to a specified precision level. This allows the measurement characteristics of an adaptive test to be dictated rather than discovered.

MANAGING QUESTION POOLS

Even the most effective exposure-control procedures will be no more successful in the long term than was the Alamo. Good exposure control can only temporarily thwart the efforts of blabber-mouthed examinees and devious test-coaching schools. The cavalry must arrive at some point to relieve a beleaguered pool or it will surely perish. Just as generals plot troop movements and maneuvers, so must testing organizations manage question pools. Strategic pool management must be used in conjunction with exposure-control methods to increase test security. Several approaches for managing pools are described.

Very Large Pools

Las Vegas knows how to deal with security problems. Reports surfaced that card players were gaining an advantage on the house by counting cards as dealt, thereby knowing which cards were left in the deck. Casinos moved quickly and simply increased the number of card decks from which dealers dealt. One deck became four. Four decks became six. Six decks became 10. Eventually, (most) players' counting efforts became overloaded and they were no longer able to judge with accuracy which cards remained undealt. The house advantage was restored. This is the basic idea behind using very large question pools.

Very large pools might contain the equivalent of 50 or more conventional forms. The hope is that no examinee would be capable of memorizing enough of this pool to gain a significant advantage. Because a pool so large essentially represents the domain being measured, the belief is that any examinee capable of memorizing enough to gain an advantage may have unwittingly acquired knowledge of that domain.

One problem with developing very large item pools is the equally large cost. However, a high-volume, high-stakes test that has been around a while will have established a bank of thousands of questions from previously administered forms developed over the years. How many of these questions would remain relevant to and suitable for today's examinees is the issue. A second problem is pretesting. As mentioned earlier, the way examinees respond to a question must be modeled before that question can be added to the pool. Whether historical data collected on old forms would be acceptable for this purpose is a question. These objections notwithstanding, the idea of very large pools holds considerable merit, at least intuitively.

Pool Rotation

The street corners of many large cities feature sportsmen who offer interested passersby the opportunity to participate in a game of chance. The game is a simple one, involving only three playing cards, usually two red and one black. The dealer places the cards side-by-side face down on a table and briefly reveals the black card to establish its position. The player makes an even-money bet that he or she can track the location of the black card as the dealer slides all three cards around the table in a quick and irregular fashion. That dealers persist in offering this wager is evidence they are generally successful in thwarting the player's tracking efforts. This, in a nutshell, is the goal of question pool rotation. The idea to alternately use any of several smaller question pools that would rotate into and out of action in an unpredictable pattern. An examinee well prepared with prior information about one pool may discover with dismay that his or her test is drawn from another pool, which is not familiar.

Pools could rotate not just over time, but over geography as well. A pool used one day in Chicago may be swapped with one used in Cleveland the next day. The ensuing chaos may buy testing organizations enough time to develop and pretest new pools. These pools would be rotated into the mix and replace other pools that had served long enough to merit retirement.

The Vat

This approach combines elements of the large pool and rotating pool strategies (Patsula & Steffen, 1997). It starts with a fairly large pool called a *vat* that might contain the equivalent of 25 to 30 conventional forms. Several smaller pools are then created by drawing questions (with replacement) from the vat either randomly or systematically, the latter being used to produce pools with specific content characteristics. The pools produced are rotated in and out of service as described previously. However, in addition to the usual rotation, new pools are periodically drawn from the vat and added to the shuffle.

ENHANCING THE SELF-CORRECTING NATURE OF ADAPTIVE TESTING

Question preexposure is a problem only to the extent that examinees can artificially inflate their scores by answering correctly on review questions that they would have answered incorrectly on first viewing. The effects of preexposure on conventional tests are simple to determine: An examinee's score is increased by the number of questions spuriously answered correctly. The effects on an adaptive test are less clear. There is at least some evidence that the adaptive testing process is robust to the effects of a few isolated spuriously correct responses (Davey & Miller, 1992). An important question is whether steps can be taken to increase the robustness of the process.

Two categories of such steps are described. The first category consists of what are termed *active* procedures. These procedures work to identify or correct test scores believed to be tainted by question preexposure. The second category consists of *passive* procedures, which work to increase the robustness of the test administration and scoring process without regard to question preexposure or any other specific sort of model misfit.

Active Procedures

A large number and variety of statistics have been developed to identify when the responses of an examinee are inconsistent with an assumed prediction model (see Meijer & Sijtsma, 1995, for a review). Two general classes of these *person-fit* statistics are important to the sort of models used to select, administer, and score adaptive tests (Nering, 1997). Statistics of the first type are based on the *likelihood functions* associated with the patterns of correct and incorrect responses (Drasgow, Levine, & Williams, 1985; Levine & Rubin, 1979). The likelihood function traces the probabilities of examinees at various proficiency levels, producing an observed response pattern. The most common type of statistic looks at the height or ordinate of the likelihood function at its maximum. Response patterns that produce nicely peaked likelihood functions that attain high values are considered properly modeled, whereas patterns that produce disperse, flat likelihood functions are considered suspect.

Statistics of the second type look at discrepancies or residuals between observed responses and responses expected under the assumed prediction model (Tatsuoka, 1984; Trabin & Weiss, 1983). Response patterns with small residuals are considered well fitting, whereas those with large residuals are again suspect.

Although several person-fit statistics have been found to work well with conventionally administered tests (Li & Olejnik, 1997), results with adaptive tests have been less promising. Nering (1997) found that none of the common person-fit statistics were good at identifying misfitting examinees in a CAT environment. Furthermore, the distributional properties of the statistics were not as expected.

More recent work by Mcleod and Lewis (1998) and van Krimpen-Stoop and Meijer (1998) largely confirmed these results. Various statistics were evaluated on their ability to detect examinees who did not fit generally, and examinees who had prior exposure to certain questions in particular. Although none of the statistics worked especially well, there was an encouraging result. Statistics that worked best tended to have the most specific hypotheses as to what caused the model misfit. Just as weaker parameter estimates are stabilized by strong prior assumptions, so are weaker test statistics strengthened by specific alternative hypotheses. The trick, of course, will be in properly specifying strong hypotheses that adequately characterize the response patterns expected from examinees who have memorized part of a question pool.

A limitation of using person-fit statistics to identify poorly modeled examinees is that it is not immediately clear what to do with this information. Why an examinee was poorly modeled and what can be done about it are questions left unanswered (Nering & Meijer, 1998). Poorly modeled examinees could simply be flagged as such. The approaches described in the following take a step beyond this and attempt to rectify model misfit rather than simply identify it.

Passive Procedures

As noted earlier, poor model fit is a problem to the extent that it influences the quality or meaning of observed test scores, which with CAT take the form of proficiency or trait estimates. The statistical techniques most commonly used to produce these trait estimates are based on certain assumptions regarding both examinees and items. Estimation quality is optimal when these assumptions are met and degraded when they are not. But different estimation procedures differ in their degree of tolerance of unmet assumptions. Some procedures are seriously affected when the observed data deviate only slightly from the assumed model. Other procedures can maintain acceptable quality even when faced with misfitting data. These procedures are termed *robust*.

The statistics literature is replete with descriptions of robust estimation methods (see Andrews et al., 1972, Hampel, Ronchetti, Rousseeuw & Staehl, 1986, for a review). These methods acknowledge that the models underlying statistical procedures are at best approximations to reality. Assumptions are usually, if not uniformly, violated to some extent. The goal is to minimize the effects of these violations on the quality of the procedures. With perfectly modeled data, robust procedures may not work as well as traditional procedures optimized for ideal circumstances. However, robust procedures are resilient under duress and will generally prevail in the more typical case where data are less than ideal.

Most robust estimation procedures employ one or more of the following principles:

1. Base estimates on the ranks, rather than the values, of observed data points. The rank order of a data set is more likely to be stable than the actual values taken on. For example, the median of a distribution is ordinarily less variable than the mean. Estimates based on ranked observations are termed *L estimates*.

2. Minimize loss functions that are tolerant of outlying data values. Model misfit will likely result in some number of outlying data points. These points should not be allowed to unduly influence parameter estimates. Estimates based on tolerant loss functions that implicitly down weight these points are called *m estimates*.

3. Explicitly weight observations differentially. A simpler way to make estimates less sensitive to outlying data points is to explicitly exclude or down weight observations thought to be outliers. The α-trimmed mean is perhaps the most common example of this strategy. Here, the mean is computed only from those observations that fall between the α and $1 - \alpha$ percentiles; that is, the largest and smallest observations are removed from the sample.

These ideas have been used to develop numerous robust estimation procedures for trait or proficiency estimate parameters. Most have been evaluated by comparing their performance with that of the standard MLE. The comparison has usually been in the context of conventional rather than adaptive testing. Brief summaries of some notable studies follow.

Wainer and Wright (1980). This study compared four alternative estimation methods to the MLE under conditions where an assumed 1P logistic or Rasch model either held or failed to hold. The latter conditions assumed that examinees guessed correctly on occasion, a circumstance the standard Rasch model does not provide for. Results supported use of a modified jackknife estimation procedure, an implementation of Principles 2 and 3. This procedure proved superior to the MLE even under the ideal circumstances when the assumed model was true, a finding unexpected given the known asymptotic efficiency of the MLE. The answer to this seeming paradox is that the 40 question tests simulated were not long enough to allow the MLE to reach asymptotic performance levels.

Mislevy and Bock (1982). The authors evaluated the performance of an estimation procedure called *biweight*, which had been described by Mosteller and Tukey (1977). The biweight is an *m*-estimator that implicitly down weights responses to questions believed to be too difficult or too easy for an examinee. Ideally, this will mitigate the influence of guessed correct responses and careless incorrect responses. Grounds for evaluation were again data simulated both under and outside the Rasch model. Results favored the biweight.

Jones (1982a, 1982b). In a series of reports, Jones developed an m-estimator similar to that of the biweight (Jones, 1982a, 1982b; Jones, Wainer, & Kaplan, 1984). This procedure weights the contribution of a response by the product $P_i(\theta)Q_i(\theta)$, where P_i and Q_i are the probabilities of the examinee's responding to a question correctly and incorrectly, respectively. The effect is again to down weight responses to questions that are too easy or too difficult for an examinee. This estimator was compared theoretically with the biweight and the MLE, and judged superior to both.

Yi and Nering (1998). This study compared the biweight with MLE under adaptive testing. The simulations providing the basis of comparison were designed to realistically characterize how actual examinees respond to actual test questions, which is ordinarily not in strict accord with any assumed model. Although the biweight was expected to thrive in the presence of the noisy data that resulted, this was not the case. Little improvement over the MLE was noted.

Research on robust proficiency estimation is therefore a mixed bag. Although some procedures have shown promise in limited contexts, the Yi and Nering (1998) study was disappointing. More discouraging is the fact that this was the only study that assessed performance with adaptive tests and under realistic simulation procedures. A possible bright spot was identified by Reise (1995), who found that nonmodel-fitting response patterns are more easily detected when biweight rather than MLE proficiency estimates are used.

CONCLUSIONS

If economics is the dismal science, the study of exposure control in adaptive testing can be characterized as being no better than gloomy. The fight for pool security is ultimately a losing battle, with a temporary holding action or stalemate being the best that can be hoped for. In some way, on some day, examinees will inevitably learn enough about a pool to render it useless. Whether they learn from each other or from a coaching school is unimportant. A pool is just as useless either way.

The sense of despair only deepens the more things are considered. For example, consider the following: The accepted goal of exposure control is to minimize the extent to which tests overlap across examinees. Unhappily, this only makes it easier for a team of examinees working together to learn an entire pool. The less tests overlap, the less redundant will be the information provided by each examinee about the questions they have seen. Fewer examinees could plunder more questions more efficiently.

It could be argued that minimal overlap is instead a positive thing because a question must be seen and memorized by several examinees to be reliably learned. However, technology has an answer to this problem. Examinees could test wearing miniature cameras that are virtually undetectable but capable of recording everything the examinee sees on the screen. Memorization is not necessary.

The danger is not that question pools will be disclosed. As stated, that much is a given—they will be. The danger is they will be disclosed so quickly that economics, logistics, and pretest requirements make it impossible to develop replacement pools fast enough to keep up. At this point a testing program would become either invalid or unviable.

That the CBT has grown rapidly over the last decade is not evidence that long-term success is ensured. Figure 8.1 is instructive in this regard. The steeply ascending solid line shows the number of a certain make of automobile sold in the years shortly after its introduction. The record of sales growth must have been as heartening to General Motors executives as the increase in CATs delivered is to testing programs. The grisly plot twist in this story is that the car in question was, of course, the infamous Corvair. Allegations concerning its roadworthiness quickly drove sales to zero (the dashed line) and the make was out of production soon thereafter.

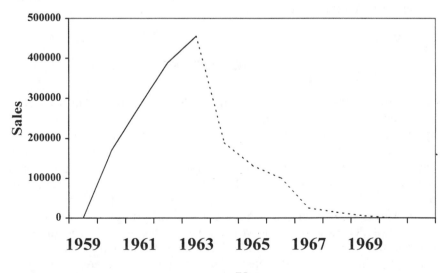

FIG. 8.1.   Car sales by year.

Are there any bright spots on this otherwise dark horizon? A few appear, perhaps. The first is that something in the operational environment changes enough that continuous testing from the same pool is no longer necessary. Computers will someday be as common as pencils. Adaptive testing will no longer have to take place at dedicated sites. Mass testing on limited occasions will again become possible. Pools could be used once or twice and discarded like conventional test forms. Adaptive tests will still retain many of their advantages under these conditions. Measurement will still be better, faster, and maybe more authentic. Score reporting can still be immediate. The loss of scheduling flexibility may not even be that serious. In many cases, most examinees would prefer to test during a fairly narrow window but are forced to distribute themselves more uniformly by the limited peak capacity of testing sites.

A second prospect is that the adaptive testing process may itself hold the key to its salvation. A CAT is smarter than a conventional test, but it can be made a lot smarter still. It must be taught to recognize the unusual response patterns produced by examinees who have been exposed to some of a pool. It must be taught to treat these examinees fairly but differently from examinees who are responding in more predictable ways. The psychometrics underlying adaptive testing can and must be substantially improved. It is a human trait to believe today's problems will be solved by tomorrow's technology. It is just possible that adaptive testing may turn out to be one of the few cases where this faith is warranted.

REFERENCES

Anastasi, A. (1976). *Psychological Testing* (4th ed.). New York: Macmillan.

Andrews, D. F., Bickel, P. J., Hampel, F. R., Huber, P. J., Rogers, W. H., & Tukey, J. W. (1972). *Robust estimates of location*. Princeton, NJ: Princeton University Press.

Chang, H. H., & Ying, Z. (1997, June). *Multi-stage CAT with stratification design*. Paper presented at the annual meeting of the Psychometric Society, Gatlinburg, TN.

Davey, T., & Fan, M. (1999, July). *Specific information item selection for adaptive testing*. Paper presented at the European meeting of the Psychometric Society. Luneburg, Germany.

Davey, T., & Miller, T. R. (1992, July). *Effects of item bias and item disclosure on adaptive testing*. Paper presented at the annual meeting of the Psychometric Society, Columbus, OH.

Davey, T., & Parshall, C. G. (1995, April). *New algorithms for item selection and exposure control with computerized adaptive testing*. Paper presented at the annual meeting of the American Educational Research Association, San Francisco.

Donlon, T. F., & Angoff, W. H. (1984). The scholastic aptitude test. In W. H. Angoff (Ed.), *The college board admissions testing program: A technical report on research and development activities relating to the scholastic aptitude test and achievement* (pp. 15–48). New York: College Entrance Exam Board.

Drasgow, F., Levine, M. V., & Williams, E. A. (1985). Appropriateness measurement with polychotomous item response models and standardized indicies. *British Journal of Mathematical and Statistical Psychology, 38*, 67–86.

DuBois, P. H. (1970). *A history of psychological testing*. Boston: Allyn & Bacon.

Hampel, F. R., Ronchetti, E. M., Rousseeuw, P. J., & Staehl, W. A. (1986). *Robust statistics*. New York: Wiley.

Jones, D. H. (1982a). *Redescending M-type estimators of latent ability* (ETS Research Report 82-30). Princeton, NJ: Educational Testing Service.

Jones, D. H. (1982b). *Tools of robustness for item response theory* (ETS Research Report 82-36). Princeton, NJ: Educational Testing Service.

Jones, D. H., Wainer, H., & Kaplan, B. (1984). *Estimating ability with three item response models when the models are wrong and their parameters are inaccurate* (ETS Research Report 84-26). Princeton, NJ: Educational Testing Service.

Levine, M. V., & Rubin, D. B. (1979). Measuring the appropriateness of multiple-choice test scores. *Journal of Educational Statistics, 4*, 269–290.

Li, M. F., & Olejnik, S. (1997). The power of Rasch person-fit statistics in detecting unusual response patterns. *Applied Psychological Measurement, 21*, 215–231.

Lord, F. M. (1980). *Applications of item response theory to practical testing problems*. Hillsdale, NJ: Lawrence Erlbaum Associates.

McBride, J. R., & Martin, J. T. (1983). Reliability and validity of adaptive ability tests in a military setting. In D. J. Weiss (Ed.), *New horizons in testing* (pp. 223–226). New York: Academic Press.

McLeod, L. D., & Lewis, C. (1998). Detecting item memorization in the CAT environment. *Applied Psychological Measurement, 23*, 147–160.

Meijer, R. R., & Sijtsma, K. (1995). Detection of aberrant item score patterns: A review of recent developments. *Applied Measurement in Education, 8*, 261–272.

Mislevy, R. J., & Bock, R. D. (1982). Biweight estimators of latent ability. *Educational and Psychological Measurement, 42*, 725–737.

Mosteller, F., & Tukey, J. T. (1977). *Data analysis and regression: A second course in statistics*. Reading, MA: Addison-Wesley.

Nering, M. L. (1997). The distribution of person fit in the computerized adaptive testing environment. *Applied Psychological Measurement, 21*, 115–127.

Nering, M. L., Davey, T., & Thompson, T. (1998, July). *A hybrid method for controlling item exposure in computerized adaptive testing*. Paper presented at the annual meeting of the Psychometric Society, Urbana, IL.

Nering, M. L., & Meijer, R. R. (1998). A comparison of the person response function and the l_z person-fit statistic. *Applied Psychological Measurement, 22*, 53–69.

Patsula, L. N., & Steffen, M. (1997, April). *Maintaining item and test security in a CAT environment: A simulation study*. Paper presented at the annual meeting of the National Council on Measurement in Education, Chicago.

Peterson, J. J. (1983). *The Iowa testing program*. Iowa City, IA: University of Iowa Press.

Reise, S. P. (1995). Scoring method and the detection of person misfit in a personality assessment context. *Applied Psychological Measurement, 19*, 213–229.

Stocking, M. L., & Lewis, C. (1995a). *A new method of controlling item exposure in computerized adaptive testing* (ETS Research Report 95-25). Princeton, NJ: Educational Testing Service.

Stocking, M. L., & Lewis, C. (1995b). *Controlling item exposure conditional on ability in computerized adaptive testing* (ETS Research Report 95-24). Princeton, NJ: Educational Testing Service.

Sympson, J. B., & Hetter, R. D. (1985). Controlling item-exposure rates in computerized adaptive testing. *Proceedings of the 27th annual meeting of the Military Testing Association* (pp. 973–977). San Diego, CA: Navy Personnel Research and Development Center.

Tatsuoka, K. K. (1984). Caution indices based on item response theory. *Psychometrika, 49*, 95–110.

Thomasson, G. L. (1995, June). *New item exposure control algorithms for computerized adaptive testing*. Paper presented at the annual meeting of the Psychometric Society, Minneapolis, MN.

Trabin, T. E., & Weiss, D. J. (1983). *The person response curve: Fit of individuals to item characteristic curve models*. In D. J. Weiss (Ed.), New horizons in testing: Latent trait test theory and computerized adaptive testing. New York: Academic Press.

van Krimpen-Stoop, E. M. L. A., & Meijer, R. R. (1998, April). *The use of person-fit in CAT*. Paper presented at the National Council on Measurement in Education, San Diego, CA.

Wainer, H., & Wright, B. D. (1980). Robust ability estimation in the Rasch model. *Psychometrika, 45*, 373–391.

Yi, Q., & Nering, M. (1998, April). The impact of nonmodel-fitting responses in a realistic CAT environment. In M. L. Nering (Moderator), *Innovations in Person-fit Research*. Related papers session at the meeting of the National Council on Measurement in Education, San Diego, CA.

New CBT Technical Issues: Developing Items, Pretesting, Test Security, and Item Exposure[1]

Ronald K. Hambleton
University of Massachusetts at Amherst

The topics addressed in the chapters by Parshall; Way, Steffen, and Anderson; and Davey and Nering are new to the CBT field. In fact, 26 of the papers in the list of 47 references in the three chapters are unpublished. Newcomers to the field may be surprised, but the fact is the topics were never part of the pioneering conferences on CBT held in the late 1970s by Weiss and the military organizations who were funding CAT research (Weiss, 1983). Even in the most significant book on the topic of CAT published in the last 10 years—the book by Wainer and his colleagues at ETS—less than 10 pages of 300 were devoted to these four topics (Wainer et al., 1990)!

The CAT topics of great interest in publications and conferences before 1990 were such things as choosing IRT models, estimating model parameters, choosing CAT design features such as starting and stopping rules and step sizes, bank size, scaling, equating, reliability and validity issues, and so on. Content considerations were rarely important, exposure controls were never an issue, and pretesting designs were rarely of interest. Since 1990, the field has moved on to a consideration of these topics—pretesting, item development, item replacement (or more broadly,

---

[1]*Laboratory of Psychometric and Evaluative Research Report No. 355.* Amherst, MA: University of Massachusetts, School of Education.

item bank maintenance), and item and test security. All of these topics have arisen as testing agencies have attempted to implement CBTs and CATs into their test delivery systems.

The topics are presented in separate chapters in this book, but they are highly related: Item and test security is enhanced by having many good items in an item bank. Replacing these items periodically requires many content-appropriate and statistically sound items being available to serve as replacements. At the same time, with many good items, the demand for field-testing is increased, and appropriate item calibrations require, in general, many examinees. But with many examinees involved in field-testing, there is an increased threat to item and test security. And, we start over again. Item and test security is enhanced by having many good items, and so on. Item and test security, pretesting, item development, item bank maintenance, and examinee sample sizes used in item calibration are inextricably linked.

Simulation methods introduced by Way, Steffan, and Anderson (chap. 7, this volume) provide an excellent framework for looking at some of the consequences of item bank sizes, vats, pools, replacement rates, exposure rates, pretesting, and so on. But to date, available simulation models represent only part of the complex process of CBT, specifically CAT, and at best provide only incomplete results on which to base practical decisions. A number of doctoral theses could be completed by continuing to work on these simulation models. At the same time, the psychological aspects associated with testing at a computer require further study. Who is disadvantaged, and how can the disadvantages be overcome?

I find myself in agreement with the authors of the chapters, and where I have disagreements, they are generally minor with one exception that I mention later. I reinforce some of the points made by the authors, and in several areas, share some of my thoughts about promising directions for CBT and CAT research and development.

ITEM PRETESTING

Parshall's (chap. 6, this volume) chapter on pretesting items begins with a plea for good items, a plea that everyone can support. The quality of items and their associated item statistics can be identified from suitable pretesting. The big question is: Can technically sound item statistics be obtained without big examinee samples, because big samples contribute to item exposure and increase the costs of test delivery?

One line of research that has not received much attention from measurement specialists involves using item writers to estimate item statistics. This topic was given little attention by Parshall, and Davey and Nering (chap. 8, this volume) in their discussions of pretesting. Perhaps they have reservations about this line of research.

Research by Bejar (1983) at ETS and some of his colleagues working on the TOEFL over the years (e.g., Freedle & Kostin, 1993) is impressive. Earlier research by others has not produced useful results, but the research itself seemed flawed in one or more of the following ways:

1. Little or no training was given to judges. Without training and feedback a judge does not have an opportunity to recenter his or her ratings, learn about the factors affecting item difficulty (such as the role of distractors, item stem length and readability, the nature of the skills being assessed, etc.).
2. Confusing item difficulty scales—such as the delta, ability, or 1 to 10 rating scale (without clear descriptors of the numbers)—have been used. For example, it is hard to explain the latent ability scale used in IRT modeling of test data to item writers and to get them to use this scale successfully in estimating item difficulty.
3. No feedback to judges is given on how they are doing, compared with, say, other judges or a gold standard (items with known item statistics). Feedback seems important for generating valid ratings. Consider, for example, that feedback to panelists is common in the standard-setting process, feedback about both intra- and interjudge consistency.

It seems that for item writers to be able to estimate item statistics well, they need to:

1. be given extensive training and feedback,
2. work with scales they understand (e.g., the conventional item difficulty scale is easy to explain to item writers, and these estimates can be transformed later to the latent ability scale, if needed),
3. provide judgments on a scale that is meaningful (e.g., it would be possible to characterize the skills reflected in items that have p values of .25, 50, and .75 much as descriptors of basic, proficient, and advanced levels of performance are developed in standard-setting studies),
4. consider exemplary items with known item statistics as anchors to help define the scales on which item statistics are estimated, and
5. provide opportunities for judges to discuss their ratings with other item writers to come to a group consensus or simply to permit discussions among the judges before obtaining final individual judgments (influenced by group discussion).

My recently completed research for the Law School Admissions Council has convinced me that item writers can be trained to provide judgments, at least of item difficulties (Hambleton, Sireci, Swaminathan, Xing, & Rizavi, 1998), that are accurate enough to be useful in the item-calibration process. The advantage is that the size of field-test samples and the resultant item exposure rates can be reduced.

I have applied some of the research ideas from the work in standard setting: training of judges, feedback to judges, extensive practice, clear descriptions of the scale on which the judgments about items are being made (e.g., descriptions of basic, proficient, and advanced), and iterations of ratings in my work to the estimation of item statistics. Although there is some skepticism about the ability of item writers to estimate item statistics, the methodology associated with previous studies has fallen short of what is needed. With improved methodology, the results are better and seemingly useful in the item statistics estimation process.

Judgmental estimates of item difficulty (and possibly other item statistics) can be incorporated into an IRT Bayesian estimation procedure (e.g., Swaminathan & Gifford, 1986). In our simulation research, we can reduce the size of examinee samples by 50% using the item writers' estimates of item statistics; a sample of 200 examinees and the prior information about item difficulty provided by the judges functions equivalently to a sample of 400 examinees (Swaminathan, Hambleton, Sireci, Xing, & Rizavi, in press). The b values (in the IRT model) can be estimated by the panelists, and with a 3P model the c parameters can be set to a suitable chance level (e.g., number of alternatives in a multiple-choice item), and the a values can be chosen to be the average of the a values for items already in the item bank (the assumption is that the new items will be about as discriminating as those already in the item bank).

Sample sizes probably can be reduced considerably from those proposed by Davey and Nering (chap. 8, this volume) when Bayesian priors on the item parameters are used. If the errors in the item parameter estimates are random, even when they are large they have relatively little effect on ability estimates if the tests are not short (e.g., Hambleton & Cook, 1983). Ability estimates are robust to random item parameter estimation errors. One consequence of the larger errors in the item parameter estimates is that CATs need to be longer to reach a desired level of measurement precision, but the required test length will still be substantially less than a full test.

PRODUCING TEST ITEMS

I am convinced we can do better in writing more high-quality test items. Cloning items is one promising direction. Everything from some fairly superficial changes, mainly aimed at disguising items (and this seems especially desirable with more memorable problems), to more substantive changes in items, while preserving their basic structure, is possible.

For example, consider an item from one of the securities industry credentialing exams: A candidate is presented with a potential client—a semiretired person with an income of $60,000 per year, investments worth $5,000,000, two children, and a desire to invest to pay for their education in 10 years. The question is, "What would be a suitable investment strategy?" followed by four possible investments. This type of question can be cloned to produce hundreds of questions by changing the client's characteristics and investment goals, tax bracket, the economic climate, and the nature of the available investments. In my experience in the credentialing exam area, most test items can be cloned, and many can be used to produce 10 to 20 more items. For more information on item writing and item shells, see Haladyna and Shindoll (1989) and Roid and Haladyna (1982).

Cloning, or milking, items is a promising direction for expanding the sizes of item banks. Depending on the nature of the cloning, item statistics compiled on some of the items may be generalizable to other items from the same cloning family. This is another good research topic. What types of cloning preserve item statistics and what types do not?

There is also the important theoretical work of Embretson, Bejar, and others in theory-based item generation that, if done properly, can produce estimates of item statistics as well (e.g., Embretson, in press).

I was pleased to see Parshall (chap. 6, this volume) mention some of my research on test development and item information functions and the problem of capitalizing on chance (Hambleton & Jones, 1994). This problem was popular in the study of classical test theory and regression analysis in the 1940s (recall developments in cross-validation and correlation shrinkage in that period), but this line of research has not attracted much interest from IRT researchers. Item parameter estimates such as high a parameter estimates are almost certainly high because of positive error. These statistics inflate the test information function and result in error estimates of ability that are too low. More focus on cross-validation and item-selection algorithms that do not select the statistically best items can minimize the problem of capitalizing on chance.

The work of Berger and van der Linden (1992), Stocking (1990), and others from the United States on optimal sampling of examinees makes sense and will result in the need for smaller sample sizes in calibrating test items. Just as testing can be made more efficient by optimally sampling items, item calibration can be made more efficient by optimally drawing examinee samples. One of my students, Sharon Slater, is looking at these problems in her dissertation, and I expect she will find that sample sizes needed for precise item calibration will be smaller when the samples are drawn to optimize parameter estimation. Note that with

CBTs ability information can be used as the testing is proceeding to decide which examinees will see which pretest items.

DEVELOPING, MAINTAINING, AND RENEWING ITEMS IN AN ITEM BANK

Way, Steffen, and Anderson (chap. 7, this volume) describe an important concept in their chapter: vats. The idea of creating small item pools from a big bank of items (a vat), using them for a while, and resampling to make new item pools makes sense. The full bank is never disclosed and the rotation of items protects against the effect of some items being overexposed within a given item pool. By the time the information about these items may be shared, a new item pool is already in place. With some of the new software, item pools can be replaced electronically overnight. We have seen this demonstrated with a number of the credentialing exams in the information technology industry when flawed items have been detected.

For the concept of vats and item pools to have value, lots of test items with known item statistics are needed. This brings me back to cloning, algorithmic item writing, improved training of item writers, investing more funds in item writers, and so on. The book by Roid and Haladyna (1982) on generating items, which has been one of the best contributions to the criterion-referenced testing literature, needs to be reread, and some of their suggestions for writing items adopted.

Way et al. address the topic of rotating items in and out of pools using a series of arbitrary rules. For example, items administered 500 times within 3 months need to be shelved for a month, or the overlap in item pools should not exceed 10%. The idea is to keep exposure rates at an acceptable level. But it takes only one person to expose an item to others. I think it was Mike Kolen from the University of Iowa who made the astute comment that the most serious problem may not be the number of persons who see an item but the length of time an item has been exposed.

Who knows what the acceptable exposure rates should be? Until we have more experience, these exposure controls will be set based on a complex set of interactions among bank size, number of examinees, expected ability distribution, expected test lengths, cost of developing test items, and more. This makes simulation modeling especially important.

One step I would like to see added to the ETS model is an increased effort to spot items that have been exposed to examinees before the test administration. Monitoring item statistics over time, for changes not predicted by shifts in the ability distribution, is a promising direction for future research. Davey and Nering (chap. 8, this volume) are not optimistic about being able to detect very small shifts, but these small shifts are likely of minimal consequence. It is the bigger shifts in item statistics that need to be detected, and these can be detected with sufficient amounts of examinee data. If there is even a suspicion of a problem, items can be rotated out of an item pool immediately.

More research attention should be given to the detection of candidates who may have been exposed to a substantial number of the test items. This might be done in much the same way as cheaters are detected on conventionally administered tests. When a problem is detected, a special pool of items (which is secure) might be used for the remainder of a test administration. At least the size of the bias in an ability estimate can be reduced. The research of Meijer from the Netherlands and Nering from Measured Progress in the United States seems especially relevant (Meijer & Nering, 1997).

Three additional topics deserve comment: new item formats (and implications for scoring and test delivery), automated test construction (and implications of item sets), and alternate test designs. First, the power of the computer, in addition to permitting test scheduling to be flexible and providing immediate score reports, adds the capability to permit new item formats for assessing some skills in a more valid way: free response, options ranking, multiple right answers, sequential testing, audio and video use, and so on. But current delivery systems may not be ready, and some of these new formats require polytomous IRT models, which create their own problems in model parameter estimation and become complex to use. The areas of new item formats and the use of polytomous IRT models are promising areas for additional research.

Second, Way et al. highlight one of the most important advances in testing practices—the concept of automated test development or optimal test design. The work of researchers such as Stocking and Swanson (1998) and van der Linden and colleagues (van der Linden & Glas, 2000) is promising. At the same time, I am not sure the software is readily available for handling all new item formats, item sets, and polytomous response data in test design in a cost effective way.

Third, let me add a comment on an understudied test design—a test design that was not mentioned by Way et al.—multistage testing. It is being overlooked by many researchers (for an exception see Luecht & Clauser, chap. 3, this volume). Although not fully adaptive, it is partially adaptive, and it permits blocks of items to be designed in advance and reviewed by committees and it allows examinees to revise their answers within blocks. Both of these features are responsive to the main criticisms of CAT. Patsula (1999) recently completed a thesis on multistage testing. Her research will help others decide on test design parameters such as number of stages, number of modules at a stage, statistical composition of items in a module, and so on. Lord (1980) is another resource for technical information about multistage test designs.

ITEM AND TEST EXPOSURE

Davey and Nering (chap. 8, this volume) provide an excellent review of the approaches for making tests secure, including an extensive review of the work on exposure controls. But they conclude by saying, "The fight for pool security is ultimately a losing battle, with a temporary holding action or stalemate being the best that can be hoped for" (p. 187). They go on to say,

> The danger is not that question pools will be disclosed. As stated, that much is a given—they will be. The danger is they will be disclosed so quickly that economics, logistics, and pretest requirements make it impossible to develop replacement pools fast enough to keep up. (p. 188)

Although I respect the experiences and insight of these two researchers, my view is more positive about the future for CBT and CAT. I argue that (a) pretesting does not need to be as examinee sample dependent as they have described, (b) there are ways to expand item banks in cost-effective and successful ways, and (c) several testing agencies are demonstrating they can deliver valid and reliable CBTs. The New York Stock Exchange, Municipal Securities Rule-Making Board, and the National Association of Security Dealers have been delivering computer-based credentialing exams to more than 50,000 candidates a year for more than 15 years and there have been no breakdowns in the quality of the exams. Other promising CBT examples were mentioned earlier in the chapter.

Interest is increasing, not decreasing, and by and large the large organizations delivering CATs and CBTs such as ETS, Graduate Management Admissions Council, Professional Examination Service, The Chauncey Group International, Microsoft, and Novell seem to be doing a fine job. At the same time, test agencies need to be continually updating their banks or they are going to have serious validity problems with their tests.

With respect to the first point, I would like to see more research on new methods for item writers to provide usable information in the estimation of item statistics. The Bayesian IRT parameter estimation methodology already is in place (e.g., Mislevy, 1986; Swaminathan & Gifford, 1986).

CONCLUDING REMARKS

The field of CBT is filled with technical problems, dilemmas, conflicts, and trade-offs. We can expand sample sizes for item calibration and hire more item writers but costs will increase. We can increase the number of items in a bank but more pretesting will be needed and overexposure of test items can become a problem. There are no easy answers in choosing a design for a valid and defensible CBT system, and difficult decisions need to be made. The decision points and factors that enter into these decisions were outlined by the researchers in this book.

The authors have made thoughtful and important contributions. They have done a superb job of organizing a diverse literature. Among the important points they have made are the following:

1. Paper-and-pencil IRT parameter estimates often are applicable to CBTs, but there are exceptions. For example, if speed is introduced as a factor in test performance with CBT, item statistics will not be comparable.
2. Volunteer samples are problematic in pretesting.
3. Bayesian parameter estimation does reduce the size of samples needed in pretesting.
4. There are optimal designs for drawing examinee samples in item calibration studies.
5. Simulation models are an effective way to investigate many questions about item bank maintenance, item replacement, exposure rates, item bank size, and so on.
6. There is a host of statistics for controlling exposure rates and spotting examinees who may have had access to some of the items in an item bank.

Despite some of the researchers' cautions, CBT has been successful and should be even more successful in the future when there is more competition among providers of test delivery systems, when more information about the strengths and weaknesses of various test designs is known, and when new item formats and associated scoring models are available to test developers.

I am impressed with the GRE (despite the early problem with a breach in test security), the nurses' credentialing exams (NCLEX), exams in the securities field, the ASVAB, and the Graduate Management Admissions Test. There is important work being done at Microsoft and Novell, and many more examples could be added to the list. We have sufficient technical knowledge to move forward with CBTs. At the same time, we can do better technically in the areas of pretesting, item security, and item development.

I believe the most useful and important directions for additional research at this time include the following:

1. The exploration of new methods for writing test items should continue. Cloning items, algorithmic item writing, expanded efforts to train item writers, and so on should continue to receive research attention. Some of this work was mentioned by Parshall, but there is much more work being done at ETS and elsewhere. Many of our CAT problems

will vanish if item banks can be expanded significantly in a cost-effective way without loss of quality.

2. More research on methods for obtaining estimates of item statistics from item writers is needed: Training, use of exemplars, meaningful judgmental scales, iterations, discussion among item writers, and feedback are all promising additions to current methods for item parameter estimation. I am convinced we can do better, and my recent research with the Law School Admissions Council is my evidence. At the same time, the method I implemented was time consuming for judges and would need to be streamlined were it to be implemented on an ongoing basis. Item judgments combined with IRT Bayesian estimation procedures can go a long way to improving the pretest sample problem. Embretson's (1998) work on theory-generated items and item statistics appears promising as well.

3. Expanded simulation research of variables in the CBT and CAT environment to guide key decisions about test design is needed.

It is going to be interesting to reassess the CBT field in 20 years and see the progress that has been made, the new problems that have emerged, and the solutions that have been found to address the topics raised by the authors of the three chapters in this section. I believe it is safe to predict CBT will be the industry standard in higher education selection and credentialing exams in 20 years, the number of new assessment formats will be huge, and automated scoring of free-response data will be common. It is research along the lines described in chapters of this book that will insure CBT leads to valid inferences about individuals and programs.

REFERENCES

Bejar, I. I. (1983). Subject matter experts/assessment of item statistics. *Applied Psychological Measurement, 7*, 303–310.

Berger, M. P. F., & van der Linden, W. J. (1992). Optimality of sampling designs in item response theory models. In M. Wilson (Ed.), *Objective measurement: Theory into practice* (Vol. 1, pp. 274–288). Norwood, NJ: Ablex.

Embretson, S. E. (1998). A cognitive design system approach to generating valid tests: Application to abstract reasoning. *Psychological Methods, 3*, 300–326.

Freedle, R., & Kostin, I. (1993). *The prediction of TOEFL reading comprehension item difficulty for expository prose passages for three item types: main idea, inference, and supporting ideas items* (ETS Research Report 93-13). Princeton, NJ: Educational Testing Service.

Haladyna, T. M., & Shindoll, R. R. (1989). Item shells: A method for writing effective multiple-choice test items. *Evaluation and the Health Professions, 12*(1), 97–106.

Hambleton, R. K., & Cook, L. (1983). Robustness of item response models and effects of test length and sample size on the precision of ability estimates. In D. Weiss (Ed.), *New horizons in testing* (pp. 31–49). New York: Academic Publishers.

Hambleton, R. K., & Jones, R. W. (1994). Item parameter estimation errors and their influence on test information functions. *Applied Measurement in Education, 7,* 171–186.

Hambleton, R. K., Sireci, S. G., Swaminathan, H., Xing, D., & Rizavi, S. (1998). *Anchor-based
methods for judgmentally estimating item difficulty parameters* (Laboratory of Psychometric and Evaluative Research Report No. 310). Amherst, MA: University of Massachusetts, School of Education.

Lord, F. M. (1980). *Applications of item response theory to practical testing problems.*
Hillsdale, NJ: Lawrence Erlbaum Associates.

Meijer, R. R., & Nering, M. L. (1997). Trait level estimation for nonfitting response vectors.
Applied Psychological Measurement, 21, 321–336.

Mislevy, R. J. (1986). Bayes modal estimation in item response models. *Psychometrika, 51,*
177–195.

Patsula, L. (1999). *Comparative study of multi-stage and computer-adaptive test designs.*
Unpublished doctoral dissertation, University of Massachusetts, Amherst.

Roid, G. H., & Haladyna, T. M. (1982). *A technology for test-item writing.* New York: Academic Press.

Stocking, M. L. (1990). Specifying optimum examinees for item parameter estimation in
item response theory. *Psychometrika, 55,* 461–475.

Stocking, M. L., & Swanson, L. (1998). Optimal design of item banks for computerized adaptive tests. *Applied Psychological Measurement, 22*(3), 271–279.

Swaminathan, H., & Gifford, J. A. (1986). Bayesian estimation in the three-parameter logistic
model. *Psychometrika, 51,* 589–601.

Swaminathan, H., Hambleton, R. K., Sireci, S. G., Xing, D., & Rizavi, S. M. (in press). Small
sample estimation in dichotomous item response models: Effects of priors based on
judgmental information on the accuracy of item parameter estimates. *Applied Psychological Measurement.*

van der Linden, W. J., & Glas, C. (Eds.). (2000). *Computerized adaptive testing: Theory and
practice.* Boston: Kluwer.

Wainer, H., Dorans, N. J., Flaugher, R., Green, B. F., Mislevy, F. J., Steinberg, L., & Thissen, D.
(1990). *Computerized adaptive testing: A primer.* Hillsdale, NJ: Lawrence Erlbaum Associates.

Weiss, D. (1983). *New horizons in testing.* New York: Academic Press.

Issues in CBT Administration

Linda Crocker
University of Florida

After reading these informative and thought-provoking chapters, I felt we might be witnessing the birth of a "microprofession" within the field of psychometrics. Typically a profession is recognized as a skilled occupation characterized by: (a) specialized vocabulary, (b) an arcane body of knowledge, (c) practices based and advanced through research conducted by its members, (d) a code of ethics to protect client and public interests, and (e) regulation of entry. Although CBT has not yet acquired all of these formal trappings, it seems to be making remarkable strides toward becoming a distinct psychometric specialization.

First, the chapters on CBT administration presented here provide us with an extensive set of new vocabulary terms and acronyms that are commonly used by the various authors, illustrating "shared insider language" that does not occur in other areas of psychometrics. From these chapters collectively, I compiled the following list of terms that savvy readers should master to follow the authors' presentations: base forecast, CAT, CBT, CCT, CMT, disclosure, dock, docking rule threshold, docking window, exposure rate, max fraction, pool, retirement, SDM, and vat. Students of psychometrics will not find these terms in the general literature of the field unless they are reading on the topic of CBT.

Second, and more important, these terms are not simply catchy new phrases for communicating about standard practices in traditional psychometrics or test administration of paper-and-pencil assessments. These terms represent new concepts in item development and test administration that owe their origin to the emergence of new computer technology for delivery of test items to examinees that goes beyond the large-group test administration that has long been standard in the industry. The concepts underlying these terms simply did not exist in the era of paper-and-pencil testing. Hence, they represent a nascent body of knowledge that all who plan to work in this field must acquire.

Third, though not swearing an oath to a credo for standards of practice, the authors of these chapters clearly share a commitment to several common guiding principles that serve client and public interests. Namely, these principles are the following:

1. Client service requires convenience of continuously available testing.
2. Item security must be maintained.
3. Psychometric quality of items and scores is critically important.
4. Costs of test development must be contained.

At this point, it may be difficult for those of us schooled in traditional testing practices and psychometrics to envision CBT as more than a topic for a few lectures in an introductory test theory course or perhaps a single advanced seminar. After reading these works, I began to wonder if some recently emerging, but accepted, academic fields of study shared comparable beginnings (packaging sciences, sports medicine, environmental law, and television broadcasting, to name a few.)

Turning from this philosophical musing, I would like to direct attention to each of the chapters in turn. I attempted to view the contents of each of these three chapters through a common lens of traditional psychometric principles. I focused on content sampling, score equivalence, and fairness. My comments on each of the chapters follow from this perspective.

Way, Steffen, and Anderson (chap. 7, this volume) provide readers with a good source for learning the new vocabulary of CBT. They also do an excellent job of highlighting the magnitude of the item-production problem test developers will encounter as they deal with maintaining an item inventory in a live testing situation. I was particularly interested in the range of correlation cited for exposure rates for the same items in different pools: for the Verbal subtest, .60 to .90 and for the Quantitative subtest, .05 to .73. Way et al.'s description of SDM is critical. With respect to my focus on content sampling, equivalence, and fairness, I found three points in this chapter of great interest. First, exposure rate for an item depends in part on the other items in the pool. Second, items retired first tend to have psychometric characteristics that are in short supply. Does this mean examinees in common ability ranges who test later in the cycle may encounter greater percentages of items with poorer psychometric quality? Third, SDM at present does not make qualitative distinctions between items from different content areas. This can be troubling from the perspective of content validity. A pool of items may sample a content domain well, but content representativeness should not be argued at the pool or vat level, but at the individual test form level, as the examinee encounters it. Taken together, these points pose challenges to the argument that must be made to examinees and client users of admissions tests; that is, scores from different examinees taking different test forms at different testing occasions can still be compared with confidence. Way et al.'s work provides us with food for thought about the current state of the art with respect to meeting this concern.

Parshall's (chap. 6, this volume) comprehensive literature review focuses on pool development pragmatics. She simplifies the underlying rationale for periodic recalibration of item parameters in a CBT pool by offering three causes of parameter shift: changes in mode of administration, use of volunteers versus use of examinees with a stake in the outcome, and changes in the trait over time. Her identification of the developing literature on sparse and data-free approaches to calibration reminds us of the realities of live testing programs and the need for further research into methods for "rebuilding the plane while it is flying." Perhaps the only thing missing from this complete review is treatment of recalibration for performance-assessment items. From the perspectives of content sampling, equivalence, and fairness, Parshalls' review highlights several areas to which test developers and users must be vigilant. First is the need to assess content-by-mode interactions. Second is the recognition that volunteers may have different degrees of content exposure from regular examinees. Third is that a select few items will be seen by many examinees, but most items will be seen by relatively few. One begins to wonder whether meeting professional assessment standards for evidence of sound equating, substantive and structural aspects of validity, and generalizability of scores while trying to meet the demands placed on test developers by the CBT environment is an attainable goal.

Davey and Nering (chap. 8, this volume) frame well the issues of test security for CBTs. These authors are so straightforward and compelling as they lay out the concerns of test company professionals that I found myself envisioning them as cyberspace heroes who defend the treasured item content from damaging exposure and develop a repertoire of algorithms for outsmarting the relentless onslaught of forces of the dark side. Of course, my sympathies began to waver as I realized the foot soldiers in this army of intruders are, in fact, the examinees—our students who have committed no breach of ethics other than seeking admission to college or graduate school! With that in mind, I returned to my original focus on content sampling, equivalence, and fairness. The following points made by Davey and Nering seem relevant: (a) the most discriminating items will be the most popular in terms of priority selection for administration, (b) security is compromised as tests overlap, (c) frequency of administration of the most discriminating items must be limited, (d) the best questions should be administered to only a specified portion of the pool of examinees (perhaps as few as 15%), and (e) the number of questions and quality of items will vary for examinees. Although all of these points make sense from the perspective of a test developer concerned with test security, the effects on fairness, score equivalence, and content sampling seem to have been relegated to the sidelines. Of course, these problems would not vanish if we ignored the issues raised by Davey and Nering; they would, in fact, be exacerbated. Nevertheless, this chapter should make us ponder the trade-offs that are made as we pursue CBT in high-stakes situations.

Finally, it might facilitate insight to remove our psychometric hat and step momentarily into the role of a college-level administrator who is concerned with graduate school admission issues. What message do these chapters convey to such a user of scores from a large-scale CBT program, such as the GRE? From the information and discussion provided in these excellent chapters, the admissions office may be reminded of the old adage, "Be careful what you wish for." Both applicants to graduate school and admissions officers longed for the convenience of continuously available testing, and now we have it. However, although the testing is continuously available, the fact remains that most institutions admit new students only one to three times per year. As a consequence, we now see some applicants who test again and again and again trying to hit the minimum required admission for some selective programs. Are scores from these repeated testings more valid predictors of their academic performance? Furthermore, most institutions that use the GRE for admissions decisions have selected that test because of its psychometric qualities, particularly that it offered a common yardstick for comparing applicants whose transcripts, undergraduate majors, past institutions attended, and letters of recommendation could not be readily compared. In addition, use of the GRE in admissions has always been a comfort to harried admissions administrators who must ward off legal challenges to the process, provide evidence of validity of their admissions process to accreditation boards, and believe their selection instruments are relatively immune to coaching. If psychometric quality is eroded to meet the demand for convenience of continuously available testing, the value of the selection tool could be diminished.

I conclude by commending the authors of the chapters in this section on a remarkable job. These informative papers highlight the complex technical and conceptual challenges that must be addressed if we are to balance the competing needs of large-scale, on-demand testing and test score information that is useful, valid, and fair to all in high-stakes situations.

TEST ANALYSIS AND SCORING

Craig N. Mills
American Institute of Certified Public Accountants

CBT is having a substantial impact on our profession. In the previous parts of this book, authors focus on current operational issues and the development of new assessment forms. As CBT has been widely adopted, operational issues have arisen, solutions have been generated, and new procedures have been developed to implement the solutions. In addition, CBT has provided an opportunity for new forms of assessment, and the previous parts document much of the work that is under way to develop those new forms of assessment. The previous chapters illuminate many of the issues associated with the design of tests and testing programs and the maintenance of those programs once they are operational.

CBT also poses problems and opportunities for test interpretation. Consider, for example, the challenge of explaining adaptive testing to students, legislators, parents, and the public at large. Mathematical explanations are not useful because much of the audience is not mathematically trained. Simple explanations, though easily understood, are usually inaccurate and occasionally misleading. One simple explanation of adaptive testing includes the assertion that examinees who answer a question correctly are next administered a harder question. Unfortunately, this simple statement misstates how adaptive testing works. Questions are not selected based solely on an examinee's response to a single question. Responses to all prior questions are considered in the selection of additional questions for administration. Furthermore, the test design has to be taken into account. As a result, although it is generally true that harder items are administered following a correct response, it is not always the case.

The use of complex models becomes even harder to explain when the discussion shifts from test administration and item selection to scoring and score interpretation. The general public tends to accept that scores of different individuals can be compared when they take the same test. The concept of adjusting test scores to account for minor variations in the difficulty of test forms is also generally, albeit not completely, accepted. These features of testing programs are so well established that most score users probably do not even think to question them. However, it is different when many different test forms are administered and the forms vary widely in difficulty. Among the questions that arise are the following:

- Will someone who does well on an easy test get the same score as someone who does equally well on a hard test?
- Isn't it unfair to assign a low score to someone who takes an easy test because they never had the opportunity to take hard questions and earn a higher score?
- Isn't it unfair to give someone who correctly answers many hard questions more credit for answering a particular item correctly than you give to someone who answers the same item correctly, but who misses the other hard questions?

Dodd and Fitzpatrick (chap. 11, this volume) address these types of questions in the first portion of their chapter. They question the assumption that score users truly understand test scores derived using classical test theory. They go on to explain that the likelihood of misunderstanding is higher when complex theories such as IRT are used to generate scores. Dodd and Fitzpatrick review several scoring methods that might be easier to explain than optimal IRT scoring, comparing the results of those methods with optimal scoring procedures. Strengths and weaknesses of the methods are documented.

Dodd and Fitzpatrick then turn their attention to a relatively new area of investigation: the automated scoring of responses to complex assessment tasks. They point out that one of the obstacles to more widespread use of complex assessment tasks is the time and expense of scoring the responses. Automated scoring systems, if successfully developed, could make scoring of complex responses both rapid and economical. Dodd and Fitzpatrick review scoring systems developed both for general writing skills and for more complex responses to professional simulation exercises. They point out that none of the automated scoring systems are sufficiently well developed at this time to be used without extensive quality control and human checks on the performance of the scoring system. In addition to improvements in the scoring systems, development of more structured item formats may be required before automated scoring can be deployed independently in high-stakes testing programs.

Dodd and Fitzpatrick conclude their chapter with a summary of the research reviewed and suggestions for additional research. They identify studies that are needed not only to further investigate the methods that exist, but to move into new areas for scoring and analysis.

Schnipke and Scrams (chap. 12, this volume) provide a view of the promise of CBT to provide new interpretations of examinee performance. CBT greatly enhances the ability of researchers to investigate the role of response time in test-taking behavior and interpretation of results.

For many measurement professionals, response-time analysis is a new area of interest. The Schnipke and Scrams chapter will be an important resource for them, providing an extensive (albeit not comprehensive, the authors caution) review of research on response time. Seven areas are covered: scoring models, speed–accuracy relationships, strategy usage, speededness, pacing, predicting finishing times and setting time limits, and subgroup differences. In addition to their application of response-time research to the analysis of CBT data, Schnipke and Scrams place their work in the context of the long tradition of response-time research in psychology generally.

Plake (chap. 13, this volume) establishes a unique context for her remarks by citing recent developments in the word of the psychometric police! Plake is generally optimistic. She sees applications for alternate scoring methods that are more easily explained than optimal scoring, that may provide better control of test content, and that provide better protection against inadvertent cuing of the answer to one question by content of another question. Plake's optimism extends to automated scoring, although she cautions that automated scoring is not sufficiently well developed to detect glib or faked responses. She also advocates construct validation studies to ensure that new item formats do not alter the construct being measured when they are substituted for more traditional forms of assessments.

With regard to response-time analysis, Plake sees potential applications to test administration and item analysis. Timing data could be incorporated into item-selection algorithms to lessen the effects of speededness. These data could also be used before conducting item analysis to remove data from examinees whose response is so rapid as to indicate they did not attempt the item.

Plake identifies other data that could be collected during CBT adminis-trations, such as the pressure exerted on the keyboard or other biometric information that could provide insights into, for example, examinees' level of anxiety. However, she cautions against collecting the data simply because they are available; instead, she advocates collecting them for a better theoretical understanding of performance.

Camara (chap. 14, this volume) adds his perspectives on the Dodd and Fitzpatrick and the Schnipke and Scrams chapters. Camara's comments focus on the educational policy implications associated with the techni-cal issues discussed in these chapters and on the possible reactions of the public. He reviews common methods of score reporting and pro-poses criteria for evaluating new scoring methodologies. Camara pro-poses that additional criteria—transparency, usability, and intended use of the scores—be used to evaluate alternate scoring methods.

Camara suggests automated scoring of complex responses is an im-portant area for development because the expense of scoring these re-sponses currently limits their use in large testing programs. He lists sev-eral questions and research initiatives that should be undertaken to improve the technology and increase the likelihood it will be accepted by score users and the public. Camara is not optimistic that automated scor-ing will replace manual scoring in the near future. He does, however, en-vision it as a means to reduce the reliance on human graders and to score practice tests.

Camara summarizes the difficulties of drawing meaningful inferences from response-time analysis in his comments on the chapter by Schnipke and Scrams. Unlike his comments on the previous chapter, Camara does not envision practical applications for response-time analysis in the short term. Rather, he points out the inconsistencies across different studies and the confounding of speed with ability, content, and other factors. Re-search that disentangles the different factors affecting response time is high on his list of priorities in this field. Camara concludes by setting the following high standard for the introduction of response time as a sepa-rate test score or a component of a score: "Test scores based on any cur-rent or proposed model must be valid and generalizable, be useful to test users, and be understood by test takers."

Alternatives for Scoring CBTs

Barbara G. Dodd
Steven J. Fitzpatrick
University of Texas at Austin

INTRODUCTION

Two areas of research regarding alternatives for scoring CBTs are discussed in this chapter. The first area has received much attention in the last several years: the development of scoring methods that use the raw score on the test rather than the pattern of item responses as is common in IRT. The goal in the development of alternative methods of scoring is to produce a scoring method that is easier to explain to examinees and other interested parties. Psychometrically, optimal or item response pattern scoring results in differential weighting of items under some IRT models (Lord, 1980). Such differential weighting of items is considered by some to be too difficult a concept to explain to examinees and other constituents who use test scores. It may also be perceived as unfair by some of these parties, particularly in the context of CAT.

The second area of research concerns the use of automated scoring systems for performance-based tasks that typically require human judgments about the quality of the responses. Researchers in this area have developed automated scoring systems to replace or reduce the number of human graders to reduce the cost of complex, performance-based assessments. Furthermore, advancements in computer technology also have allowed for the development of new item types that are easier to score than the more complex, performance-based assessments but that are more cognitively complex than traditional multiple-choice items.

A related line of research that will not be directly addressed in this chapter is CMT. The scoring of these tests typically uses an NC score or an item pattern (IP) score derived using IRT. The research on methods for ability estimation to be discussed in this chapter addresses these scoring options. However, the various procedures used to obtain the final pass–fail or competency-level decision in computer-based mastery testing are not discussed here.

REVIEW OF RESEARCH AND DEVELOPMENTS

Methods of Ability Estimation

In this part of the chapter we review some of the interpretation problems in explaining test scores based on either classical test theory or IRT. In particular, we focus on alternative procedures to produce a score that may be easier for consumers to understand than those used by optimal IRT methods. This part begins with a brief discussion of the difficulties associated with explaining scoring using either classical test theory or IRT with optimal scoring. It then describes alternative scoring methods using IRT. Alternative scoring procedures are reviewed last.

Classical Test Theory. Tests that are scored using classical test theory methodology typically use either an NC score or a formula score that is then transformed to a scaled score. Because these procedures have been accepted for several decades, we think that test takers and test users have some understanding of the meaning of scaled scores. We assume they understand that the NC scores or the formula scores have been equated to other forms of the same test via linear, equipercentile, or some type of true score equating procedure. Yet, it is doubtful that test users, and especially test takers, fully understand all of the steps in the scoring and reporting process.

IRT. In recent years there has been research on alternative scoring procedures for CATs because of concerns that examinees will not understand the item pattern scoring procedures used to obtain the test score. For example, Stocking (1996) stated that "test sponsors are also obliged to ensure that the understanding of this testing paradigm [CAT] by test takers, test score users, legislative and/or regulatory institutions, and other interested parties is as complete as their current understanding of conventional testing" (p. 365). Although Stocking has limited her concerns to CAT, these issues have also been investigated for paper-and-pencil tests that are scored using IRT (Thissen, Pommerich, Billeaud, & Williams, 1995). Thus, this research has implications for linear CBTs.

In this part we review the literature on alternatives to IP scoring of fixed-length tests and CATs. IP scoring refers to MLE or Bayesian trait estimates based on the pattern of responses to the items administered. This is the optimal IRT scoring method from a psychometric perspective (Lord, 1980). If a Rasch model is used for a linear, fixed-length test, all examinees with the same raw score receive the same trait estimate because the raw score is a sufficient statistic for trait estimation in these models. When other models, such as the 3PL model, are used, the trait estimate is a weighted combination of the item responses, and for any given raw score there may be as many different trait estimates as there are ways of obtaining that raw score. Under the 3PL model the item weights depend on the trait level. A low-ability examinee receives less credit for a correct response to a difficult item than does a high-ability examinee. Even under the 2PL model, a given raw score can result in different ability estimates. There is concern this may not be perceived as fair by examinees (Stocking, 1996).

In response, several researchers have investigated ways of obtaining an IRT ability estimate that is based on NC scoring rather than IP scoring. Maximum likelihood (Stocking, 1996; Thissen et al., 1995; Yen, 1984) and Bayesian (Schnipke & Reese, 1997; Thissen, 1998) methods have been proposed. The resulting ability estimate for a given raw score is approximately a weighted average of the IP trait estimates for that raw score.

NC Scoring on Linear, Fixed-Length Tests. Yen (1984) described a procedure for obtaining an MLE from an NC score on linear, fixed-length tests. The procedure results in a look-up table where the NC score is used to find an examinee's estimated trait level based on the 3PL model. She implemented an approximation to the compound binomial distribution that was initially proposed by Lord and Novick (1968) and compared trait estimates from NC scores with MLEs from IP scoring. Several simulated and real data sets were used to make comparisons among known and estimated trait values as well as estimated true scores.

Yen's (1984) study reported that NC scoring produced results similar to IP scoring except in the lower two quintiles of the trait scale. In the simulated data sets, there was a 0% to 10% increase in the average standard error of measurement on the theta scale when going from IP to NC scoring. When the trait estimates were compared within quintiles, there was a 6% decrease to an 18% increase in the standard error of measurement. The two methods produced nearly identical results in the upper two quintiles, and the NC method was least accurate at the lowest quintile. There was little difference between the two methods in the overall and local bias. Yen also compared the empirical standard errors of measurement with those predicted by the 3PL model, which predicts higher standard errors of measurement for IP scoring than for NC scoring. Yen found the predicted standard errors were accurate for moderate trait values, but the model overpredicted the standard errors for the lowest quintile.

Comparison of the two estimation methods on the estimated true score scale revealed high correlations and little or no overall or local bias in the simulated data sets. The NC estimated true scores were accurate in that they had standard errors of measurement ranging from 0% to 7% larger than the standard errors of measurement associated with the IP estimated true scores. Once again, the largest differences in the two methods were at the lower end of the estimated true score scale. This was attributed in large part to floor effects on the tests.

Yen (1984) concluded that although the NC scoring method produced good trait estimates and estimated true scores in both the simulated and real data sets,

> The estimated true scores were more accurate estimates of true scores than the estimated trait values were of true trait values. The estimated true scores also tended to be more stable over test forms than did the trait estimates, and the IP and NC estimated true scores were more similar than the IP and NC trait estimates. In general, the estimated true score scale was a more accurate and stable scale than the trait scale. (p. 109)

This suggests that, if Yen's NC estimation method is used, reported scale scores should be converted from the estimated true score scale rather than from the trait estimate scale.

NC Scoring for Polytomous Response Data.   Thissen et al. (1995) described another method for obtaining a trait estimate from NC scoring. They noted that the approximation used by Yen (1984) applies only to dichotomous response data and is still relatively computationally intensive. They proposed a recursive algorithm to estimate the likelihood of theta, given raw score, that can be applied to dichotomous or polytomous response data or a combination of both types of data. Whereas Yen examined the MLE of theta and the corresponding estimated true score, Thissen et al. used the estimated likelihood function to obtain an EAP estimate of theta. They presented two examples of the method: one using real data from an exam consisting of three open-ended items, each scored polytomously, and another using a data set consisting of two forms of an exam containing 80 multiple-choice items each. The items in the first example were calibrated using Samejima's (1969) graded response model, and the items in two forms of the exam in the second example were calibrated using the 3PL model.

They reported their results corresponded with Yen's (1984) in that the summed score estimation produces slightly larger standard errors than does IP scoring, but the difference has no practical importance because of the number of decimals with which results are typically reported. They also noted the EAP summed score estimate for a given raw score is approximately a weighted average of the pattern-scored estimates for that same raw score.

The Thissen et al. (1995) procedure appears to have two advantages over MLEs based on summed scores: First, the EAP estimates have much less variability for scores at the extremes of the distribution, and, second, the EAP method allows for estimation of the raw score distribution on a test, which can be used as a check on the fit of the model. Yen (1984) found that, although both the theta estimates and the estimated true scores were variable at the low end of the ability scale, the estimated true scores were less variable than the theta estimates in that region. Thissen et al. did not examine the estimated true scores resulting from the EAP method.

The procedures described by Yen (1984) and Thissen et al. (1995) both address the issue of estimating the likelihood function for an NC or summed score on a fixed-length, nonadaptive test. In this situation, the NC scores and the ability estimates based on NC scores will have the same order for a given test. The relation between the NC score on a CAT and the IRT ability estimate is much different.

NC Scoring for Fixed-Length CATs.   Stocking (1996) proposed a method for scoring fixed-length CATs based on the NC score on the CAT. Whereas examinees have various NC scores on a fixed-length test, they all have approximately the same raw score on a CAT; the difference is in the difficulty of the items administered. Stocking's method uses an equated NC scoring method based on IRT true score equating (Lord, 1980). Once the adaptive test has been administered, with any desired constraints such as content balancing and item exposure control, a reduced information trait estimate is obtained by solving for θ in the equation:

$$\sum_{i=1}^{n} (u_i - P_i(\theta)) = 0. \tag{1}$$

In Equation 1, u_i is the response (correct or incorrect) to item i, n is the number of items administered, and $P_i(\theta)$ is the probability of a correct response under the 3PL model. It can be seen by distributing the summation inside the parentheses that this estimate of theta is the one that makes the estimated true score equal to the raw score. Stocking referred to this as a reduced information trait estimate because Equation 1 is the likelihood equation for estimating theta if the 1PL model is used, but in her procedure the 3PL is used. The likelihood equation for estimating theta under the 3PL model, which uses the values of information at theta as weights for each item, is:

$$\sum_{i=1}^{n} \left(u_i - P_i(\theta) \right) \frac{P_i(\theta)'}{P_i(\theta)Q_i(\theta)} = 0, \qquad (2)$$

where $P_i(\theta)'$ is the first derivative of the 3PL model with respect to θ, and $Q_i(\theta)$ is the probability of an incorrect response. Equation 2 uses all of the available information about the items, whereas Equation 1 does not, and is referred to by Stocking as a full information estimate of theta.

After a trait estimate is obtained from Equation 1, it is transformed to an estimated true score on a reference test with item parameter estimates on the same scale as those used in the CAT. The reference test is used for each examinee. So, for each CAT a table of correspondence between raw scores on the CAT and estimated true scores on the reference test may be constructed.

The study reported by Stocking (1996) was a Monte Carlo experiment designed to investigate the loss of accuracy in estimated true scores on the reference test when the full- and reduced-information estimation procedures are used in CAT. These estimates were also compared with the NC and estimated true score on a linear, fixed-length reference test. Data sets were simulated from item parameter estimates from six real tests.

The equated NC scoring performed well. Stocking reported that, in four of the six data sets, the equated NC scores had less bias than the estimated true scores, based on the full-information trait estimate. In all cases, however, the equated NC scores were more variable. The reliabilities of the reduced-information equated NC scores were only slightly lower than the reliabilities of the full-information estimated true scores, and in only one data set was the reliability of the equated NC score lower than the reliability of the reference test scored as NC. The reliability of the NC scores on the reference test was considered to be the minimum acceptable reliability. The difference in the conditional standard errors of the two scoring methods was small enough to be considered unimportant.

Stocking's (1996) equated NC scoring method was investigated by Potenza (1994) using data from both experimental and operational administrations of the GRE. Two studies were conducted. The first used data from a prior study conducted by Schaeffer, Reese, McKinley, and

Mills in 1993 (cited in Potenza, 1994) that concluded that scores on linearly administered computer-based GREs (GRE-CBT) and scores on fixed-length GRE-CATs scored using the 3PL model were comparable. The goal of the first study was to rescore the data and examine the comparability of equated NC scores with scores based on linearly and adaptively administered tests. The second study used data from operational versions of the computerized adaptive GRE, and compared scores derived from the 3PL model with those from the equated NC procedure.

In the first study, Potenza (1994) found that the patterns of differences between linear, computer-based scores and CAT full-information scores were similar to the patterns of differences between the linear, computer-based scores and the reduced-information equated NC scores. Based on the results of the second study, Potenza concluded that Stocking's (1996) equated NC scoring is interchangeable with MLE scoring of CATS based on the 3PL. She noted that, when there were large differences between the two scoring methods, the 3PL model did not fit the examinee response data, and therefore neither method was appropriate.

Scoring Multistage Tests.   The methods described thus far attempt to obtain an IRT-based ability estimate from a raw score for either a linear, fixed-length test or an adaptive test. The items are considered to be locally independent and, in an adaptive test, item responses cannot be reviewed by the examinee. In some situations it is desirable to administer items in groups. This may be because sets of items are not locally independent, or a testlet approach may be preferred because it can allow for some limited item review by the examinee. Schnipke and Reese (1997) and Thissen (1998) described procedures that may be used in two-stage or multistage testing with routing between stages based on NC scores.

Schnipke and Reese (1997) conducted a simulation study to investigate two-stage and multistage testlet designs for adaptive testing. Response data were simulated according to the 3PL model, and items were grouped into 5-item testlets with varying average levels of difficulty. The number of levels of testlet difficulty used depended on the test design. There were several adaptive testlet designs, all of which resulted in 25 items being administered (in five testlets of 5 items). After five testlets had been administered, a Bayes modal estimate of theta was obtained using the 3PL model.

The simplest testlet design was a two-stage design in which each simulee was first administered two randomly selected testlets. The raw score on the combined testlets was used to branch to the second stage in which three more testlets of low, medium, or high difficulty were administered. A two-stage design with changing levels in the second stage also was examined. As in the simple two-stage design, two randomly selected testlets were first administered and the raw score was used to route the simulee to a low, medium, or high difficulty stage-two testlet. After taking the first stage-two testlet, the simulee was routed to a low-, medium-, or high-difficulty second stage-two testlet. A third stage-two testlet of low, medium, or high difficulty was then administered depending on the raw score (and the difficulty level) of the second stage-two testlet.

The third test design was a multistage design that had four levels. In this design the simulee first was administered two randomly selected testlets and routed to a testlet with one of three difficulty levels. In the next stage, the simulee was routed, on the basis of the raw score on the stage-two testlet, to a stage-three testlet with one of five levels of difficulty. The simulee's raw score on the stage-three testlet was then used for routing to a stage-four testlet with one of five levels of difficulty that were more widely spread out than the difficulties of the stage-three testlets. Schnipke and Reese described how they determined which raw scores at each stage would route simulees to the appropriate difficulty-level testlet at the next stage.

For comparison purposes, Schnipke and Reese also simulated a standard maximum-information CAT with item exposure controls and they chose for administration a testlet-based CAT with the highest total information summed over the 5 items. The testlet-based CAT also used testlet exposure control. Finally, theta estimates were obtained for all simulees on fixed 25-item and 51-item tests designed to provide the best measurement in the middle of the ability distribution.

Schnipke and Reese (1997) reported that, as expected, the maximum-information CAT recovered known ability values with the least error and bias, and the 25-item fixed test had the most error and bias. Regarding the other designs, they stated:

> The two-stage, multistage, and maximum-information testlet-based designs (which were all 25 items in length) led to ability estimates that were very similar in terms of RMSE and bias to the 51-item paper-and-pencil design for θ's [with absolute value] less than 1.5. For θ's [with absolute value] greater than 1.5, the 51-item paper-and-pencil design led to θ's with less error and bias than the two-stage and multistage designs. . . . The maximum-information testlet-based design led to θ's that had slightly less error and bias than the 51-item paper-and-pencil design, especially in the tails of the ability distribution. (p. 10)

Whereas Schnipke and Reese computed a Bayes modal estimate of theta after all 25 items had been administered, Thissen (1998) built on the work of Thissen et al. (1995) by extending the procedure for obtaining an EAP ability estimate from a summed score to obtaining an EAP ability estimate from a pattern of two or more summed scores. He also described a Gaussian approximation to the EAP estimate of ability based on a pair (or set) of summed scores that is a weighted linear combination of the EAP estimates of ability from the separate summed scores. The procedure can be used to combine ability estimates from multiple-choice and constructed-response sections of a test, or it can be used to estimate ability from patterns of raw scores on testlets in multistage testing.

Thissen (1998) demonstrated the procedure with a simulation study in the context of two-stage testing. Data were simulated to fit the 3PL model, and the two-stage procedure used a 5-item routing testlet and two 5-item second-stage testlets. The Gaussian approximation of the EAP ability estimate and the EAP ability estimate were compared with known ability parameters. Furthermore, the relation between the nature of the first- and second-stage testlets and the accuracy of the ability estimates were examined. This was accomplished by constructing all possible combinations of the 15 items across the three testlets and the five possible cut scores on the first testlet.

Thissen concluded that the Gaussian linear approximation of the EAP estimate performed as well as the EAP estimate. He also reported there was no single arrangement of items into first- and second-stage testlets that outperformed all of the others in recovering known ability parameters. For example, certain unusual arrangements of items into testlets with a cut score on the routing testlet between 0 and 1 performed statistically as well as more intuitive arrangements of items and routing testlet cut scores.

Non-IRT Scoring. All of the research discussed so far involves the estimation of an ability estimate according to some IRT model. Green (1997) proposed a method for scoring adaptive tests, called fixed-weight scoring, that does not produce a theta estimate using any IRT model. His procedure is a weighted sum of the responses to the items administered during a fixed-length CAT. The weight for each item is the value of theta that maximizes the information of that item under the 3PL model. A theta estimate for each examinee must be computed during the CAT after each item is administered, but this is not used to determine the final reported score. The procedure was demonstrated using data simulated to fit the 3PL model.

Green examined several possible scoring schemes using different combinations of weights: the average of the weights for the items answered correctly, the average of the weights for the items answered incorrectly, the average of the weights of the correctly answered items plus one half of the weights of the incorrectly answered items (referred to as partial credit), and the average of the weights of all of the items administered regardless of the response (referred to as average weights—all). Fixed-length CATs were simulated with 30 items using known item parameters, maximum-information item selection, and an approximation to Bayes model theta estimation. Two types of item pools were used: one with uniformly distributed item difficulty and discrimination parameters, and one with uniform difficulty and negatively skewed discrimination parameters. Both item pools used a constant guessing parameter of 0.15. The CATs were then IP scored with MLE, Stocking's (1996) equated NC, and the four scoring procedures mentioned earlier. Green found that the fixed-weight methods resulted in overestimation of thetas below −1.5 and underestimation of thetas above 1.5. To minimize this effect, he applied a quadratic correction to the estimates of the thetas outside this range.

The partial credit and average weights—all fixed-weight scoring schemes performed equally well in terms of root mean squared error (RMSE) and bias in the recovery of known ability parameters. The equated NC and IP scored CATs had almost identical RMSEs. However, the fixed-weight scoring methods had RMSEs ranging from 10% to more than 30% larger than those resulting from the IP and equated NC methods, depending on the level of ability. The performance of IP and equated NC was similar in the two item pools, but the fixed-weight procedures had different patterns of RMSEs across levels of theta in the two pools. This suggests the fixed-weight procedures may be sensitive to the characteristics of the item pools.

Automated Scoring Systems

This part of the chapter moves from the mathematical IRT model-based scoring of CATs to the use of computers to automate the scoring of complex, performance-based tasks that traditionally require human graders. It addresses the degree of agreement between the scores from the automated systems and human graders, the use of graders in the development of the scoring engine, the number of features employed in scoring, and the algorithms used to combine feature scores to produce a final score. Issues of quality control are also discussed. Finally, the use of unique item types, which are easier to score than complex performance tasks, is reviewed.

Complex Performance Tasks. Over the last decade, the inclusion of performance tasks has increased on both paper-and-pencil tests and CBTs. The use of such tasks as part or all of the assessment has posed a major implementation problem for large-scale testing programs (Hardy, 1995; Wainer & Thissen, 1993). The cost of scoring performance tasks is greater than machine scoring multiple-choice items because several graders must rate each task. As a consequence, more automated scoring systems have been developed for performance tasks used in different types of assessments. Early prototype systems have been developed in mathematics (Sebrechts, Bennett, & Rock, 1991), architectural design problems (Bejar, 1991), computer programming (Braun, Bennett, Frye, & Soloway, 1990), physicians' patient management (Clauser et al., 1995), and writing (Burstein, Braden-Harder, et al., 1998; Elliot, Chernoff, & Burnham, 1997; Landauer, Laham, Rehder, & Schreiner, 1997; Page & Peterson, 1995). Some of the automated scoring systems have been developed to remove graders from the scoring process, whereas other systems have been developed to reduce the number of graders needed for the scoring process.

The goal of all of these automated scoring systems is to emulate the best aspects of the graders and at the same time minimize the errors made by the graders, thus yielding an automated scoring system that might handle responses that are difficult for graders to judge (Williamson, Hone, Miller, & Bejar, 1998). Williamson, Bejar, and Hone in 1997 (cited in Williamson et al., 1998) investigated differences between graders and automated scoring for an architectural design test and found that the automated system produced scores that were consistent with those of the graders. They also found that the automated system scored more consistently and extracted more information than the graders. When the graders were shown the analyses from the automated scoring system, most of them elected to let the automated score stand.

Good agreement between the scores produced by an automated scoring system and graders has been found in other content areas as well. Burstein, Kukich, et al. (1998) found an 87% to 94% agreement between the essay scores produced by an automated scoring system and the scores graders awarded for the same essay responses. This finding was comparable to the accuracy found between two graders of the same essays. Similar results have been found for automated systems developed to assess physicians' patient management (Clauser, Margolis, Clyman, & Ross, 1997; Clauser, Ross, et al., 1997). These promising results have resulted in the use of an automated scoring system for one of two readings of essay responses on the GMAT as of January 1999.

All of the automated scoring systems developed to date have incorporated graders to identify the scoring algorithms. Clauser et al. (1995), Clauser, Margolis, et al. (1997), and Clauser, Ross, et al. (1997) relied heavily on panels consisting of five expert clinicians to develop two scoring systems for physicians' patient management. The experts tried to reach consensus as a group. Similarly, Burstein, Kukich, et al. (1998) used essays scored by graders to develop the automated scoring system for essays. Williamson et al. (1998) employed six graders to develop the scoring algorithm for the architectural design scoring system. The number of actual examinees' performances rated by the graders in the studies varied from 200 to 326, and this set of performances is typically referred to as the training set. In all of these studies graders also were used to evaluate the accuracy of the automated scoring system.

The type and number of features analyzed initially by the automated scoring system were determined by the graders in the studies cited here. In the physicians' case management task, graders classified all actions into various levels of potential benefit or risk to the patient. The automated scoring system for the essay responses developed by Burstein, Kukich et al. (1998) relied on advanced computational linguistics techniques for scoring constructed writing responses. More than 60 features, which were either syntactic, rhetorical, or topical content features, were extracted and scored using the computational linguistic techniques. The architectural design automated scoring system (Williamson et al., 1998) analyzes actual candidates' solutions on a feature-by-feature basis according to the degree of acceptability of the solution.

Various approaches have been used to combine the scores on the features into a score that resembles the score given by a grader. For the architectural design test, the feature scores were aggregated to produce a final solution score on a 3-point acceptability scale. Burstein, Kukich et al. (1998) and Clauser et al. (1995) have used regression-based approaches to determine the weights given various feature scores to produce the final test score. Generally, the regression-based approach produced scores that were highly correlated with the scores given by graders. At least one generalizability study (Clauser, Swanson, & Clyman, 1998) has shown that automated scores produced by a regression-based approach are as reliable as those produced by graders.

Clauser, Ross, et al. (1997) investigated another automated scoring procedure that is based on the policies used by graders rather than on empirically derived weights used in the regression-based method. For the complex rule-based method, specific features are mapped into specific scores using the logical rules graders have identified as being used to assign final scores. Correlation coefficients of .70 to .86 were found for scores yielded by the rule-based automated system and scores given by graders. Agreement in pass–fail classifications based on scores produced by the automated system and those given by graders was found to be comparable to the agreement coefficients obtained for two graders. In other content areas such as computer science (Sebrechts et al., 1991), the scoring algorithms used by the graders also determined the automated scoring system and thus can be viewed as another example of the rule-based method.

Clauser, Margolis, et al. (1997) compared the regression-based approach with the rule-based approach. Two independent committees of graders also rated the performances of 200 examinees on several physicians' patient management cases. Ratings given by the second independent committee of graders were correlated with the ratings given by the first committee of graders, the regression-based scores, and the rule-based scores for each case. The correlation coefficients obtained for the original committee of graders were the highest (.63–.93). The regression-based scores yielded a slightly lower degree of correspondence, followed by the rule-based scores. Clauser, Margolis, et al. concluded that the regression-based approach was superior to the rule-based approach.

Quality control is critical to the success of any automated scoring system. Clyman and Clauser (1998) stated that the accuracy of the scoring algorithm is a function of the care taken by the graders in identifying the features to be used and by the programmers responsible for translating the features into computer code. The validity of the scoring rules is typically assessed using graders to assign scores to the same responses that were scored by the automated scoring system. Williamson et al. (1998) used classification trees to automate the identification of performances that might result in scores given by the graders that would be different from those produced by the automated scoring system. The classification trees were shown to identify future cases likely to need review and to reduce the review process by 68%.

Unique Item Types.   It is unlikely the automated systems developed to handle complex performance tasks will operate as stand-alone systems in the near feature. The nature of high-stakes testing programs means graders will still be needed to handle atypical responses and maintain quality control. To achieve a stand-alone system that can be made operational immediately, several researchers have investigated new item types that require more structured, constructed responses than some of the complex performance-based tasks, but less structured than responses to traditional multiple-choice items. Several item types have been developed to assess writing and mathematics skills.

Editing skills on writing tests traditionally have been measured with multiple-choice type items where the examinee selects from among various alternatives the most appropriate rewritten section of the underlined text in the reading passage. The criticism of this type of test is that, in real editing tasks, the section of the text to be revised is never identified. In an attempt to overcome the artificial nature of this type of task, Davey, Godwin, and Mittelholtz (1997) developed a more realistic task to measure editing skills. Passages to be edited are presented to the examinee with no part of the text marked for editing. Examinees are told to highlight the section of the text they think should be revised and press the enter key, whereupon the examinee is presented a list of alternative rewrites of the segment of text. In essence, the task becomes one of multiple choice at this point.

Davey et al. (1997) used an iterative procedure developed by Sympson and Haladyna (1988) to assign scoring weights to the various response alternatives. Initially, each incorrect-response option is assigned a weight of 0.0 and the correct-response option is assigned a weight of 1.0. Each examinee's score is computed by summing the weighted responses selected. These scores are then converted to percentile ranks. The scoring weights are revised by assigning the mean score of the examinees selecting that alternative. The new weights are collapsed into four categories and used in combination with the sequential probability ratio test to assign examinees into one of several ability groups for placement purposes. This scoring procedure appears complicated and might not be easily understood by examinees or other interested parties.

Breland (1998) described the development of an automated editing task that, unlike the one developed by Davey et al. (1997), requires the examinee to construct the replacement phrase rather than select from among alternatives that are provided. The task represents a computerized version of the interlinear exercise used by the College Board in the 1950s and 1960s. Although the interlinear exercise had good reliability (above .80) and predictive validity (above .60), the scoring was time consuming. The computer prototype developed by Breland identifies the text that can be changed, but there are plans to remove this feature in the future. Scoring of the task consists of matching the examinees' constructed responses with solutions provided by experts. Both the Davey et al. study and the Breland research represent an attempt to measure the revision skills of writing.

Bennett, Steffen, Singley, Morley, and Jacquemin (1997) investigated a new open-ended item type for mathematics where the responses are mathematical expressions. Correct solutions to a given problem can be expressed in many forms. The purpose of the new item type is to expand the assessment of mathematical skills to include mathematical modeling problems. Whether an examinee's response is algebraically equivalent to the keyed response is evaluated using established symbolic computational principles. Results showed the automated scoring algorithm agreed with graders 99.62% of the time. This degree of accuracy is only slightly less than that found for scanning of multiple-choice answers (99.95%).

Bennett, Morley, and Quardt (1998) compared the symbolic scoring of responses to the mathematical expression items with another evaluation method that solves the mathematical equations for a specified number of points for the particular problem. Results showed that both automated scoring methods produced the same errors when compared with scores given by graders for real data. Differences between the two automated scoring methods were found, however, when they were applied to deliberately constructed hard expressions and difficult paraphrases. The symbolic scoring method correctly scored 70% of the paraphrases, whereas the evaluation method correctly scored all of the paraphrases.

Two other new item types were investigated by Bennett et al. (1998): generating examples and graphical modeling. The generating-examples item type requires examinees to produce examples that yield a correct solution to the mathematical problem. Responses are scored using the evaluation methodology used for the mathematical expression items discussed earlier. Scoring keys are created given the constraints of the problem. A pilot study of the accuracy of the automated scoring algorithm showed it has produced 100% accuracy rates. The graphical modeling item type requires examinees to demonstrate mathematical concepts graphically. The automated scoring system contains the conditions that must be present for a credit answer and scores the responses against these conditions. To date, no study has assessed the accuracy of this scoring algorithm in the context of graphical modeling items.

SYNTHESIS OF RESEARCH, IDENTIFICATION
OF ADDITIONAL NEEDED WORK

Methods of Ability Estimation

It appears several considerations preclude the optimal scoring of IRT-based tests, whether linear or adaptive. Stocking (1996) and Potenza (1994) both pointed out that, in modern CAT, the requirements of content balancing and protecting item security through item-exposure control necessarily result in a less than optimal CAT because item selection is not based solely on statistical criteria, that is, information. Furthermore, it is questionable whether IP scoring of CATs and linear tests will be accepted by consumers of test scores. So, less than optimal items must be administered in CATs and tests may need to be scored with less than optimal methods. The question is the extent to which these constraints affect ability estimation.

Yen (1984) and Thissen et al. (1995) presented MLE and EAP procedures, respectively, to estimate ability from summed scores rather than from IRT patterns on linear tests. Both methods resulted in acceptable ability estimation, although Yen reported excessive variability at the lower end of the scale. Linear tests exhibit greater standard errors at the extremes of the ability distribution because such tests are usually targeted near the center of the ability distribution. The Thissen et al. procedure has an advantage over Yen's procedure because it can handle dichotomous or polytomous items and, because it is an EAP procedure, it holds the extreme ability estimates in check.

Stocking (1996) and Green (1997) proposed methods for scoring fixed-length CATs using the raw score on the test. Stocking's simulation study was conducted using a less than optimal CAT because of item-exposure control, content constraints, and less than optimal scoring based on the NC score. The procedure worked well when compared with an optimally scored CAT with constraints on item exposure. In his study, Green compared Stocking's procedure with his and with an optimal CAT with no exposure control and found the equated NC procedure to work well. Stocking's equated NC procedure uses no item weights. It would be interesting to investigate whether using item discriminations as fixed weights in Stocking's procedure would improve its accuracy.

Green's (1997) fixed-weight scoring proposal is the only one than does not result in an ability estimate on the theta scale. In fact, the resulting scores must be equated before they can be compared with scores produced by other methods. The simulation study was conducted using true rather than estimated item parameters during the CAT, and no item exposure control was incorporated. Because the item weight in this procedure is the value of theta under the model used for the CAT that maximizes information, item selection based on considerations in addition to information (e.g., content balancing and item-exposure control) would probably reduce the accuracy of the procedure. This should be investigated under more realistic simulation conditions and with real data.

Green's procedure does not provide standard errors of the ability estimates. However, Thissen (1998) speculated that his Gaussian linear approximation to the EAP ability estimate from a pattern of testlet raw scores may be more similar to Green's fixed-weight method than it appears. If his procedure is used to form a weighted linear combination of the items administered in an adaptive test, the weight for each item is a product involving the EAP estimate of theta for an incorrect or correct response, whichever is appropriate. This is a fixed weight for all examinees. Thissen stated that the weights will be different from, but related to, Green's weights. If this is the case, Thissen's method provides an alternative fixed-weight scoring scheme, for which standard errors of ability estimates are available.

Schnipke and Reese (1997) and Thissen (1998) investigated two-stage and multistage testing with routing based on testlet raw scores. Schnipke and Reese reported that selecting testlets on the basis of information, even using testlet exposure control, worked better than selecting testlets of a given average difficulty based on the raw score on the previous testlet. The final score on the test in their study was an estimate of theta based on the overall item-response pattern. Thissen's procedure is designed to estimate theta from the pattern of raw scores on a set of testlets. A combination of Thissen's estimation procedure and Schnipke and Reese's testing designs would allow for an NC theta estimate to be computed after each testlet, the next testlet could be selected on the basis of information at the current estimate of theta, and the final test score would be an EAP estimate derived from the raw scores on the testlets. Also, it may be possible to use Thissen's (1998) or Stocking's (1996) procedure to obtain a theta estimate from the sum of the testlet scores. Testlet-pattern scoring may not be viewed any more favorably than IP scoring. Research should be conducted to address the interpretability of the various scoring methods discussed here. This might be done by developing prototype score reports and interpretation guides, and assessing users' reactions to them.

Automated Scoring Systems

The research on automated scoring systems for complex performance-based assessments has moved beyond the prototype phase. Many of the studies presented at the national conferences in 1998 indicated future research should investigate ways to improve the systems in terms of scoring accuracy and efficiency. Although the accuracy of the automated scoring systems has been found to be comparable to that found for graders, we still should strive to improve the scoring algorithms to increase the precision of measurement. It might be possible to increase the precision of measurement beyond the level produced by graders because automated systems can more consistently score atypical responses that are difficult for graders. One way to increase the scoring accuracy of the automated systems might be to investigate the use of additional scoring features in the scoring algorithm to determine if the precision of measurement of trait levels can be improved.

Another way scoring accuracy might be increased is to investigate alternative procedures to combine scores on the various features into a final test score. Although the regression-based approach appears to be superior to the complex rule-based method for some applications, this might not be the case for other applications. For some testing programs, the graders might be able to better verbalize the logical rules they use for assigning scores. If this is the case, the rule-based approach might produce scores that are as good as those from the regression-based approach. Even if this is not the case, some high-stakes testing programs might prefer the rule-based approach over the regression-based approach because of logical and political reasons. Each testing program should investigate alternative methods of combining the features to produce the final test score to determine which methodology best satisfies the need of the testing program. The identification of an optimal way of combining the feature scores might allow for fewer features to be scored in an automated scoring system that could still achieve a specified level of measurement precision. That is, there may be a trade-off between the number of features evaluated and the methodology used to produce the final score. More research is needed to address these issues.

A related question identified by Clyman and Clauser (1998) concerns the number of graders needed to develop the scoring algorithm that is used in an automated scoring system. Most of the research has employed panels of three to six graders to identify the features to be incorporated into the scoring algorithm. To reduce the cost of the development of such systems, would it be possible to use fewer graders at this phase of the development of the automated system? Also, is it necessary to have the graders meet as a group or could they work independently? No systematic research has addressed these issues. The answers to the questions might reveal the correct balance between cost efficiency and scoring accuracy.

If research shows that the number of graders used in the development of the automated scoring algorithm cannot be reduced, perhaps the number of performances used in developing the scoring algorithm could be reduced, thus shortening the time needed for the graders to score the training set of performances. Based on the research conducted, a training set typically consists of 200 to 300 examinees' performances that each grader must score.

More research needs to address quality control procedures. Only when adequate procedures are developed to assure the accuracy of the scoring algorithm can a testing company consider a full-scale implementation of an automated scoring system for complex performance-based assessments. The use of classification trees to automate the identification of cases that are likely to produce scoring differences between graders and an automated scoring system appears to be a useful quality control procedure. The question is whether there are other procedures that might be equally good or better.

Each testing program must decide if an automated scoring system should replace graders or merely reduce the number needed. This decision might depend on whether the testing program is high stakes or low stakes. Even if graders are eliminated from the grading of most performance-based assessments, graders will never be eliminated from the development and validation of the scoring algorithm, or from the resolution of scoring atypical cases. A related issue is how often graders should be used to check the accuracy of the automated system.

Additional research needs to be conducted to determine if the unique item types in writing and mathematics are in fact measuring the new or expanded skills they were intended to measure. That is, more validity studies need to be conducted. Issues of differential item function for the new types of items should also be investigated before these new item types are included in operational forms of CBTs.

The two new item types developed to assess editing skills appear less artificial than the item types typically used to do so. Once the procedures introduced by Breland (1998) are fully developed, it will be interesting to compare them with the procedures developed by Davey et al. (1997). Use of either type of editing task will require careful construction of the text to be edited to avoid issues of dependency among the responses. It is possible the dependency problem cannot be avoided in the constructed-response format proposed by Breland. More research is warranted to address the issue.

Early work on evaluation versus symbolic scoring methods for math items is informative, but the methods need further investigation with populations for which the test was designed. Whether polytomous scoring of these items will yield better measurement precision as compared with the dichotomous scoring currently used still needs to be addressed.

PROPOSED PRIORITIES FOR THE PSYCHOMETRIC COMMUNITY

The priority of the research that has been proposed in this chapter should be determined by the needs of the individual testing program. Testing programs that use adaptive tests will continue to investigate alternative methods for scoring adaptive tests that have been discussed in this chapter and others. Once the viable scoring procedures have been identified, prototype score reports with interpretation guides should be developed for those procedures as well as for the currently used optimal ability estimation procedures. The interpretation guides and score reports should then be given to examinees and other interested parties to determine which of the scoring options are most easily understood by the groups. If the adaptive test also includes complex performance-based tasks such as an essay or some of the unique item types, issues of competing automated scoring algorithms and validity issues also might be a priority.

Whether a testing program is high stakes or low stakes will determine the need to investigate ways to increase the accuracy of the automated scoring system. The need to improve an already satisfactory automated scoring system might not be an issue for a low-stakes testing program, but it may be paramount for a high-stakes testing program. For example, the current system may be satisfactory for low-stakes scoring of practice tests but may need to be improved for high-stakes scoring such as in admissions testing.

Similarly, the importance of some of the research areas identified in this chapter might be determined by the size of the testing program. Large-scale testing programs might look at the effect of decreasing the number of experts, the size of the training set, or reducing or eliminating the number of graders involved in the scoring process after the automated system is in place. Such research might make the inclusion of performance-based tasks less costly and therefore more feasible. Smaller scale testing programs on the other hand might not be so concerned with these issues.

Perhaps in the future it will be possible to construct tests, possibly IRT-based tests, composed of a greater mixture of item types than currently exists. For example, a CBT might consist of dichotomously scored items, polytomously scored items, and performance-based tasks that are scored by an automated scoring system. Some of the unique item types require less testing time than complex performance-based tasks, yet have higher reliability. It is possible that including a variety of item types and scoring procedures could produce tests that have better reliability and validity than currently used tests. Such tests might also allow for the assessment of a broader spectrum of the cognitive domain of interest.

REFERENCES

Bejar, I. I. (1991). A methodology for scoring open-ended architectural design problems. *Journal of Applied Psychology, 76*, 522–532.

Bennett, R. E., Morley, M., & Quardt, D. (1998, April). *Three response types for broadening the conception of mathematical problem solving in computerized-adaptive tests*. Paper presented at the annual meeting of the National Council on Measurement in Education, San Diego, CA.

Bennett, R. E., Steffen, M., Singley, M. K., Morley, M., & Jacquemin, D. (1997). Evaluating an automatically scorable, open-ended response type for measuring mathematical reasoning in computer-adaptive tests. *Journal of Educational Measurement, 34*, 162–176.

Braun, H. I., Bennett, R. E., Frye, D., & Soloway, E. (1990). Scoring constructed responses using expert systems. *Journal of Educational Measurement, 27*, 93–108.

Breland, H. M. (1998, April). *Writing assessment through automated editing*. Paper presented at the annual meeting of the National Council on Measurement in Education, San Diego, CA.

Burstein, J., Braden-Harder, L., Chodrow, M., Hua, S., Kaplan, B., Kukich, K., Lu, C., Nolan, J., Rock, D., & Wolff, S. (1998). *Computer analysis of essay content for automated score prediction* (ETS Research Report RR-98-15). Princeton, NJ: Educational Testing Service.

Burstein, J., Kukich, K., Wolff, S., Lu, C., & Chodorow, M. (1998, April). *Computer analysis of essays*. Paper presented at the annual meeting of the National Council on Measurement in Education, San Diego, CA.

Clauser, B. E., Margolis, M. J., Clyman, S. G., & Ross, L. P. (1997). Development of automated scoring algorithms for complex performance assessments: A comparison of two approaches. *Journal of Educational Measurement, 34*, 141–161.

Clauser, B. E., Ross, L. P., Clyman, K. M., Rose, K. M., Margolis, M. J., Nungester, R. J., Piemme, T. E., Chang, L., El-Bayoumi, G., Malakoff, G. L., & Pincetl, P. S. (1997). Development of a scoring algorithm to replace expert rating for scoring a complex performance-based assessment. *Applied Measurement in Education, 10,* 345–358.

Clauser, B. E., Subhiyah, R. G., Nungester, R. J., Ripkey, D. R., Clyman, S. G., & McKinley, D. (1995). Scoring a performance-based assessment by modeling the judgments of experts. *Journal of Educational Measurement, 32,* 397–415.

Clauser, B. E., Swanson, D. B., & Clyman, S. G. (1998, April). *A comparison of generalizability of scores produced by expert raters and automated scoring systems.* Paper presented at the annual meeting of the National Council on Measurement in Education, San Diego, CA.

Clyman, S. G., & Clauser, B. E. (1998, April). *Practical issues in large-scale implementation of computer delivered performance assessments that use automated scoring systems.* Paper presented at the annual meeting of the National Council on Measurement in Education, San Diego, CA.

Davey, T., Godwin, J., & Mittelholtz, D. (1997). Developing and scoring an innovative computerized writing assessment. *Journal of Educational Measurement, 34,* 21–41.

Elliot, S., Chernoff, M., & Burnham, W. (1997, March). *Validating computer-based scoring of open-ended written assessments.* Paper presented at the annual meeting of the American Educational Research Association, Chicago.

Green, B. F. (1997, March). *Fixed-weight methods of scoring computer-based adaptive tests.* Paper presented at the annual meeting of the American Educational Research Association, Chicago.

Hardy, R. A. (1995). Examining the cost of performance assessment. *Applied Measurement in Education, 8,* 121–134.

Landauer, T. K., Laham, D., Rehder, B., & Schreiner, M. E. (1997). How well can passsage meaning be derrived without using word order? A comparison of Latent Semantic Analysis and humans. In G. Shafto & P. Langley (Eds.), *Proceedings of the 19th annual meeting of the Cognitive Science Society* (pp. 412–417). Mahwah, NJ: Lawrence Erlbaum Associates.

Lord, F. M. (1980). *Applications of item response theory to practical testing problems.* Hillsdale, NJ: Lawrence Erlbaum Associates.

Lord, F. M., & Novick, M. R. (1968). *Statistical theories of mental test scores.* Reading, MA: Addison-Wesley.

Page, E. B., & Peterson, N. S. (1995). The computer moves into essay grading. *Phi Delta Kappan, 76,* 561–565.

Potenza, M. T. (1994). *The exploration of an alternative method for scoring computer adaptive tests.* Unpublished doctoral dissertation, University of Nebraska, Lincoln.

Samejima, F. (1969). Estimation of latent trait ability using a response pattern of graded scores. *Psychometrika Monograph,* No. 17.

Schnipke, D. L., & Reese, L. M. (1997, March). *A comparison of testlet-based test designs for computerized adaptive testing.* Paper presented at the annual meeting of the American Educational Research Association, Chicago.

Sebrechts, M. M., Bennett, R. E., & Rock, D. A. (1991). Agreement between expert-system and human raters' scores on complex constructed-response quantitative items. *Journal of Applied Psychology, 76,* 856–862.

Stocking, M. L. (1996). An alternative method for scoring adaptive tests. *Journal of Educational and Behavioral Statistics, 21,* 365–389.

Sympson, J. B., & Haladyna, T. M. (1988, April). An evaluation of "polyweighting" in domain-referenced testing. Paper presented at the annual meeting of the National Council on Measurement in Education, New Orleans, LA.

Thissen, D. (1998, April). *Scaled scores for CATs based on linear combinations of testlet scores*. Paper presented at the annual meeting of the National Council on Measurement in Education, San Diego, CA.

Thissen, D., Pommerich, M., Billeaud, K., & Williams, V. S. (1995). Item response theory for scores on tests including polytomous items with ordered responses. *Applied Psychological Measurement, 19*, 39–49.

Wainer, H., & Thissen, D. (1993). Combining multiple-choice and constructed-response test scores: Toward a Marxist theory of test construction. *Applied Measurement in Education, 6*, 103–118.

Williamson, D. M., Hone, A. S., Miller, S., & Bejar, I. I. (1998, April). *Classification trees for quality control processes in automated constructed response scoring*. Paper presented at the annual meeting of the National Council on Measurement in Education, San Diego, CA.

Yen, W. M. (1984). Obtaining maximum likelihood trait estimates from number-correct scores for the three-parameter logistic model. *Journal of Educational Measurement, 21*, 93–111.

Exploring Issues of Examinee Behavior: Insights Gained from Response-Time Analyses

Deborah L. Schnipke
David J. Scrams
Law School Admission Council

INTRODUCTION AND DEFINITION OF THE TOPIC

Early in the history of aptitude and achievement testing, researchers believed speed and accuracy measured the same construct (e.g., Spearman, 1927), implying it does not matter whether an examinee's ability is measured on a scale of accuracy (power), a scale of speed, or some combination of the two. Starting with the Army Alpha in World War I, the use of time-limited tests has steadily increased. Such tests are often intended to be power tests but are given with time limits mainly for administrative convenience (Morrison, 1960). If speed and accuracy measure the same construct, as Spearman and others believed, time limits will not matter.

Researchers have found, however, that speed and accuracy on complex tasks do not measure the same construct.[1] For example, speed (measured by the time to finish a test) is uncorrelated with test score on an untimed test (Baxter, 1941; Bridges, 1985; Foos, 1989), and time-limit

---

[1]Simple reaction times (e.g., Jensen, 1982a, 1982b) have a small, negative correlation with simple measures of intelligence, but simple reaction times are not of interest in the present chapter and will not be considered further.

scores (number correct after a given amount of time on a test) are composed of both speed and level[2] factors (Davidson & Carroll, 1945). Speed (measured by the percentage of people who answered the last item on each page of the test) and accuracy (number right) comprise orthogonal factors in test scores (Myers, 1952).

Most psychometric research has focused on accuracy in some form. Classical test theory and IRT have also focused on accuracy. Until recently, relatively little attention has been given to response times[3] in operational tests. Now that more tests are being administered on computer, it is possible to collect response times on large numbers of examinees and use those response times in various ways. This chapter focuses on some of the many uses of response times in testing.

REVIEW OF RESEARCH AND DEVELOPMENTS

Interest in response times as a method of revealing information about mental activity is as old as the field of psychology itself. In 1868, Donders suggested that the time required to perform a mental activity could be inferred by exposing the subject to two procedures that differed only in whether that activity was used and subtracting the response times (cited in Luce, 1986). The first psychological laboratory was established 11 years later by Wundt, marking the official beginning of the field of psychology (Kendler, 1987). Eleven years after that (1890), Jastrow stated that if the mind is highly structured, different paths through that structure will require different amounts of time (which will be reflected in response times), and this is a major argument for investigating response times (cited in Luce, 1986).

Response times have been the preferred dependent variable in cognitive psychology since the mid-1950s (Luce, 1986) because how long it takes someone to process something is thought to indicate something about how the person processed it. Some early researchers in testing also used response times. For instance, Blommers and Lindquist (1944) investigated the relation between reading rate and comprehension. Subjects read a question and a paragraph that contained the answer, then

---

[2]Level refers to what the examinee's score (proficiency) would have been on an untimed test.

[3]We use the term response time rather than response latency because the latter term has generally been reserved by cognitive psychologists for unobservable processes (e.g., the duration of the decision component versus the motor component in a simple cognitive task). The term response time is used for events with observable start and stop times. We prefer to use the terms with the more established meanings from the field of cognitive psychology.

answered the question. There was a small, positive correlation between the rate of reading comprehension (mean reading rate on items answered correctly) and power of comprehension (NC score). Blommers and Lindquist also found that good comprehenders read more slowly as the difficulty of the material increased, whereas poor comprehenders read at the same rate regardless of difficulty.

Tate (1948) investigated the relationship between speed and accuracy on arithmetic reasoning, number series, sentence completion, and spatial relations questions. He found that the fastest examinees were not necessarily the most accurate and that when accuracy is controlled, fast subjects are always fast and slow subjects are always slow. This supports Kennedy's (1930) finding that individuals tend to perform at consistent rates of work across a variety of cognitive tasks, even after partialing out differences due to intelligence. Kennedy concluded that rate of work (speed) is a personality trait. These studies suggested that response time is a person parameter.

Although analysis of response times has had a long, successful history in experimental cognitive psychology, its use in testing has been limited because of the difficulties in recording response times in operational settings. Early research on response times in testing relied on cumbersome methods such as having examinees write down their start and stop times for each item or their total time per item as provided by the examiner. In addition to being intrusive, these techniques also require nonstandard test administrations, which may preclude inference to typical testing situations (Rindler, 1979).

More tests are now being administered on computers, providing easy and unobtrusive collection of response times in standard, operational settings. As response times are becoming more available, we can start making use of them. One could even argue that we are obligated to investigate response times in the interest of fairness and equity.

We organize our review of research on response times in testing into the following categories: scoring models, speed–accuracy relationships, strategy usage, speededness, pacing, predicting finishing times and setting time limits, and subgroup differences. These categories are closely related to one another. For example, whether response times should be used for scoring depends on the relationship between speed and accuracy (as well as whether speed is a valid measure of the construct being assessed). Strategy usage (and a special case—speededness) affects pacing and can be affected by time limits. Additionally, all of these issues could vary by subgroup. The following is not intended to be an exhaustive literature review, but rather an overview of the types of research that have been done.

Scoring Models

The most commonly observed examinee behavior in testing is accuracy on test items and the score examinees receive on the test based on their accuracy. Most psychometric research has concentrated on scores in some form (e.g., general test theory, reliability, validity, equity, and comparability of scores).

Given the interest in scores, it is not surprising that theorists have developed models that use response times in the scoring process. Several models have been proposed, and they differ in terms of the assumed response-time distributions (if any), the assumed relation between ability and response speed, and the nature of items for which the model was designed.

Samejima (1973, 1974, 1983b) offered an extension of IRT that can serve as a model of any continuous response, including response time. Samejima's approach can accommodate the specification of a function relating response time to latent ability; for response times, the function could take the form of a cumulative distribution function. The approach is not limited to a particular function, and Samejima argued that model checking is of utmost importance in function selection. Thus, Samejima's model could, but need not, be used with any of the distributions that have been proposed as appropriate models of response-time distributions.[4] The continuous-response generalization of IRT can also be used with a nonparametric (empirical) approximation of the function relating response time to latent ability.

The use of Samejima's (1973, 1974, 1983b) continuous-response generalization of IRT requires that response speed be the dependent variable of interest. Samejima argued that this is appropriate only when the items represent relatively simple cognitive tasks, for which response time is representative of ability. She suggested that response times for more complicated tasks would require more complicated modeling approaches because the response time will have a less straightforward relation to the cognitive process of interest.

Scheiblechner (1979, 1985) offered the linear exponential model (LEM) as a response-time model for speed test items. He envisioned relatively uncomplicated cognitive tasks such as Posner's (e.g., Posner & Boies, 1971) perceptual-matching task or Sternberg's (1970) memory-scanning task. For the uncomplicated cognitive tasks Scheiblechner described, response time may be considered a fairly straightforward index of processing. For such tasks, all examinees could probably correctly re-

---

[4]Schnipke and Scrams (1997b) evaluated several candidate functions in terms of the quality of fit to empirical response-time distributions. Their research is discussed later.

spond to each item given sufficient time, so errors are likely to be caused by time urgency rather than item difficulty as defined by IRT.

According to the LEM, the response time t for individual i responding to item j follows an exponential distribution with density given by:

$$f(t) = (\tau_i \mid \xi_j) \exp[-(\tau_i + \zeta_j)t],$$

where τ_i is an examinee speed parameter and ξ_j is an item speed parameter. The item speed parameter is further modeled in terms of the component processes that are required to solve the item. Thus,

$$\xi_j = \sum_l a_{jl} \eta_l,$$

where a_{jl} indicates the amount to which component l is present in item j, and η_l indicates the speed of component l.

Scheiblechner (1979, 1985) focused on items for which response time is often considered an appropriate measure of processing skill. Response accuracy is not considered within the model because most items would be solved correctly were there sufficient time. The applicability of Scheiblechner's model to power tests is an issue for future theory and research.

Tatsuoka and Tatsuoka (1980) offered a response-time model in which an examinee's speed is characterized by a single parameter, τ, and each item's time requirements are characterized in terms of two parameters, c and u. τ is conceptualized as the expected response time for the given examinee over an infinite set of items of the same type as those presented at test. c and u are the shape and scale parameters of the Weibull distribution. Together, these parameters determine the distribution of expected response times for a particular examinee responding to a particular item. Tatsuoka and Tatsuoka (1980) assumed a Weibull distribution on the basis of earlier research (Tatsuoka & Tatsuoka, 1978), so the cumulative distribution function representing the expected response time, t_{ij}, for examinee i responding to item j is given by:

$$F(t_{ij}) = 1 - \exp\left[-\left(\frac{\tau_i + (t_{ij} - \bar{t}_i)}{u_j)}\right)^{c_j}\right],$$

where $\bar{t}_i$ is the mean response time for examinee i over all items in the set.

Tatsuoka and Tatsuoka (1980) were interested in what might be considered a homogeneous set of items (mixed-number subtraction), and their goal was to use response-time information to classify examinees in terms of the different solution strategies employed. Applying their model to a more heterogeneous group of items would require careful consideration of which items should be included as part of a single set for the determination of $\bar{t}_i$. If test items varied considerably in format or requisite skills and strategies, Tatsuoka and Tatsuoka's (1980) model might need to be applied separately to homogeneous subsets. Also, Tatsuoka and Tatsuoka make no claim about the relationship between response speed and response accuracy; instead, they concentrate on differences in response speed due to differences in strategy usage. They do, however, limit themselves to modeling correct responses on the grounds that incorrect responses may involve various misconceptions at various processing stages, so response times may be less indicative of overall strategy.

Thissen's (1983) timed-testing model is unusual in that it is designed to capture response time and response accuracy within a single model. Thissen, building on the research of Furneaux (1961), offered a model in which response accuracy is characterized in terms of a 2PL IRT model, and the natural logarithm of response time, $\ln(t)$, is characterized as a linear function of examinee and item parameters:

$$ln(t_{ij}) = \mu + \tau_i + u_j - \rho z_{ij} + \varepsilon_{ij},$$

where μ is a grand mean across items and examinees, τ_i is a slowness parameter for examinee i, u_j is a slowness parameter for item j, ρ represents the log-linear relation between response time and ability, z_{ij} is the logit from the IRT model, and ε_{ij} is a normally distributed error term. This model assumes a lognormal distribution for the expected response-time distribution for an examinee responding to an item.

Thissen (1983) was interested in both response time and response accuracy, and his model is applicable to items typically found on large-scale, standardized achievement and aptitude tests. Thissen allowed for a log-linear relation between response speed and response accuracy in terms of ρ. Most other response-time models offered by test theorists have ignored issues of response accuracy by focusing on correctly answered items (e.g., Tatsuoka and Tatsuoka, 1980) or on relatively uncomplicated cognitive tasks (e.g., Samejima, 1973, 1974, 1983b; Scheiblechner, 1979, 1985). Thissen pointed out that his model is meant to provide a practical description of responses to typical test items rather than an explanation of the cognitive processes underlying these responses. He suggested that future theorists might develop such process models.

Similar to Samejima (1973, 1974, 1983b) and Scheiblechner (1979, 1985), Verhelst, Verstralen, and Jansen (1997) concentrated on speed tests—tests in which all items could be answered correctly given sufficient time, but time limits lead to a sense of urgency and possible errors. Ability, θ, is tied to response speed by introducing the concept of *momen-*

tary ability. Rather than assuming examinees have fixed ability levels, Verhelst et al. assumed an examinee's momentary (effective) ability is the realization of a random variable, which is influenced both by the examinee's *mental power* and by the time devoted to the item. An item is answered correctly if the examinee's momentary ability exceeds the item's difficulty (conceptualized as a fixed *cognitive weight*). Because the momentary ability distribution belongs to a shift family in which the location parameter is an increasing function of time, spending more time increases the probability of a correct response.

Verhelst et al. (1997) assumed examinees select the amount of time to devote to an item, and the resulting response times follow a 2P gamma distribution with rate considered an examinee parameter and shape considered an item parameter. They further assumed the momentary ability distribution conditioned on response time follows a generalized extreme value distribution with parameters reflecting the examinee's mental power and the item's cognitive weight. Together, these assumptions determine that the marginal distribution of momentary ability (with time integrated out) follows a generalized logistic distribution. This makes the model consistent with the prevalent use of logistic item response functions. When the shape parameter of the response-time distribution is equal to one, the distribution reduces to the exponential, and the marginal momentary ability distribution is a 1PL distribution, so the model is a version of the Rasch, 1PL, IRT model.

The model proposed by Verhelst et al. (1997) is similar to Thissen's (1983) model in that response accuracy and response speed are considered simultaneously, but the nature of the speed–accuracy relationship takes a different form in the two models. An important distinction between the two models is the type of items most appropriate for their application. Thissen was interested in items from power tests, whereas Verhelst et al. focused on items from speed tests. Verhelst et al.'s model may be applied to items from power tests, but this would likely require some modification of the assumed speed–accuracy trade-off mechanism. As proposed, the model assumes momentary ability (and hence the probability of a correct response) increases without bounds as a function of time. This is an undesirable conceptualization for power tests. Limits could be placed on the amount of time spent, but this is a theoretically unsatisfying solution.

Roskam's (1997) Rasch–Weibull model shares much in common with Verhelst et al.'s (1997) model. Both models result in Rasch models of response accuracy, but Roskam's model introduces the Rasch response-accuracy model at the level of the correct-response probability conditioned on response time, whereas Verhelst et al.'s model introduces the Rasch response-accuracy model for the marginal correct-response probability (integrating over time). Another key difference concerns the assumed response-time distribution. Verhelst et al. assumed gamma-distributed response times, and Roskam assumed Weibull distributions. Both models use an effective ability that is an increasing function of time spent, so they explicitly model the relationship between response speed and response accuracy.

Although several theorists have tested the appropriateness of their own assumed response-time distributions, few independent investigations have been conducted along these lines. One exception is the research by Schnipke and Scrams (1997b) in which they explored the empirical fit of four theoretical response-time distributions: gamma, Gaussian, lognormal, and Weibull. Response times for each of 30 items from a computerized adaptive arithmetic-reasoning test were divided into exploratory (500 observations) and confirmatory (507–6,917 observations) samples. Each candidate distribution was fit to each of the exploratory samples by means of MLE (Gaussian, lognormal), matching-moments estimation (gamma), or nonlinear regression of the cumulative distribution function (Weibull). The exploratory parameters were used to check each model's fit against the confirmatory samples. Visual inspection of double-probability plots and measures of model misfit showed a strong advantage for the lognormal distribution. The lognormal distribution was proposed by Thissen (1983) and could also be used in conjunction with Samejima's (1973, 1974, 1983b) continuous-response model.

No validity studies have been offered that address the utility of the resulting scores from response-time models. Future research on this topic is recommended. Use of the scoring models relies on the relationship between speed and accuracy, and details of empirical research along these lines are provided next.

Speed–Accuracy Relationships

An integral question raised by response-time models concerns the relationship between response speed and response accuracy. This has been an important issue raised by cognitive psychologists as well (Luce, 1986; Townsend & Ashby, 1983), but the focus of cognitive psychologists has been different from the focus of psychometricians. Cognitive psychologists have focused on the within-person relationship between speed and accuracy (the oft-mentioned speed–accuracy trade-off): When a person chooses to perform a task more quickly, the person's accuracy tends to decline. Psychometric researchers have focused more on the across-person relationship between speed and accuracy: Do the most accurate examinees tend to respond slower or faster than their less accurate counterparts? With the advent of computerized testing, the across-person relationship between speed and accuracy has been investigated by a growing number of researchers.

For clarification, both types of speed–accuracy relationships can be considered within the response-time model suggested by Verhelst et al. (1997). Speed–accuracy trade-off is modeled by making momentary ability partially dependent on the time devoted to the task—spending more time on an item increases the probability of a correct response. However, separate parameters reflect the examinee's mental power (the primary driving force behind accuracy) and mental speed (the rate parameter of the gamma distribution of response times). Any relationship between mental power and mental speed (across examinees) reflects the traditional psychometric focus for speed–accuracy relationships. The across-examinee type of speed–accuracy relationship is modeled in Thissen's (1983) timed-testing model by the coefficient relating the logarithm of response time to the IRT logit.

Thissen (1983) investigated his timed-testing model with data from 78 examinees who completed three cognitive tests: a verbal analogies test described by Whitely (1977b) and Tinsley (1971), a subset of Raven's (1956) Progressive Matrices, and part of a spatial-visualization test from the Guilford–Zimmerman (1953) Aptitude Survey, Part VI. Thissen's (1983) model allows two ways to examine the speed–accuracy relationship. First, the relationship is represented by the coefficient relating the logarithm of response time to the IRT logit. The coefficient was low (.20) for the verbal analogies, high (.80) for the progressive matrices, and near zero (.03) for the spatial-visualization test. A complementary approach is to consider the correlation between the examinee slowness and examinee ability parameters. These values were moderate (.68) for the verbal analogies, high (.94) for the progressive matrices, and near zero (–.03) for the spatial-visualization test. In all cases, a positive coefficient or correlation indicates more accurate examinees also tended to be faster.

Segall (1987) investigated the speed–accuracy relationship with data from 209 military applicants completing a pretest of the CAT-ASVAB. The relationship was investigated in terms of the correlation between total time spent answering items and estimated ability, and analyses were completed separately for nine subtests: general science, arithmetic reasoning, word knowledge, paragraph comprehension, shop information, auto information, math knowledge, mechanical comprehension, and electronic information. The four subtests that involve reasoning or computation (arithmetic reasoning, paragraph comprehension, math knowledge, and mechanical comprehension) demonstrated positive relationships: Higher scoring examinees tended to spend more time. The remaining subtests involve simple recall, and they demonstrated either no relationship (auto information, shop information, and electronic information) or a negative relationship (general science and word knowledge) between total time spent answering items and estimated ability. Examinees received different subsets of items—more able examinees received more difficult items—so the observed positive relationships could be explained by more difficult items' requiring more time.

Parshall, Mittelholtz, and Miller (1994) investigated several examinee, item, and interaction variables as predictors of item-response times (transformed onto a logarithmic scale) for an adaptive mathematics placement test. The strongest predictor was the logarithm of the examinee's mean response time across items received, indicating examinees tended to differ in their response speed. A small amount of variability was explained by estimated ability; more able examinees tended to take slightly more time, replicating Segall's (1987) findings. Parshall et al.'s results suffer from the same confound as did Segall's results—examinee ability is confounded with item difficulty; thus the observed relationship may reflect greater time requirements for more difficult items as opposed to slower processing by high-ability examinees.

Bergstrom, Gershon, and Lunz (1994) also attempted to predict item-response times (transformed onto a logarithmic scale) from examinee and item characteristics, but unlike Parshall et al. (1994), Bergstrom et al. used a hierarchical linear model with item effects nested within examinee effects. Although they found relative difficulty was a significant predictor of response time (i.e., examinees spent more time on difficult items), examinee ability was not a significant predictor of response speed. Bergstrom et al.'s test was considerably different from that used by Parshall et al. (Bergstrom et al. used an adaptive certification exam instead of an adaptive placement exam), but the results are consistent.

Swanson, Featherman, Case, Luecht, and Nungester (1997) explored the same issue using responses from approximately 20,000 examinees to a computer-administered component of the United States Medical Licensing Exam (USMLE). Consistent with Parshall et al.'s (1994) and Bergstrom et al.'s (1994) findings, Swanson et al. found no relationship between mean response time and examinee ability.

Scrams and Schnipke (1997) applied a version of Thissen's (1983) timed-testing model to responses from approximately 7,000 examinees to three nonadaptive, CBTs assessing verbal-, quantitative-, and analytical-reasoning skills. All three tests resulted in small values of the coefficient relating the logarithm of response time to the IRT logit: .19, .13, and −.02 for the verbal-, quantitative-, and analytical-reasoning tests, respectively. The correlation between examinee ability and slowness was relatively high for the verbal- and quantitative-reasoning tests ($r^2 = .39$ and .33, respectively) but nonexistent for the analytical-reasoning test ($r^2 = .00$). In general, high-scoring examinees took more time than low-scoring examinees on the verbal- and quantitative-reasoning tests, but the groups did not differ on the analytical-reasoning test. Because all examinees received the same items (the tests were nonadaptive), Scrams and Schnipke's results were not confounded by differences in item difficulty.

Swygert (1998) investigated the relationship between response time and examinee ability for three subtests of a large-scale, adaptive test. There was no substantive relationship between response time and examinee ability for the verbal-reasoning subtest. There was a modest positive relationship for the quantitative-reasoning subtest, indicating that high-scoring examinees took more time on average. There was also a positive relationship for the analytical-reasoning subtest, but this relationship was primarily due to a small group of outliers. An important difference between Swygert's analyses and others reported in the literature concerns methodology. Swygert analyzed residual effects after controlling for examinee and item differences, so her results do not suffer the confound plaguing the results of earlier adaptive testing research.

Research shows that the relationship between speed and accuracy depends on test context and content. Unfortunately, much of the research addressing this issue uses measures of accuracy that are affected by response speed. The IRT ability estimate, for example, represents the examinees' accuracy given the time constraints of the administration; this is clearly confounded with response speed. This is a serious confound, and a solution to this problem is needed. Some of the response-time scoring models may be useful in this regard, but model-checking procedures will be of considerable importance.

Research on speed–accuracy relationships has implicitly assumed that all examinees use the same strategy for responding to items. Thus, only one speed–accuracy relationship is discussed. If examinees use different strategies, however, the speed–accuracy relationship would depend on strategy.

Strategy Usage

Classical test theory (CTT) and IRT describe examinees in terms of their tendency to answer items correctly. CTT and IRT measure quantitative differences in proficiency, but neither can detect qualitative differences. CTT and IRT proficiency estimates indicate examinees' ability within a single strategy (Mislevy & Verhelst, 1990).

CTT and IRT characterize ability in terms of the amount or quantity of expertise one has in some domain. CTT and unidimensional IRT characterize expertise in the domain on a single, unidimensional scale. Multidimensional IRT characterizes expertise in the domain on multiple scales.

None of these models are appropriate for qualitative changes in ability. Recent research in cognitive and educational psychology indicates learning is not simply the collection of new knowledge. Rather, learning is an active, constructive process in which learners reconfigure their knowledge structures, incorporate new facts based on their current level of understanding, and create their own interpretations of the material (Masters & Mislevy, 1993; Mislevy, 1993). For example, expert–novice research suggests novices use inappropriate or inefficient strategies, based on internal knowledge structures they have constructed (Masters & Mislevy, 1993). Thus, we expect qualitative differences in the performance of experts and novices, or more generally, among examinees using different strategies. More important than knowing how many items examinees answer correctly is knowing what strategies examinees are using.

Another example of an important change in strategy is in children's expressive language. When children first learn to speak, they learn words as individual units. Later, as they learn the rules of language, they apply the rules in all cases, even when there are exceptions. Therefore children might switch from saying "I went to the store" to "I goed to the store" when they learn the "add -ed to a verb to make it past tense" rule. This signifies a deeper understanding of the language, even though they sound like their language skills are regressing. Assessing the child's expressive language in terms of accuracy would result in incorrectly inferring a loss of skill. Incorporating a deeper understanding of strategies would help to uncover the child's improvement.

In CTT and IRT the person either answers an item correctly or incorrectly, but how the person solved the item is ignored. To take strategy into account, new models are needed. Although models for detecting strategy usage that do not use response times have been proposed (e.g., Davey, 1990; Mislevy, 1996; Samejima, 1983a; Yamamoto & Everson, 1995), the focus here is on models that use response times to detect strategy usage.

Mislevy and Verhelst (1990) provided a mixture model that takes strategy into account. Their approach characterizes students in terms of strategy used and proficiency within that strategy. Mislevy, Wingersky, Irvine, and Dann (1991) used what has traditionally been called a mental rotation task to illustrate the mixture-model approach presented in Mislevy and Verhelst. As indicated in the visualization literature, the mental-rotation task can either be solved by mental rotation or by an analytical, rule-based strategy. Different patterns of response times are obtained depending on which strategy is used. Mislevy and Verhelst's model uses response-time patterns to determine which strategy the person most likely used.

As noted in the section on scoring models, Tatsuoka and Tatsuoka's (1980) model was designed to use response-time information to classify examinees in terms of which strategy they employed. Tatsuoka and Tatsuoka (1978) discovered that response-time distributions could be approximated as Weibull distributions if response times were fit separately for examinees using different subtraction strategies. Tatsuoka and Tatsuoka (1980) built on this finding in developing their response-time model. Examinee strategy is predicted on the basis of model-provided response-time parameters.

Holden (1993) used response times to differentiate between a lying and an honest strategy on personnel tests. Some examinees were instructed to lie and some were instructed to answer honestly. Based on schema theory, it was predicted examinees would take longer to admit to negative or delinquent behavior if they were lying than if they were answering honestly (e.g., Holden & Kroner, 1992; Holden, Kroner, Fekken, & Popham, 1992). Holden (1993) used discriminant function analysis and was able to distinguish between response times for examinees who lied and examinees who answered honestly with a classification hit rate of 64%.

Schnipke (1995) used response times to detect two response strategies on a CBT that was speeded. In *solution behavior*, examinees actively try to determine the correct answer to every item; accuracy is determined by item and examinee characteristics. In contrast, in *rapid-guessing behavior*, examinees respond rapidly to items as time expires; accuracy is at or near chance because examinees are not fully considering the items. Schnipke and Scrams (1997a) developed a mixture model to distinguish between these two response strategies on individual items. The model only used response times, but response accuracy supported the classifications. Accuracy was at or below chance for responses classified as rapid guesses. Their model could be applied to other strategy-usage issues as long as the strategies are associated with different response-time demands. For example, "stolen" items might have fast, correct responses.

One special case of strategy usage that has received considerable attention is speededness (e.g., Schnipke, 1995; Schnipke & Scrams, 1997a). Next, we discuss the use of response times to define and measure speededness in more depth.

Speededness

In testing, a distinction is made between power tests and speed tests (e. g., Gulliksen, 1950/1987). In a pure power test, the items range in difficulty and no time limit exists. The goal is to measure how accurately examinees can answer items. In a pure speed test, the items are easy and the time limit is strict. The goal is to measure how quickly examinees can answer items. In practice, most tests contain both speed and power components, and these tests are called speeded (or partially speeded) tests. Speeded tests usually result from administering a power test with a time limit, a practice that is usually required when the test is group administered.

Speededness, or the extent to which a test is speeded, has traditionally been measured on NC scored tests by the percentage of unreached (unanswered) items at the end of the test under the assumption examinees did not have time to reach these items. Indeed, on speeded tests, some examinees do not finish all of the items. Other examinees, however, rapidly mark answers as time expires, presumably in the hopes of getting some of the items right by chance. Examinees who rapidly mark answers will not have unreached items and therefore are not considered speeded in traditional measures of speededness. Thus, traditional speededness indexes almost surely underestimate the amount of speededness on most NC scored multiple-choice tests (Schnipke, 1995), and perhaps for-mula-scored tests as well. A more complete estimate of speededness would include examinees who rapidly respond to items as time expires. Thus response times provide additional information about speededness.

Some research has used average item-response times to investigate speededness. For example, Schaeffer, Reese, Steffen, McKinley, and Mills (1993) compared the average item response time for each item of the GRE-CBT with the amount of time expected if examinees spent the same amount of time on all items and answered all items in the allotted time (i.e., the total amount of time divided by the number of items on the test). Although the average response times were slightly less than the ex-pected times, fewer examinees answered the last item in the quantita-tive and analytical sections on the GRE-CBT than on the paper-and-pencil GRE. Schaeffer et al. (1993) concluded the time limits were sufficient, but "further insights into the extent of this speededness question may be gained with future examination of the item timing data" (p. 46).

Schnipke (1995) used item-response times to look at speededness. She used accuracy and response-time data from a nonadaptive CBT to look at speededness at the end of each test section. She found evidence of two types of speeded behavior. Some examinees did not finish the test; they spent more time on each item than most examinees and ran out of time before finishing. Figure 12.1 shows the behavior of such an examinee from Schnipke. The examinee's standardized natural loga-rithm of response time[5] ($z_{ln(RT)}$) is shown in Fig. 12.1 for each item on the linear (nonadaptive) CBT.

The examinee whose behavior is depicted in Fig. 12.1 responded more slowly than most examinees on the first few items (Items 1–7; 1.2 to 2.9 standard deviations above the mean, with a mean of 3 min, 10 sec per

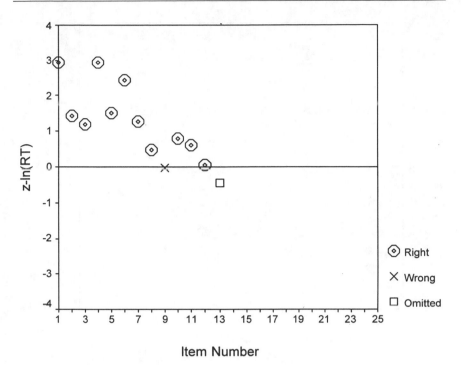

FIG. 12.1. Standardized transformed response time, $z_{ln(RT)}$, across items for a speeded examinee who did not finish the test.

item). The examinee then sped up and responded at about the same speed as most examinees on the next several items (Items 8–13; 0 to 1 standard deviation above the mean, with a mean of 1 min, 34 sec per item). The examinee did not finish the rest of the test. This examinee was slow, but accurate: Of Items 1 to 12, all were answered correctly except Item 9. The examinee did not respond to Item 13 (i.e., it was omitted— displayed on the screen but not answered), and the rest (Items 14–25) were unreached (i.e., the items were never displayed on the screen).

The other type of speeded behavior Schnipke (1995) found was rapid-guessing behavior (defined in the previous section on strategy usage). Figure 12.2, from Schnipke shows the behavior of an examinee who

---

[5] The natural logarithm is used because the response-time distributions are positively skewed; the natural logarithm transformation creates a more normal distribution. The transformed response times were then standardized, item by item, to control for item differences (e.g., long items take longer on average to answer than short items). If an examinee responded at the mean speed on an item, $z_{ln(RT)}$ would be 0. Positive values of $z_{ln(RT)}$ indicate the examinee responded slower than the average of all examinees, and negative values indicate the examinee responded faster than average.

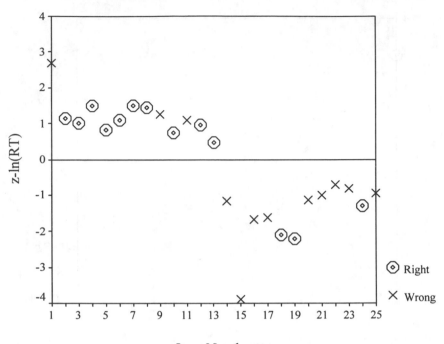

FIG. 12.2.   Standardized transformed response time, $z_{\ln(RT)}$, across items for a speeded examinee who switched strategies on the second half of the test.

switched from solution behavior to rapid-guessing behavior. At the beginning of the test, the examinee responded at a slower rate than most examinees (from .5 to 1.5 standard deviations above the mean, with a mean of 2 min and 17 sec per item). After Item 13 (when the examinee had only 2 minutes remaining), the examinee suddenly started responding much faster (from −.7 to −3.9 standard deviations below the mean, with a mean of 12.25 sec per item). The examinee's accuracy also changed—from 77% accuracy on the first 13 items to 25% accuracy on the last 12 items. The examinee engaged in solution behavior on the first half of the items, but the examinee engaged in rapid-guessing behavior on the last half of the items (and with very little time left).

Schnipke and Scrams (1997a) developed a mixture model of two lognormal distributions to distinguish between solution behavior and rapid-guessing behavior on a nonadaptive CBT. The model uses response times to determine whether a response is more likely to come from the rapid-guessing distribution or the solution distribution. Schnipke and Scrams determined the rapid-guessing distribution is essentially the same across items, supporting the claim that rapid-guessing behavior is not affected by item content.

Figure 12.3 shows the probability density functions of response times for two sample items from Schnipke and Scrams (1997a). The item on the left (the 4th item in the 25-item nonadaptive test) shows no rapid-guessing behavior, whereas the item on the right (the 17th item in the test) contains both rapid-guessing behavior and solution behavior. Schnipke and Scrams' final mixture model indicates 1% of the examinees engaged in rapid-guessing behavior on Item 4, whereas 18% engaged in rapid-guessing behavior on Item 17.

Swanson et. al (1997) investigated response times on computer-administered components of the USMLE. They investigated both a nonadaptive CBT and a testlet-based CAST. CAST adapts between testlets, but not within testlets. The testlets used by Swanson et al. contained 60 items. Both the CBT and CAST showed evidence of rapid-guessing behavior, as shown in response-time density functions (similar to Fig. 12.3, Item 17). Swanson et al. determined the CBT was speeded for less proficient examinees. The CAST design reduced speededness for less proficient examinees, but it may have increased speededness for more proficient examinees.

Hadadi and Luecht (1998) analyzed data from two CBTs—one that was speeded and one that was not speeded. They separated their data into blocks of 30 items (Positions 1–30, 31–60, etc.) and combined response times from these blocks to create stable response-time distributions to detect rapid-guessing behavior. In particular, the speeded CBT showed evidence of both omits (unanswered items) and rapid-guessing behavior (identified as response times of less than 8 seconds), especially on the last 30 items (of 180 items).

Assessing speededness in CATs is made difficult because examinees do not see the same items in the same positions and because individual items might not be seen by enough examinees to draw meaningful conclusions about response times. To look for speededness at the end of the test, results must be pooled over different items or must be done at the examinee level. Hadadi and Luecht's (1998) method is one approach. Swygert's (1998) solution for investigating response times by item position on a CAT is to remove the item and examinee effects from each item and to look at the residual response times across items for each position. Bontempo and Julian (1997) used a similar procedure for investigating speededness on a variable-length adaptive test (the NCLEX-RN™). All examinees were required to take a minimum of 60 scored items (and 15 unscored items). If a pass–fail decision could be made at that point, testing stopped. Otherwise, examinees continued to take items, up to 265 items (250 scored and 15 unscored), until a reliable pass–fail decision

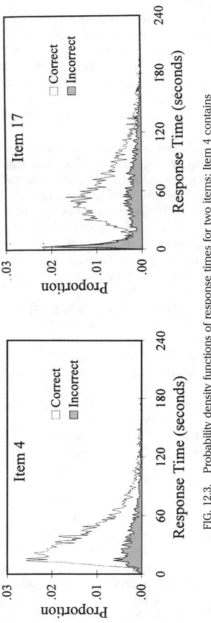

FIG. 12.3. Probability density functions of response times for two items: Item 4 contains only solution-behavior responses; Item 17 contains both solution-behavior responses and rapid-guessing-behavior responses.

could be made. Bontempo and Julian assumed the first 60 items would be unspeeded. One way they assessed speededness was by comparing examinees' relative response rate on the first 60 scored items with their relative response rate on the remaining 190 items or the last 50 items. Relative response rate, τ_i, is given by

$$\tau_i = \frac{\sum_{j=1}^{J} (t_{ij} - \bar{t}_j)}{J},$$

where τ_{ij} is the response time for examinee i to item j, $\bar{t}_j$ is the average response time on item j for all examinees who took the item, and J is the total number of items in the comparison.

Bontempo and Julian (1997) found that 88% of the examinees worked faster on the remaining 190 items, and 91% worked faster on the last 50 items, indicating that examinees had to work faster at the end of the test and that it may have been speeded. Overall, they concluded that at least 5% of the examinees were significantly affected by the time limit. However, they did not establish examinee accuracy was affected by increased speed, so their results may reflect increased efficiency or comfort with the delivery system.

Rapid-guessing behavior and not finishing a speeded test are two pacing strategies. Many other pacing strategies are possible, next section we discuss examinee pacing more generally.

Pacing

The goal of standardized testing is to assess examinee performance, usually based on the accuracy with which examinees respond to items. More able examinees are assumed to respond more accurately. Unfortunately, accuracy can be affected by factors other than ability, such as strategy usage, processing speed, or test sophistication. Examinee pacing is related to all three of these: pacing may represent strategic choices, examinee processing speed may influence pacing decisions, and more sophisticated examinees may choose more optimal pacing strategies than do less sophisticated examinees of comparable ability. For the present review, pacing issues are limited to response-time patterns across item positions, types, or difficulties. Issues related only to overall examinee speed are discussed in the sections Speed–Accuracy Relationships, Subgroup Differences, and Speededness.

Llabre and Froman (1987) investigated the pacing strategies of 38 Hispanic and 28 non-Hispanic, white examinees who completed a computer-administered version of the California Test of Mental Maturity. Although Hispanic examinees tended to spend slightly more time on each item, the more interesting finding is that non-Hispanic examinees tended to allocate their testing time according to item difficulty to a greater extent than did Hispanic examinees. Llabre and Froman argued this was a more optimal strategy and suggested non-Hispanic examinees may have been more test sophisticated than ability-matched Hispanic examinees.

Gitomer, Curtis, Glaser, and Lensky (1987) offered one of the most interesting uses of response times for psychometric tests. They investigated processing strategies for analogy problem solving by examining timed eye-fixation patterns observed with eye-tracking equipment. One of the results was that high- and low-ability examinees tended to allocate their processing time similarly on easy analogies, but high-ability examinees tended to increase processing time for more difficult items to a greater extent than did low-ability examinees. This is consistent with Llabre and Froman's (1987) findings. Unlike Llabre and Froman, Gitomer et al. determined the increased processing time was for both stem and response-option processing. It is unclear whether low-ability examinees would have benefited from using the high-ability examinees' pacing strategy. Additional research is needed.

Schaeffer et al. (1993) investigated several response-time issues using data from a field test of the GRE-CAT. They found that although low-ability examinees spent similar amounts of time on the easiest and most difficult items administered, middle-ability examinees spent more time on difficult items, and high-ability examinees spent considerably more time on difficult items. This pattern was observed for all three subtests: verbal, quantitative, and analytical reasoning. Unfortunately, item type was confounded with item difficulty, and the middle-difficulty items failed to fit the expected pattern for verbal- or quantitative-reasoning items. Examination of the mean response times by item type and examinee ability revealed that low- and high-ability examinees tended to allocate their testing time differently across item types. For some item types, high-ability examinees invested less time than did low-ability examinees; the opposite pattern was observed for other item types. Some item types showed no response-time differences across ability groups.

Swanson et al. (1997) investigated pacing differences across ability groups. Similar to Schaeffer et al.'s (1993) results, Swanson et al. found low-ability examinees tended to allocate their time equally across items of varying difficulty. High-ability examinees, on the other hand, tended to allocate more time to difficult items and less time to easy items. Swanson et al. also observed that examinees tended to speed up throughout the test; mean item response times tended to decrease across sequential 30-item test blocks. This latter finding is consistent with results reported by

Bontempo and Julian (1997) who found examinees tended to respond more slowly to the first 60 items than to the remaining items on a large-scale, CMT.

Schnipke (1995) explored pacing strategies at the examinee level for a nonadaptive CBT. She suggested plots of standardized response times against item position could be useful for investigating pacing issues. Her interest was in identifying examinees who engaged in speeded behavior. To this end, she provided examples of examinees who tended to respond more slowly than most examinees during the early part of a test and then either failed to finish (shown in Fig. 12.1) or responded very rapidly to later items (shown in Fig. 12.2).

More recent research by Scrams and Schnipke (1999) has used the same technique as Schnipke (1995) with data from a CAT to uncover additional pacing strategies including equal-allocation strategies and decreasing-speed strategies. The latter strategy was unexpected, but Scrams and Schnipke found a large minority of test takers who tended to respond quickly to early items and were then able to spend more time on later items. The advantages of such a strategy in a CAT environment should be considered in future research.

Predicting Finishing Times and Setting Time Limits

Some studies have used item-response times to determine or predict finishing times or to set time limits for CBTs. Studies that used total test times (rather than item-level response times) are not included (e.g., Segall, Moreno, Kieckhaefer, Vicino, & McBride, 1997), nor are studies that investigated the effects of different time limits on test performance.

Time limits define the task for the examinees (Mollenkopf, 1960), which is another way of saying it affects examinee behavior. Time limits also affect the meaning of scores. As Mollenkopf noted, identical material administered under speeded and power conditions may not measure the same thing, which is important to remember when interpreting scores from speeded tests, especially if the degree of speededness is unclear. Studies have attempted to specify optimal time limits based on item-response times (Bhola, Plake, & Roos, 1993), predict response times so the regression equation can be used to predict finishing times and therefore inform appropriate time limits (Bergstrom et al., 1994; Halkitis, Jones, & Pradhan, 1996; Reese, 1993), and use response-time information to constrain item selection in a CAT (van der Linden, Scrams, & Schnipke, 1999).

Bhola et al. (1993) administered a CBT without a time limit and recorded the amount of time examinees spent on each item. They calculated the median and interquartile range of response times for each item.

They suggested the optimum time limit for a nonadaptive test would be the sum of the median response time for each item, plus .5 times the interquartile range, which they suggested would allow approximately 75% of the examinees to complete the test under power conditions (and the remaining 25% under speeded conditions). They demonstrated that two test forms matched on difficulty, discrimination, and lower asymptote (from the 3PL IRT model) can have different optimal time limits (according to their formula). One of Bhola et al.'s hypothetical forms required 28% more time than the other, suggesting item-time requirements need to be balanced across test forms along with statistical and content constraints.

For the GRE-CAT, time limits were established initially by building a regression model that predicted response times (from a nonadaptive computer-administered field-test version of the GRE) based on examinee ability and item characteristic (Reese, 1993). The model was used with simulated CAT data to predict finishing times on the CAT. Time limits for the CAT were selected to insure that virtually all examinees were predicted to have enough time to finish the CAT. The time limits were found to be appropriate after actual CAT timing data were collected (Schaeffer, Steffen, Golub-Smith, Mills, & Durso, 1995).

Halkitis et al. (1996) investigated the relationship between response times and item characteristics (item length, difficulty, and discrimination) on a nonadaptive CBT. Item length was defined as the number of words in the item. Item difficulty was defined as the percentage of examinees who answered correctly. Item discrimination was defined as the point biserial correlation coefficient between the item score (right–wrong) and total test score. Halkitis et al. predicted the logarithm of response times from item length, difficulty, and discrimination and found that 50.18% of the variance in log response times could be predicted by these three variables. They suggest their results provide a preliminary model that can be used to provide an initial estimate of the total testing time required.

Bergstrom et al. (1994) investigated the relationship between response times and examinee and item characteristic on a CAT. They used hierarchical linear modeling to predict the logarithm of response times from examinee characteristics (gender, ethnicity, ability, and anxiety) and item characteristics (item position, item length, relative item difficulty, key position, and figure inclusion). Gender, ethnicity, and ability did not affect response times, although all other variables did. Bergstrom et al. explained at least one third of the variation in log response times. They suggested that to control total testing time, items with characteristics that make them especially time consuming could be removed from the item bank or balanced across examinees during test administration. Furthermore, they suggested that understanding how item characteristics affect response times may allow test developers to predict the amount of time required for test administration. Such predictions can be based on the response-time history of test items.

van der Linden et al. (1999) proposed a model for incorporating response-time information into item selection for CAT. They used a model that describes response times using both item and examinee speed parameters. The examinee speed parameter is updated after every response and is used to guide item selection (based on IRT parameters and item speed) to ensure that all examinees will have enough time to finish the test. They found the algorithm was able to reduce speededness for examinees who otherwise would have suffered from the time limit. This algorithm controls finishing times for each examinee to make sure examinees have enough time to work on all items.

Research on setting time limits (or predicting finishing times) has included investigating subgroup differences as time limits should be set, in part, to limit differential subgroup speededness. Additional research on subgroup differences in response times is discussed next.

Subgroup Differences

There is evidence speed and time are perceived differently by different cultures (Klineberg, 1935; Roberts & Greene, 1971; Shannon, 1976). Therefore, subgroups may have different patterns of response times and may be differentially affected by time limits on tests. In addition, other factors such as language skills may differentially affect response times across subgroups. Thus, it is relevant to investigate response times for subgroups of the population, as well as for the overall examinee population.

Differential access to computers has been documented for members of different gender and ethnic subgroups and social classes (Sutton, 1991), although more recent research has not found such differences in some populations (e.g., Jenkins & Holmes, 1997). If subgroups differ in computer access, low-access groups may be disadvantaged on CBTs. Even if subgroups do not have less access to computers, their scores could be affected in irrelevant ways because of the computer delivery of the test. Thus, subgroup analyses are especially important in CBTs.

Some researchers have found gender and ethnicity not to be significant predictors of response times on CBTs (Bergstrom et al., 1994; Parshall et al., 1994; Schnipke, 1995), although anxiety was found to significantly predict response times (Bergstrom et al., 1994).

Other researchers have found small differences in response times for some subgroups. Llabre and Froman (1987) found Hispanic examinees consistently spent more time on items than White examinees. O'Neill and Powers (1993) found male and female test takers differed little on the amount of time spent on tutorials[6] and tests, although African American, Hispanic, and Native American examinees generally spent more time on tutorials and test sections than did White examinees. Schaeffer et al. (1993) found female examinees spent slightly longer on tutorials than did male examinees, but the differences were small and both groups saw and answered almost every item. African American examinees, however, spent more time on tutorials than did White examinees, and they saw and answered one fewer item on average than did White examinees. Schnipke (1995) found that rapid-guessing behavior was more common among male examinees on an analytical test, more common among female examinees on a quantitative test, and equally common on a verbal test. Female examinees were slightly more likely to have unreached items on all three tests. Some of these differences may be related to differences in courses taken by male and female examinees.

Most researchers who have investigated subgroup differences in response times have compared median or mean response times. Schnipke and Pashley (1997) suggested a more powerful approach of looking at the entire distribution of response times for each item. They used survival analysis methodology and demonstrated the approach with CBT data comparing response times for primary and nonprimary speakers of English. They found nonprimary speakers responded slower on items at the beginning of the test and faster on items toward the end of the test, suggesting the nonprimary speakers were more affected by the speed component than were primary speakers.

Overall, there is evidence of small response-time differences among subgroups, but these small differences tend to be masked by stronger predictors in regression analyses. Such differences could result in differential speededness, differential finishing rates (e.g., O'Neill & Powers, 1993; Schaeffer et al., 1993; Schnipke, 1995), or different test-taking strategies. As noted by O'Neill and Powers (1993), subgroup timing information should be taken into account when time limits are set to ensure that no subgroups are disadvantaged. Examining subgroup differences in response time is not only possible but necessary to ensure equity.

SUMMARY AND RECOMMENDATIONS FOR FUTURE RESEARCH

Interest in response times as a method of revealing information about mental activity is as old as psychology itself. Response times have been

---

[6]Many researchers have compared subgroup response times on both items and tutorials. Presumably, time on tutorials is compared under the assumption that if speed is a personality trait, subgroup differences would also appear on time spent on tutorials.

found to be useful in cognitive psychology, where they have been the preferred dependent variable since the mid-1950s (Luce, 1986). Some early researchers in testing also have been interested in the use of response times, although their use in testing has been limited because of the difficulties in recording them in operational settings. When tests are administered on computers, however, recording response times is trivial.

Research on response times in testing is in its infancy. This chapter organizes the research into scoring models, speed–accuracy relationship, strategy usage, speededness, pacing, predicting finishing times and setting time limits, and subgroup differences. All of these areas need additional research. For instance, in scoring models, no validity studies have been offered that address the utility of scores resulting from response-time models. Without assessing the validity of the scores, they are of no practical use. Research shows that the relationship between speed and accuracy depends on test context and content. Unfortunately, much of the research addressing this issue uses measures of accuracy that are affected by response speed. This is a serious confound, and a solution to this problem is needed. Some of the response-time scoring models may be useful in this regard, but model-checking procedures will be important. Research on speed–accuracy relationships has implicitly assumed all examinees use the same strategy for responding to items. If examinees use different strategies, however, the speed–accuracy relationship would depend on strategy, and additional research is needed to address this issue. Much of the research on subgroup differences has been done with relatively small, possibly unrepresentative sample of subgroups. Additionally, subgroup differences could affect all of the other topics (e.g., strategy usage), and additional research is needed to investigate those possibilities.

Over the past few decades, cognitive perspectives have become dominant in psychology, and several theorists have argued for a similar paradigm shift within psychometrics (Embretson, 1983, 1997; Frederiksen, Mislevy, & Bejar, 1993; Mislevy, 1994, 1996; Snow & Lohman, 1989; K. K. Tatsuoka, 1990; Yamamoto, 1989). Applying a cognitive psychology perspective to response-time research is highly recommended.

Although most of the psychometric response-time models rely at least partially on research from cognitive psychology, little of the empirical research has used either these models or other approaches from the cognitive psychology literature. Two exceptions are the research by Whitely (1977a) and Gitomer et al. (1987). Whitely tested a multiple-component model of analogical reasoning using conformatory factor analysis. The model was based on theory concerning the cognitive-processing demands of analogies, and Whitely tested the model against both accuracy and response-time data. The model appeared adequate for accuracy data but was insufficient to explain the response-time data. Whitely argued that a more detailed model of cognition might be needed.

Gitomer et al. (1987) also investigated the processes underlying analogy performance. They used eye-tracking equipment to monitor the amount and proportion of time spent on the initial encoding of the problem stem, subsequent encoding of the stem, and encoding of the response options. Similar to Whitely (1977a), Gitomer et al. were motivated by cognitive theories of analogical reasoning. They found that both low- and high-ability examinees tended to increase their processing time as items became more difficult, but low-ability examinees tended to increase the time spent on initial encoding of the stem whereas high-ability examinees increased their subsequent processing time. Gitomer et al. inferred that high-ability examinees focus on response options for difficult items whereas low-ability examinees focus on initial encoding of the stem. This suggests a fundamental difference in how the two group process items.

Research such as that done by Whitely (1977a) and Gitomer et al. (1987) is valuable and makes excellent use of response-time information. Response times have been the preferred dependent variable among cognitive psychologists because they believe response times provide information about how individuals process information (Luce, 1986; Townsend & Ashby, 1983). Such a perspective would benefit psychometricians who are interested in going beyond the relatively simple scores derived from CTT and IRT, but the nature of such research may demand closer interactions among psychometricians and cognitive psychologists. Fortunately, such interactions are likely to offer benefits for other issues in psychometrics such as complex assessment, diagnostic feedback, and construct validity.

ACKNOWLEDGMENTS

We would like to thank Lori McLeod, Craig Mills, Peter Pashley, Chris Scarlata, and Kimberly Swygert for their helpful comments and suggestions on an earlier draft of this paper.

REFERENCES

Baxter, B. (1941). An experimental analysis of the contributions of speed and level in an intelligence test. *Journal of Educational Psychology, 32*, 285–296.

Bergstrom, B., Gershon, R., & Lunz, M. E. (1994, April). *Computer adaptive testing: Exploring examinee response time using hierarchical linear modeling*. Paper presented at the annual meeting of the National Council on Measurement in Education, New Orleans, LA.

Bhola, D. S., Plake, B. S., & Roos, L. L. (1993, October). *Setting an optimum time limit for a computer-administered test*. Paper presented at the meeting of the Midwestern Educational Research Association, Chicago.

Blommers, P. & Lindquist, E. F. (1944). Rate of comprehension of reading: Its measurement and its relation to comprehension. *Journal of Educational Psychology, 35*(8), 449–473.

Bontempo, B. D., & Julian, E. R. (1997, March). *Assessing speededness in variable-length computer adaptive testing*. Paper presented at the annual meeting of the National Council on Measurement in Education, Chicago.

Bridges, K. R. (1985). Test-completion speed: Its relationship to performance on three course-based objective examinations. *Educational and Psychological Measurement, 45*, 29–35.

Davey, T. (1990, April). *Modeling timed test performance*. Paper presented at the meeting of the American Educational Research Association, Boston.

Davidson, W. M., & Carroll, J. B. (1945). Speed and level components in time-limit scores: A factor analysis. *Educational and Psychological Measurement, 5*, 411–427.

Embretson, S. E. (1983). Construct validity: Construct representation versus nomothetic span. *Psychological Bulletin, 93*, 179–197.

Embretson, S. E. (1997). Multicomponent response models. In W. J. van der Linden and R. K. Hambleton (Eds.), *Handbook of modern item response theory* (pp. 305–322). New York: Springer.

Foos, P. W. (1989). Completion time and performance on multiple-choice and essay tests. *Bulletin of the Psychonomic Society, 27*, 179–180.

Frederiksen, N., Mislevy, R. J., & Bejar, I. I. (Eds.). (1993). *Test theory for a new generation of tests*. Hillsdale, NJ: Lawrence Erlbaum Associates.

Furneaux, W. D. (1961). Intellectual abilities and problem solving behavior. In H. J. Eysenck (Ed.), *The handbook of abnormal psychology* (pp. 167–192). London: Pitman.

Gitomer, D. H., Curtis, M. E., Glaser, R., & Lensky, D. B. (1987). Processing differences as a function of item difficulty in verbal analogy performance. *Journal of Educational Psychology, 79*, 212–219.

Guilford, J. P., & Zimmerman, W. F. (1953). *The Guilford–Zimmerman aptitude survey. IV. Spatial Visualization Form B*. Beverly Hills, CA: Sheridan Supply Company.

Gulliksen, H. (1950/1987). *Theory of mental tests*. Hillsdale, NJ: Lawrence Erlbaum Associates.

Hadadi, A., & Luecht, R. M. (1998, April). *Effects of assessing speededness/non-speededness in computerized tests*. Paper presented at the annual meeting of the National Council on Measurement in Education, San Diego, CA.

Halkitis, P. N., Jones, J. P., & Pradhan, J. (1996, April). *Estimating testing time: The effects of item characteristics on response latency*. Paper presented at the annual meeting of the American Educational Research Association, New York.

Holden, R. R. (1993, August). *Response latency detection of lying on personnel tests*. Paper presented at the annual meeting of the American Psychological Association, Toronto, Canada.

Holden, R. R., & Kroner, D. G. (1992). Relative efficacy of differential response latencies for detecting faking on a self-report measure of psychopathology. *Psychological Assessment: A Journal of Consulting and Clinical Psychology, 4*, 170–173.

Holden, R. R., Kroner, D. G., Fekken, G. C., & Popham, S. M. (1992). A model of personality test item response dissimulation. *Journal of Personality and Social Psychology, 63*, 272–279.

Jenkins, S. M., & Holmes, S. D. (1997). *Computer usage and access patterns of actual and potential LSAT takers*. (LSAC Computerized Testing Report 97-10). Newtown, PA: Law School Admission Council.

Jensen, A. R. (1982a). Reaction time and psychometric *g*. In H. J. Eysenck (Ed.), *A model for intelligence*. New York: Springer.

Jensen, A. R. (1982b). The chronometry of intelligence. In R. J. Sternberg (Ed.), *Advances in the psychology of human intelligence* (Vol. 1). London: Lawrence Erlbaum Associates.

Kendler, H. H. (1987). *Historical foundations of modern psychology*. Pacific Grove, CA: Brooks/Cole.

Kennedy, M. (1930). Speed as a personality trait. *Journal of Social Psychology, 1*, 286–292.

Klineberg, O. (1935). *Race differences*. New York: Harper.

Llabre, M. M., & Froman, T. W. (1987). Allocation of time to test items: A study of ethnic differences. *Journal of Experimental Education, 55*, 137–140.

Luce, R. D. (1986). *Response times: Their role in inferring elementary mental organization*. New York: Oxford University Press.

Masters, G. N., & Mislevy, R. J. (1993). New views of student learning: Implications for educational measurement. In N. Frederiksen, R. J. Mislevy, & I. I. Bejar (Eds.), *Test theory for a new generation of tests* (pp. 219–242). Hillsdale, NJ: Lawrence Erlbaum Associates.

Mislevy, R. J. (1993). Foundations of a new test theory. In N. Frederiksen, R. J. Mislevy, & I. I. Bejar (Eds.), *Test theory for a new generation of tests* (pp. 19–39). Hillsdale, NJ: Lawrence Erlbaum Associates.

Mislevy, R. J. (1994). Evidence and inference in educational assessment. *Psychometrika, 59*, 439–483.

Mislevy, R. J. (1996). Test theory reconceived. *Journal of Educational Measurement, 33*, 379–416.

Mislevy, R. J., & Verhelst, N. (1990). Modeling item responses when different subjects employ different solution strategies. *Psychometrika, 55*, 195–215.

Mislevy, R. J., Wingersky, M. S., Irvine, S. H., & Dann, P. L. (1991). Resolving mixtures of strategies in spatial visualization tasks. *British Journal of Mathematical and Statistical Psychology, 44*, 265–288.

Mollenkopf, W. G. (1960). Time limits and the behavior of test takers. *Educational and Psychological Measurement, 20*, 223–230.

Morrison, E. J. (1960). On test variance and the dimensions of the measurement situation. *Educational and Psychological Measurement, 20*, 231–250.

Myers, C. T. (1952). The factorial composition and validity of differently speeded tests. *Psychometrika, 17*(3), 347–352.

O'Neill, K., & Powers, D. E. (1993, April). *The performance of examinee subgroups on a computer-administered test of basic academic skills*. Paper presented at the meeting of the National Council on Measurement in Education, Atlanta, GA.

Parshall, C. G., Mittelholtz, D., & Miller, T. R. (1994, April). Response time: An investigation into determinants of item-level timing. In C. G. Parshall (Ed.), *Issues in the development of a computer adaptive placement test*. Symposium conducted at the meeting of the National Council on Measurement in Education, New Orleans, LA.

Posner, M. I., & Boies, S. (1971). Components of attention. *Psychological Review, 78*, 391–408.

Rasch, G. (1960). *Probabilistic models for some intelligence and attainment tests*. Copenhagen: Danish Institute for Educational Research.

Raven, J. (1956). *Progressive matrices*. London: Lewis.

Reese, C. M. (1993, April). Establishing time limits for the GRE computer adaptive tests. In W. D. Way (Chair), *Practical problems in the development of large scale computer adaptive tests*. Symposium conducted at the meeting of the National Council on Measurement in Education, Atlanta, GA.

Rindler, S. E. (1979). Pitfalls in assessing test speededness. *Journal of Educational Measurement, 16*(4), 261–270.

Roberts, A. H., & Greene, J. E. (1971). Cross-cultural study of relationships among four dimensions of time perspective. *Perceptual and Motor Skills, 33,* 163–173.

Roskam, E. E. (1997). Models for speed and time-limit tests. In W. J. van der Linden and R. K. Hambleton (Eds.), *Handbook of modern item response theory* (pp. 187–208). New York: Springer.

Samejima, F. (1973). Homogeneous case of the continuous response level. *Psychometrika, 38,* 203–219.

Samejima, F. (1974). Normal ogive model on the continuous response level in the multidimensional latent space. *Psychometrika, 39,* 111–121.

Samejima, F. (1983a). *A latent trait model for differential strategies in cognitive processes* (Technical Report ONR/RR-81-1). Knoxville, TN: University of Tennessee.

Samejima, F. (1983b). *A general model for the homogeneous case of the continuous response* (ONR Research Report 83-3). Arlington, VA: Office of Nsval Research, Personnel and Training Research Programs.

Schaeffer, G. A., Reese, C. M., Steffen, M., McKinley, R. L., & Mills, C. N. (1993). *Field test of a computer-based GRE General Test* (ETS Research Report 93-07). Princeton, NJ: Educational Testing Service.

Schaeffer, G. A., Steffen, M., Golub-Smith, M. L., Mills, C. N., & Durso, R. (1995). *The introduction and comparability of the computer adaptive GRE General Test* (ETS Research Report 95-20). Princeton, NJ: Educational Testing Service.

Scheiblechner, H. (1979). Specific objective stochastic latency mechanisms. *Journal of Mathematical Psychology, 19,* 18–38.

Scheiblechner, H. (1985). Psychometric models for speed-test construction: The linear exponential model. In S. E. Embretson (Ed.), *Test design: Developments in psychology and psychometrics* (pp. 219–244). Orlando, FL: Academic Press.

Schnipke, D. L. (1995). Assessing speededness in computer-based tests using item response times (Doctoral dissertation, Johns Hopkins University, 1995). *Dissertation Abstracts International, 57,* B759.

Schnipke, D. L., & Pashley, P. J. (1997, March). *Assessing subgroup differences in item response times.* Paper presented at the meeting of the National Council on Measurement in Education, Chicago.

Schnipke, D. L., & Scrams, D. J. (1997a). Modeling item response times with a two-state mixture model: A new method of measuring speededness. *Journal of Educational Measurement, 34,* 213–232.

Schnipke, D. L., & Scrams, D. J. (1997b). *Representing response-time information in item banks* (LSAC Computerized Testing Report 97-09). Newtown, PA: Law School Admission Council.

Scrams, D. J., & Schnipke, D. L. (1997). *Making use of response times in standardized tests: Are accuracy and speed measuring the same thing?* Paper presented at the meeting of the National Council on Measurement in Education, Chicago.

Scrams, D. J., & Schnipke, D. L. (1999, April). *Response-time feedback on computer-administered tests.* Paper presented at the meeting of the National Council on Measurement in Education, Montreal, Canada.

Segall, D. O. (1987). *Relation between estimated ability and test time on the CAT-ASVAB.* Unpublished manuscript.

Segall, D. O., Moreno, K. E., Kieckhaefer, W. F., Vicino, F. L., & McBride, J. R. (1997). Validation of the experimental CAT-ASVAB system. In W. A. Sands, B. K. Waters, & J. R. McBride (Eds.), *Computerized adaptive testing: From inquiry to operation* (pp. 103–114). Washington, DC: American Psychological Association.

Shannon, L. (1976). Age change in time perception in Native Americans, Mexican Americans, and Anglo-Americans. *Journal of Cross-Cultural Psychology, 7*, 117–122.

Snow, R. E., & Lohman, D. F. (1989). Implications of cognitive psychology for educational measurement. In R. L. Linn (Ed.), *Educational Measurement* (3rd ed., pp. 263–331). New York: American Council on Education and Macmillan.

Spearman, C. (1927). *The abilities of man*. New York: Macmillan.

Sternberg, S. (1970). Memory scanning: Mental processes revealed by reaction time experiments. In J. S. Antrobus (Ed.), *Cognition and affect* (pp. 13–58). Boston: Little, Brown.

Sutton, R. E. (1991). Equity and computers in the schools: A decade of research. *Review of Educational Research, 61*(4), 475–503.

Swanson, D. B., Featherman, C. M., Case, S. M., Luecht, R., & Nungester, R. (1997, March). *Relationship of response latency to test design, examinee proficiency and item difficulty in computer-based test administration*. Paper presented at the meeting of the National Council on Measurement in Education, Chicago.

Swygert, K. A. (1998). *An examination of item response times on the GRE-CAT*. Unpublished doctoral dissertation, University of North Carolina, Chapel Hill.

Tate, M. W. (1948). Individual differences in speed of response in mental test materials of varying degrees of difficulty. *Educational and Psychological Measurement, 8*, 353–374.

Tatsuoka, K. K. (1990). Toward an integration of item-response theory and cognitive error diagnosis. In N. Frederiksen, R. Glaser, A. Lesgold, & M. G. Shafto (Eds.), *Diagnostic monitoring of skill and knowledge acquisition*. Hillsdale, NJ: Lawrence Erlbaum Associates.

Tatsuoka, K. K., & Tatsuoka, M. M. (1978). *Time-score analysis in criterion-referenced tests* (CERL Report E-1). Urbana, IL: University of Illinois, Computer-Based Education Research Laboratory.

Tatsuoka, K. K., & Tatsuoka, M. M. (1980). A model for incorporating response-time data in scoring achievement tests. In D. J. Weiss (Ed.), *Proceedings of the 1979 Computerized Adaptive Testing Conference* (pp. 236–256). Minneapolis, MN: University of Minnesota, Department of Psychology, Psychometric Methods Program.

Thissen, D. (1983). Timed testing: An approach using item response theory. In D. J. Weiss (Ed.), *New horizons in testing: Latent trait test theory and computerized adaptive testing* (pp. 179–203). New York: Academic Press.

Tinsley, H. E. (1971). *An investigation of the Rasch simple logistic model for tests of Intelligence or attainment*. Unpublished doctoral dissertation, University of Minnesota.

Townsend, J. T., & Ashby, F. G. (1983). *The stochastic modeling of elementary psychological processes*. Cambridge: Cambridge University Press.

van der Linden, W. J., Scrams, D. J., & Schnipke, D. L. (1999). Using response-time constraints to control for differential speededness in computerized adaptive testing. *Applied Psychological Measurement, 23*, 195–210.

Verhelst, N. D., Verstralen, H. H. F. M., & Jansen, M. G. H. (1997). A logistic model for time-limit tests. In W. J. van der Linden & R. K. Hambleton (Eds.), *Handbook of modern item response theory* (pp. 169–185). New York: Springer.

Whitely, S. E. (1977a). Information-processing on intelligence test items: Some response components. *Applied Psychological Measurement, 1*, 465–476.

Whitely, S. E. (1977b). Relationships in analogy items: A semantic component of a psychometric task. *Educational and Psychological Measurement, 37*, 725–739.

Yamamoto, K. (1989). *Hybrid model of IRT and latent class models* (ETS Research Report 89-41). Princeton, NJ: Educational Testing Service.

Yamamoto, K., & Everson, H. T. (1995). *Modeling the mixture of IRT and pattern responses by a modified hybrid model* (ETS Research Report 95-16). Princeton, NJ: Educational Testing Service.

Alternatives for Scoring CBTs and Analyzing Examinee Behavior

Barbara S. Plake
University of Nebraska–Lincoln

PREAMBLE: THREE ERAS OF INTERPRETATIONS

We here at the office of the Psychometric Police have experienced a transition over the last couple of decades. In the early years of our operation, back in the mid-70s, we had few calls. When we did hear from disgruntled examinees, they'd send us letters asking whether their test administration had been fair or if their test scores were meaningful. We had it pretty easy back then as we could rely on comparability of scores derived from examinees taking basically the same test under exactly the same conditions. The examinee may not have liked all the strict rules and regulations, but there weren't many reasons for score challenges as long as these administrative conditions were satisfied.

Then came the early- to mid-90s, with the start of some tailored administrations, and things got a little more exciting at the Psychometric Police Office. For one thing, we got our toll free number: 1-800-TEST-COP. That made us a whole lot more accessible and we did get more interesting calls. Some of the folks seemed concerned their scores weren't fair, or it wasn't OK to compare their test score with that of someone who may have taken an easier test. We were able to forestall legal challenges, though, by explaining to the callers that their "score" was adjusted so that those folks who took harder questions and got them right were given a higher score than test takers who answered easier questions correctly. Logic prevailed!

Things have gotten a whole lot more challenging though since we installed our website: www.psychocop.com. Speaking of your Y2K problems, we are prepared for additional issues and concerns being raised with the increased use of CBT and increased sophistication of test takers. Those logical (but not exactly true) answers that were sufficient for the 90s probably won't cut the mustard at the turn of the century. We expect to be answering questions, not just from the individual test taker, but from his or her legal representatives as well. It's a good thing we have our liability insurance paid up!

INTRODUCTION

In this chapter I discuss chaps. 11 and 12 in this book. In chap. 11, Dodd and Fitzpatrick focus on issues of summarizing examinees' performances to assessments delivered by computer, whether they be multiple choice or constructed response. These types of tests are already in existence, and represent state-of-the-art CBT scoring. In chap. 12, Schnipke and Scrams address the potential for capturing additional information from an examinee as he or she responds to questions delivered on the computer. Principally, Schnipke and Scrams consider the usefulness of item-response time as a source of performance information from examinees. Their chapter, therefore, represents a possible additional source of performance information that is not currently routinely used in summarizing examinee performance on CBTs.

ALTERNATIVES FOR SCORING CBTs

In their chapter, Dodd and Fitzpatrick (chap. 11, this volume) identify two issues in scoring CBTs. The first issue focuses on the use of pattern scoring for CATs with a 3P item-response model. The second issue deals with automated scoring of constructed responses. The first, therefore, is an issue with multiple-choice items delivered in an adaptive framework. The second is an issue faced when attempting to use algorithms for scoring compositions created by the examinee.

Pattern Scoring Versus Raw Scores

With a 3P item-response model, higher ability examinees who answer the same item correctly as their lower ability counterparts receive more credit in their score. This is because, based on the inclusion of the pseudoguessing parameter (c), the lower ability examinee's correct answer is attributed more to guessing than to a higher level of ability on the latent trait. Although this is inherent in the mathematics of the 3P item-response model, it is difficult to justify on logical grounds. After all, these examinees took exactly the same item, answered it exactly the same way, so wouldn't logic suggest they should get the same credit (or, as one colleague suggested, the lower ability examinee may in fact deserve more credit for getting this harder item right as it was more challenging because of his or her lower ability!)? I believe there have not been any legal challenges over this issue because this fact isn't well known. There have been threats of legal challenges over CAT scoring, but this problem with pattern scoring hasn't been the basis for any legal challenges.

This issue has been addressed empirically, though, and a promising method has been identified through research by Stocking (1996) and Potenza (1994). In their research, pattern scoring is used dynamically for theta estimation in CAT administration. At the conclusion of the CAT, however, the vector of item responses (0s and 1s) is used to compute the examinee's NC score. This NC score is converted to the test scale using true score equating. Therefore, the conversion to the score scale takes into account the difficulty of the test administered. In addition, the test is administered dynamically and adaptively using the 3P item-response theory model. The studies by Stocking and Potenza indicated the method yields scale scores close to the scaled score based on pattern scoring. The scoring method, though, may seem fairer to examinees and therefore may be less likely to face legal challenges.

Another proposed solution to this problem with pattern scoring is to use multistage testing instead of CAT administration. In this approach, examinees are still given different sets of test questions, but the examinees take a restricted number of test forms, which are predetermined. Examinees who take the same predetermined forms are given the same credit for answering the same number of items correctly, because NC scoring is the basis for their test score. Research by Kim and Plake (1993, 1994) and Castle (1997) have shown close results to CAT administrations. Not only does multistage testing reduce concerns about pattern scoring, but it allows for more control over the test content in the administered test forms. Unlike the fully adaptive test where the computer is preprogrammed to select the next test question to be administered, with multistage tests, the test forms are preassembled. This allows the test developer to ensure the test form complies with test specifications while watching for cuing and other test-assembly issues.

Automated Scoring

As early as the mid-60s with the introduction of the Project Essay Grade (PEG) scoring system (Page, 1994), researchers and practitioners have been looking for a means to use the computer to score essays. The purposes for these scoring systems have been both theoretical (to understand what features influence test scores) and practical (to reduce the costs, both in human raters and time). The early attempts were dust-bowl empiricism at its raging best—whatever fit the regression model was what was used in the scoring algorithm. It was a heyday for regression zealots! One of my favorite examples is the use in the scoring algorithm of the fourth root of the number of words as a predictor of test score.

Recent research by Burstein, Kukich, Wolff, Lu, and Chodorow (1998) is a good example of the more modern, conceptually sophisticated approach to automated scoring of essays. In their work, the computation of test scores is based on linguistic theory, not simply regression coefficients. This approach adds construct validity to these automated scores.

However, caution needs to be used in interpreting evidence provided by researchers on the comparability of essay scores provided by human raters and an automated scoring system. These data are promising, indicating in some instances that the computer may even outperform humans in the accuracy of scores (Williamson, Hone, Miller, & Bejar, 1998). These studies have been based on experimental applications where the examinees are naive about the potential for automated scoring. When these programs become operational (which is the case in a modified use of automated scoring with the Graduate Management Admission Test, GMAT), the potential for examinees obtaining enhanced scores by second-guessing the algorithm must be considered.

Studies are needed on the detection of "glib" responses, ones that have all the right "buzz words" but don't really say anything. Examinees may be able to "fake" good responses by knowing some features of the scoring system, like "just make it long" or "use lots of adjectives, even if they aren't relevant." It is essential that the research program examining the utility of automated scoring include studies that test the sensitivity of the scoring system to the possibility of faked or undeserved high scores earned by outsmarting the system.

So are human raters likely to become an endangered species? Not likely, at least not until studies can demonstrate the robustness of the automated scoring system to faking. Until then, there will be a need for a verification that the essay is "on task." Perhaps a human rater will be used to provide a "quick screen" to verify the essay is legitimate, and after this screen, the score would be based on computer scoring.

Automated scoring has also been used in the medical arena with patient-management tasks. The scoring algorithm used in the medical arena still poses serious challenges to these automated scores, but progress is being made using regression-based approaches, based on cognitively coherent predictor variables (Clauser, Margolis, Clyman, & Ross,

1997). As with automated scoring of essays, though, there is still the need for verification by human raters.

New Item Formats

Computer delivery of test questions has opened the opportunity to present different item formats that were infeasible using paper-and-pencil administrations. In some ways, this is where the frontier of CBT begins. There is the need, though, to conduct validity studies to verify that the construct being assessed is the same (if the intent is to measure the same construct as before) using a new item format. For example, in the work by Bennett, Steffen, Singley, Morley, and Jacquemin (1997) on new mathematics item formats, they use a format that requires the examinee to generate a mathematical expression as an alternative to having the examinee solve a mathematical problem. Is generating a mathematical expression the same construct as solving a mathematical problem using that expression? A validity study would need to be conducted to address this question. I see this as a promising and important area of research.

EXPLORING ISSUES OF EXAMINEE BEHAVIOR: INSIGHTS GAINED FROM RESPONSE TIME DATA

In their chapter, Schnipke and Scrams (chap. 12, this volume) focus on the amount of time examinees take to process and answer questions, information not readily available through paper-and-pencil administrations. Like the new item formats discussed earlier, this is an important direction for CBT interpretation. Notice that the phrase "CBT interpretation" was used, not the more typical "test score interpretation." Although some researchers are interested in pursuing how time and processing information complements test score results, another possible usefulness of response data may be in understanding the cognitive processing of test questions by examinees. For example, if examinees take more time to complete items with graphs or pictures, it may be that other cognitive processes are being engaged when answering the item. Time to respond to items may be used as a proxy for depth of processes of text passages.

Another use of item response data could be to investigate differential speededness of adaptive tests. Items that exhibit the same IRT parameters may require substantially different average response times. Current item-selection algorithms focus on preprogrammed item features (such as the item's a, b, and c parameters and other characteristics that have been predetermined as important to meetings the adaptive test's psychometric and content specifications). However, time to process the item is not among the characteristics that have been programmed into these item-selection algorithms. It is possible examinees could be administered CATs that are equivalent in the variables used in the item-selection algorithm but are administered tests that vary substantially in item-response-time requirements. The comparability of the CAT scores could be compromised because of the speededness differences in the test forms. Bhola and Plake (1993) compared administration times for items when they appeared in a traditional CAT. Items with comparable b parameter values showed substantial variations in examinee processing time. Bhola and Plake demonstrated that 20-item "equivalent" CATs could be constructed that had expected administration differences of 30 minutes!

Use of Item Response Data to Purge Nonvalid Item Responses

Item-response data could also be used in a preliminary step when performing item analyses. Bhola (1994) investigated the utility of purging from the item-response data set responses that were probably based on random guessing or less than serious item consideration. To identify which items were likely not responded to with reasonable consideration, Bhola generated a decision rule on the item-response time that incorporated both the typical response rate of the individual examinee (idiosyncratic response time) and the average response time for the individual item. When the item response by an individual examinee was both significantly lower than his or her typical item response and significantly lower than that of other examinees for an item, the Bhola criteria would identify that item response as a likely unrealistic attempt to respond (either random marking or less than serious consideration). Because these item responses represent noise in the item data, the removal of these item responses from the item data would probably provide more accurate information about the items.

Other Examinee Behaviors

In addition to item response time, there is other information that can be obtained through computer administration. It would be fairly simple to measure pressure differences in keystrokes (would harder keystrokes be indicative of more "confident" answers?) or galvanic skin response (to monitor anxiety?). A critically important question to keep in mind when considering these (and additional examinee response information) variables is their relationship to the construct being assessed. There is a concern these variables would be gathered simply because they can be, rather than because they serve theoretical purpose in understanding the examinees' test performance. It is one thing to gather this information for research purposes, and another when this information is used in the score reports.

CONCLUSION

Cole (1986) commented that what has been most remarkable about the last several decades of testing was how little things have changed. CBT has changed a lot of things in testing! And these changes are likely to continue. Change, in the abstract, is neutral; what needs to be monitored is whether the changes are positive, negative, or neutral. Will the changes result in more useful, accurate, valid, and reliable test performance interpretations?

Unlike the controversies of the 60s to 80s, stimulating as they were, the growth of CBT represents an assessment frontier. Because this is a frontier, we need to assess the usefulness of our previous understandings and assessment tools. As we have already seen, to understand this new territory, new tools are needed. Research looking at the appropriateness of score interpretations is important to meet the goals of verifying that what we've done in the past is still appropriate, or adjusting what was done before to fit better with the new technology. The two chapters discussed here help us identify the major issues and understand the conflicting priorities that must be considered when new scoring models are considered for CBTs.

REFERENCES

Bennett, R. E., Steffen, M., Singley, M. K., Morley, M., & Jacquemin, D. (1997). Evaluating an automatically scorable, open-ended response type for measuring mathematical reasoning in computer-adaptive tests. *Journal of Educational Measurement, 34*, 162–176.

Bhola, D. B. (1994). *An investigation to determine whether an algorithm based on response latencies and number of words can be used in a prescribed manner to reduce measurement error.* Unpublished doctoral dissertation, University of Nebraska-Lincoln.

Bhola, D. B., & Plake, B. S. (1993, October). *Setting an optimum time limit for a computerized-adaptive test.* Paper presented at the annual meeting of the Mid Western Educational Research Association, Chicago.

Burstein, J., Kukich, K., Wolff, S., Lu, C., & Chodorow, M. (1998, April). *Computer analysis of essays.* Paper presented at the annual meeting of the National Council on Measurement in Education, San Diego, CA.

Castle, R. A. (1997). *The relative efficiency of two-stage testing versus traditional multiple choice testing using item response theory in licensure.* Unpublished doctoral dissertation, University of Nebraska-Lincoln.

Clauser, B. E., Margolis, M. J., Clyman, S. G., & Ross, L. P. (1997). Development of automated scoring algorithms for complex performance assessments: A comparison of two approaches. *Journal of Educational Measurement, 34*, 141–161.

Cole, N. S. (1986). Future directions of educational achievement and ability testing. In B. S. Plake & J. C. Witt (Eds.), *The future of testing. Buros-Nebraska Series on Measurement and Testing* (pp. 73–88). Hillsdale, NJ: Lawrence Erlbaum Associates.

Kim, H., & Plake, B. S. (1993, April). *Monte-Carlo comparison of an IRT-based two stage testing and computerized adaptive testing*. Paper presented at the annual meeting of the National Council on Measurement in Education, Atlanta, GA.

Kim, H., & Plake, B. S. (1994, April). *The effect of overlapping items on measurement accuracy and efficiency of two stage testing in comparison to CAT*. Paper presented at the annual meeting of the National Council on Measurement in Education, New Orleans, LA.

Page, E. B. (1994). Computer grading of student prose, using modern concepts and software. *Journal of Experimental Education, 62*, 27–42.

Potenza, M. (1994). *The exploration of an alternative method of scoring computer adaptive tests*. Unpublished doctoral dissertation, University of Nebraska-Lincoln.

Stocking, M. L. (1996). An alternative method for scoring adaptive tests. *Journal of Educational and Behavioral Statistics, 21*, 365–389.

Williamson, D. M., Hone, A. S., Miller, S., & Bejar, I. I. (1998, April). *Classification trees for quality control processes in automated constructed response*. Paper presented at the annual meeting of the National Council on Measurement in Education, San Diego, CA.

Examinee Behavior and Scoring of CBTs

Wayne Camara
The College Board

INTRODUCTION

Research on CBTs has generally focused on issues of design, development, and delivery. Only in the last several years has there been serious attention by researchers to examinee behavior and scoring of CBTs. The chapters by Dodd and Fitzpatrick (chap. 11, this volume) and Schnipke and Scrams (chap. 12, this volume) shift attention to these critical issues in CBT. In this chapter I discuss the major issues and implications for research on and operation of CBTs raised in these chapters.

ISSUES IN SCORING CATS

Traditionally, optimal scoring weights have been used for the three logistic models in IRT. The 1P model follows classical test theory in this regard and assumes all items are equally discriminating, weighting items equally. The 2PL model applies optimal scoring weights for each item based on the item's discrimination power. Items with progressively greater discriminating power receive greater weights than items with less discriminating power. However, most CATs use the 3PL model, which generates differential optimal weights for examines as a function of the latent trait (theta) or their ability estimate. That is, the same response to an item will generate a different weight for examinees with different thetas. These weights discount responses that are more likely to be guesses and emphasizes responses to items where guessing is less likely (Hulin, Drasgow, & Parsons, 1983).

In the current educational environment, policymakers and the general public are endorsing assessment-based accountability. However, many stakeholders remain skeptical of the fairness and relevance of testing, especially when group differences are reported. The differential weighting of items that occurs with optimal ability estimates is difficult to explain to examinees and other key stakeholders in high-stakes testing programs. Concepts such as item-pattern scoring or Bayesian trait estimates used in generating test scores for many CATs are complex and not easily understood or conveyed to test takers and the general public. In fact the Code of Fair Testing Practices in Education (1988) noted that test developers should provide test scores that are easily understood and describe test performance clearly and accurately. Similarly, the *Standards for Educational and Psychological Testing* (American Educational Research Association, 1999) state that "test documents should provide test users with clear explanations of the meaning and intended interpretations of derived score scales, as well as their limitations" (Standard 4.1).

Today, test developers and users routinely produce alternative types of test scores. Some methods of reporting scores are much less susceptible to misuse than others, and some scoring methods are more transparent to test users than are other methods. Figure 14.1 illustrates some common methods of reporting test scores in educational L4 and psychological testing programs.

Raw scores are typically reported as the number of items correct, or they may be transformed to a scale worth 100 points. For example, teacher-made tests might report a student grade as 17 of 20, indicating the student had 17 correct items out of 20 test items. The scoring method is clear and transparent, but interpreting that score may be difficult. Raw scores are most frequently used in teacher grading and other simple tests (e.g., driving tests). Often, raw scores may be transformed to a letter grade or a 100-point scale to aid in interpretation. In the former example, the student with a raw score of 17 of 20 may better understand his or her performance once that grade is transformed to a B or 85. Formula scores are another variation or transformation of raw scores and incorporate a penalty for guessing. The SAT is the most well-known test using formula scores. Scoring is still relatively straightforward. The formula score is calculated by dividing the number of incorrect questions by the number of incorrect response options and subtracting the result from the number of

➤ Raw Scores (e.g.,…Number correct)

➤ Formula Scores (e.g.,…Number correct – Number wrong/ Number of response options –1)

➤ Percentile (e.g., …45th%)

➤ Rank (e.g.,…15th in class, in top 5%)

➤ Norms (e.g,… adjusted by group)

➤ Standard Scores (distance from mean in standard deviation units, t-score)

➤ Grade Equivalent Scores (e.g.,…grade 4.5)

➤ Scaled / Equated Score (e.g., …200-800 SAT Scale)

FIG. 14.1.   Types of test scores.

correct items. If a student answers 17 questions correctly and 2 questions incorrectly, and omits one question on a four-option multiple-choice test, his or her formula score would equal:

$$17 - (2/4 - 1) = 16.33 = 16$$

Formula scores and raw scores simply report the performance of a single student on a test with no reference to the scores of other examines. A second form of test scores is based on the performance of all examines. Percentiles, percentile ranks, norms, standard scores, or grade equivalent scores are each derived through reference to some normative group. These scores may have greater meaning and aid in interpretation for most test takers, yet the calculations used for these derived scores are not as straightforward as raw and formula scores. Percentiles are the most frequently used scores, whereas grade-equivalent scores remain a difficult concept for many to understand. The *Standards for Educational and Psychological Testing* (American Educational Research Association, 1999) noted that grade-equivalent scores have often been criticized because the scale is subject to misinterpretation and the number of data points associated with the scale is small (Comment for Standard 4.1).

A third form of test scores, scaled or equated scores, maintains the consistency of test difficulty across multiple forms (and often years) of a test. Scaling and equating methods may be no more easily understood than optimal ability estimation, yet the assumptions behind the scale scores are more transparent and logical. The same scale score on two different forms of the same test may result from slight differences in the absolute number of items answered correctly on two forms. On the SAT Verbal scale, an examinee who misses four or five questions could receive a scaled score of 760 on one form, whereas the same number of incorrect questions could result in a score of 740 on another form. Even larger disparities in raw scores could result in the same scaled score if the equating forms are less precise.

Dodd and Fitzpatrick (chap. 11, this volume) describe several alternative methods for obtaining an IRT ability estimation. Because optimal ability estimation results in different weights for different examines on the same items, several questions concerning the procedural and outcome fairness of traditional CAT scoring models may be raised. For example, under some models and operational constraints, examines may receive different numbers of items or examinees with the same number and proportion of correct responses may receive different ability estimates or test scores. Such obvious procedural and operational differences are difficult to explain when test users have been convinced about the virtues of standardization in paper-and-pencil test administration. Furthermore, concerns may arise it there are noticeable differences in item exposure or weighting across subgroups. Because examinees within particular subgroups may be more homogeneous on a trait (e.g., ability or personality trait) than examines across the general population, it is likely that students within a subgroup will have different exposure rates to some items from students in other subgroups, or even that differential weights may be more similar within subgroups than across subgroups. Dodd and Fitzpatrick are appropriately concerned about the public's ability to understand these technicalities and accept these psychometric methods in large-scale programs. Although public concern with IRT-based scoring methods has generally not surfaced in current CAT programs such as the CAT-GRE, CAT-GMAT, and various licensing and credentialing tests, public attention and concern might grow with a CAT-SAT or CAT-state graduation test.

Alternative approaches for obtaining an ability estimate from the number of correct items or the summed score for a fixed-length nonadaptive CBT have been proposed by Thissen, Pommerich, Billeaud, and Williams (1995) and Yen (1984). However, these approaches would not be applicable to adaptive testing. Dodd and Fitzpatrick note that two-stage, NC scoring models employed with adaptive testlets may be promising, as items would relate to a passage or common stimuli and permit additional content specifications to be met, while sacrificing little in the way of precision. Unresolved is whether testlet pattern scoring would be better understood and interpretable.

Item-pattern scoring and Bayesian procedures currently employed in CAT environments also appear to constrain the types of items and content specifications used in assessments. CAT imposes limitations on the range and scope of content represented on moderate-length tests. Fewer items are typically administered in a CAT, and there is less opportunity to sample across a broad domain of skills and competencies. Although this may not be viewed as a psychometric weakness of CAT because theta can be accurately estimated with fewer items, it may be considered an educational weakness because the full range of content standards or specifications valued by educators may not be represented in all CATs. State testing programs increasingly include a large domain of content standards and competencies that are viewed as essential for the instructional validity of the instruments. It is doubtful that a CAT could cover such broad content domains, and if it did, the costs of developing such large item pools and the ability to satisfy content constraints consistently would become an increasing concern. A related concern is the tension between maximizing IRT information and item-exposure rates in operational CATs. This is especially a challenge at specific levels of difficulty or within narrow content domains where item pools may be insufficient.

Mills and Stocking (1996) and Wightman (1998) have discussed several additional practical concerns with scoring examinee responses on CAT that could be of increasing concern with a highly visible high-stakes CATs. Issues such as examinee control of reviewing, skipping and deferring items, speededness of a CAT, and penalties imposed for incomplete testing may take on greater importance in a CAT-SAT or CAT-state assessment program.

In addition to the psychometric criteria for evaluating alternative scoring methods, score reports, and score scales, criteria are needed to assist test users in evaluating the usability and utility of test scores. Several additional criteria could be proposed for evaluating the extent that test scores are easily understood and clearly and accurately described:

1. *Transparency.* Can the test user see how the score is computed and transformed to the final score? As is the case with the face validity of the test, if you cannot see the computation and transformation you must trust the test developer. Test developers and users must realize trust is not given when it comes to test scores in today's environment.

2. *Understanding of score information (usability).* Do you get the types of information needed? Users are demanding more information from tests today. Different users need different types of information. Increasingly, the same test is being used for school and student accountability; to improve instruction; and for selection, placement, and remediation.

3. *Intended use.* Is the type of score produced responsive to the intended use(s) of the test? The score scale chosen by the test developer should complement the intended use of

the test. When the test is designed and intended to provide diagnostic information to aid in instruction or remediation, more discrete information about the examinees' competencies are required. When the test is designed for placement, greater precision is needed at the cut point, and information on likely success in alternative programs or courses is desired. Finally, when selection, sorting, or accountability are the main purpose of testing, comparative information across test takers and over years of testing may be needed.

AUTOMATED SCORING OF CONSTRUCTED-RESPONSE ITEMS

Dodd and Fitzpatrick (chap. 11, this volume) devote the second half of their chapter to a discussion of automated scoring methods for constructed-response items. This is an increasingly important issue for large-scale testing programs, as the demand for more authentic assessments grows. Free- or constructed-response items are increasingly used in educational assessments and these items can incorporate multidimensionality, can be standardized, can be scored reliably with disciplined holistic rubrics, and are viewed as more direct measures of skills or knowledge associated with the performance criteria However, these item types have not been universally adopted in many educational testing programs because of costs and the difficulties and time associated with scoring (Camara, 1998). Automated scoring is represented under Inouye and Bunderson's (1986) fourth generation of CBT, *intelligent measurement*, when technology affects test development, item generation, scoring, and interpretation.

Several operational and public policy questions emerge in both the chapter by Dodd and Fitzpatrick and other discussions of automated scoring technology. For example, should such scoring systems seek to replace or supplant human readers? Do scoring systems emulate readers or extend beyond expert judgment to score papers on additional dimensions that may not enter into human judgments? Can these systems support holistic scoring rubrics, or are they most effective in mechanistic scoring processes? Currently, automated scoring systems are based on (a) computational linguistics, (b) intelligent tutoring systems, and (c) process and content analyses. Is one of these methods more effective for different open-ended tasks or content areas? Would multimethod systems be more effective? What limitations to the task are imposed by automated scoring systems? How open ended can tasks be and still provide reliable scores from such systems?

Five areas of additional research emerge from Dodd and Fitzpatrick's review. First, additional research on rater agreement and classification accuracy is required. Existing studies report comparable levels of reliability between automated scoring methods and interrater agreement with human raters (Burstein et al., 1998; Elliott, 1997). However, there is still disagreement about the appropriate indexes to use in comparing reliability of these systems with existing human ratings. Often, rater agreement or adjacent ratings are used that treat scores that are within 1 point (+/–1) of each other as comparable. Yet, if the scoring scale is not sufficiently broad (e.g., a 4-point scale is used), this may result in artificially high reliability estimates. In such cases, exact agreement is a preferable indicator of reliability. Consensus among the research community is needed about the appropriate indexes to use, and under what circumstances they should be used, in comparing the rater reliability of automated scoring systems with existing human ratings. In addition, research is required that examines the effect of classification accuracy at specific cut points if automated scoring is to be used in assessments designed to make placement decisions or to generate proficiency scores.

Second, Dodd and Fitzpatrick distinguish between rater agreement and the validity or precision of measurement associated with such scoring systems. They note that the objective of automated scoring systems is not necessarily to match human graders but to increase the precision of measurement, through improved scoring algorithms, beyond that produced by graders. In addition to research that examines the utility of complex, rule-based scoring approaches suggested by Dodd and Fitzpatrick, research applying policy-capturing approaches may also improve existing regression-based approaches.

Third, operational research that determines the number of graders required in the development of such systems and other ways of reducing development costs is recommended. Among the research issues that should be addressed is whether graders could conduct such studies from remote locations and meet in real time via the Web to reduce the costs associated with in-person meetings and gradings. Currently, ETS and the College Board are examining the use of remote expert panels in setting proficiency and scoring levels for College Level Examination Program (CLEP) examinations as they migrate to a CBT environment.

It is doubtful that automated scoring will replace human scores in high-stakes assessments any time soon. Too many educators and other stakeholders are skeptical of this technology or believe it can be compromised (Schwartz, 1998). However it holds promise for reducing time and costs associated with large paper gradings for low-stakes tests or replace the second grader in some high-stakes testing programs. Researchers at ETS and the College Board are exploring ways of including an automated scoring system on CD-ROMS for the Advanced Placement that could score several practice papers. Additional uses for an automated scoring network may be to conduct a preliminary review of papers and route certain papers to specific graders based on features detected by the system.

Additionally, automated scoring may provide an estimated score on papers in real time, and a human reader could then conduct the reading at
a later time. This appears most useful for conducting state testing-pro-
grams that are designed for school- and district-level accountability
rather than for producing student level scores.

Fourth, the coachability or fakeability of automated scoring systems is
likely to be the area of greatest scrutiny for a program that employs this
method to score or partially score (along with a grader) operational tests.
Existing systems go well beyond the surface features of essays (word
counts, average length of sentences, complexity of vocabulary used,
keywords) in scoring papers, yet the inclusion of any surface features in
arriving at a grade appears troubling to many (Schwartz, 1998). Can students be coached or tutored to beat the system? The developers of automated scoring systems need to determine how successful they can be in
coaching students to do well based on their knowledge of the algorithms,
and rigorous studies of the fakeability of these systems are needed across
settings where this system may be employed. A program of research similar to that proposed for evaluating the fakeability of biographical data in
personnel assessment is needed before any automated scoring system is
operationally employed without a human check in a high-stakes testing
program (Lautenschlager, 1994).

Finally, how effective can algorithms be in scoring cognitive processes
used in arriving at answers and providing diagnostic information to examines? One useful application of such technology would be in low-
stakes practice or diagnostic testing. Automated scoring systems may
have greatest utility in low-stakes contexts if they can provide detailed diagnostic information, with sufficient levels of accuracy, to assist examinees in improving their skills.

Ultimately, the immediate success of automated scoring systems will
largely depend on their acceptability and efficiency, and on quality control. If educators and stakeholders can be convinced these scoring systems are valid (meaning they focus on deep meaning rather than surface
features), reliable, generalizable across stimuli, secure, and resistant to
faking, the scoring systems may be more widely accepted than many crit-
ics envision. In addition, they must also be cost effective and efficient.
Quality control issues will be central for any large-scale program that introduces automated scoring for operational use. Finally, the economics
of the technology must be considered. If development costs match or exceed current operational costs for human graders, there is no incentive to
replace the current human grading systems. However, if algorithms generalize both across both stimuli and domain with minimal development
work, the economic incentives of automated scoring will likely fuel additional research and development work in this area.

RESPONSE TIME AS AN INDICATOR OF EXAMINEE BEHAVIOR

The remainder of this chapter addresses research on response time in CBT described by Schnipke and Scrams (chap. 12, this volume). Better understanding of the complex speed–accuracy relationship remains one of the most important research issues in cognitive ability testing, because few such tests are untimed. Early test theory assumed speed and accuracy measured the same construct in general intelligence testing (Spearman, 1927). Schnipke and Scramms note that response time has been the primary dependent variable in the cognitive psychology literature because the time required to complete a task is considered an indication of the processes used. However, many factors mediate cognitive processing and response time, and the relationship between these two variables is by no means causal or as direct as some research may imply.

The speed–accuracy relationship appears to be moderated by the constructs measured and the content of test items. Scrams and Schnipke (1997), Segall (1987), and Thissen (1983) examine this relationship across different constructs. The results reviewed by Schnipke and Scrams indicate that inconsistencies exist across studies. Certain strategies associated with expert behavior may reduce response times, but these strategies may not have a direct linear relationship with performance. That is, some strategies may increase response time and not response accuracy, whereas other strategies may improve accuracy and not response time. One of the pressing research questions in this area addresses how to disentangle such effects. Do these effects differ across contexts and situations? Do these effects differ by contextual factors associated with the process, task, or examinee (e.g., gender, ethnicity, experience)? More research is required before we can determine the extent to which strategies and processes used by experts and novices generalize across contexts and the extent to which response time remains stable.

Response-time research using CAT is confounded by examinee ability, item difficulty, and optimal ability estimation, making such research problematic. Greater time is often required for more difficult items and exposure differs by ability across examines in CAT. Linear CBT is ideal for response-time research.

Response time or speed may not be directly related to most constructs, including ability in some domains. Educators have been increasingly critical of on-demand tests that impose time limits on problem-solving tasks, especially in writing. Yet, speed may be related to performance on some tests. Most observers would agree that typing speed and typing accuracy are both related to competencies in typing or word processing. In other areas, employment tests may include a speeded component not because it is related to the underlying construct, but because it is related to successful job performance.

Speed may not be directly related to constructs such as writing, mechanical skills, or interpersonal relations. Yet, workers may be required to write business correspondence quickly and efficiently in an office environment, perform mechanical tasks rapidly in a production job, or deal with customers efficiently but diplomatically in a store. The National Council of Teachers of English has focused on writing as an iterative process, best measured with examples of student work that capture editing and revision. However, in some occupations (e.g., journalism) and other professional environments, writing clearly and quickly are both demanded.

Schnipke and Scrams discuss strategy and pacing as it affects test performance. How the person solves the problem or completes the task may be of secondary interest to his or her expertise in a domain. If the relationship between strategy used and performance is weaker than the relationship between the predictor and criterion, the former may not offer much utility for tests used in sorting and selecting, yet it may be of great relevance for tests used in placement and diagnosis. Some of the promising research cited by Schnipke and Scrams appears too imprecise to use as the basis of inferences about examinee behavior. For example, they cite Holden and Kroner's (1992) use of response time in completing an employment test as indicating the extent to which examinees were truthful in response to the test. The reported classification rate of 64% may be impressive in studies of cognitive processes, but it is inadequate for judging applicants' actual honesty.

Pacing may be related to speed, ability, strategy, and test sophistication. Research in this area may be promising in evaluating examinees' skills in test taking and providing instruction for improved test performance. Some of the pacing strategies reported in the research are certain to be techniques used by coaching and test prep firms today, blurring the line between instruction and learning versus test prep and coaching.

It is instructive to compare response-time research largely derived from cognitive psychology with the more traditional research on test speededness derived from psychometric research. Traditional speededness indexes likely underestimate the speededness of a test. Additional time results in small to moderate score gains on both constructed-response tasks and multiple-choice items (Evans, 1980; Wild and Durso, 1979). The speed–accuracy relationship varies by content area and by individual ability, style, and strategy. Score differences are more pronounced when highly speeded conditions exist. In addition, timing does not differentially affect ethnic or racial groups in these studies, and findings regarding gender differences are inconsistent (Camara, Copeland, &

Rothchild, 1998). Response-time research conducted on CBTs has generally failed to examine such contextual effects and individual and group differences. Contextual factors such as content or domain, construct, complexity of stimuli, familiarity, examinee ability, social cues, examinee experience, and demographic variables must be considered before operational testing programs can benefit from research in these areas.

CBT provides an ideal platform to examine response time and other examinee behaviors that are not available with paper-and-pencil tests. Research in this area should go beyond traditional psychometric techniques and small sample experimental efforts in cognitive labs if it is to offer utility for testing programs. In addition, as Schnipke and Scrams point out, validity studies that examine the utility of resulting scores based on various models have been neglected in the current research using response time for inferences of examinee behavior. Test scores based on any current or proposed model must be valid and generalizable, be useful to test users, and be understood by test takers.

REFERENCES

American Educational Research Association, American Psychological Association, & National Council for Measurement in Education. (1999). *Standards for Educational and Psychological Testing*. Washington, DC: American Educational Research Association.

Burnstein, J. C., Braden-Harder, L., Chodorow, M., Hua, S., Kaplan, B., Kukich, K., Lu, C., Nolan, J., Rock, D., & Wolff, S. (1998). *Computer analysis of essay content for automated score prediction* (ETS Research Report RR-98-15). Princeton, NJ: Educational Testing Service.

Camara, W. J. (1998, April). *Generational changes in future assessments: Capabilities emerging from new technologies*. Paper presented at the Annual Conference of the Society for Industrial and Organizational Psychology, Dallas, TX.

Camara, W. J., Copeland, T., & Rothchild, B. (1998). *Effects of extended time on the SAT I Reasoning Test: Score growth for students with learning disabilities* (CBRR 98-7). New York: College Board.

Code of Fair Testing Practices in Education. (1988). Washington, DC. Joint Committee on Testing Practices.

Elliott, S. (1997). *Validation of the computerized scoring of open-ended assessments* (Vantage Technologies Research Report IM-103). Yardley, PA: Vantage Technologies.

Evans, F. R. (1980). *A study of the relationship among speed and power test scores and ethnic identity* (College Board Research and Development Report RDR 80-81, No. 2). New York: College Board.

Holden, R. R., & Kroner, D. G. (1992). Relative efficacy of differential response latencies for detecting faking on a self-report measure of psychopathology. *Psychological Assessment: A Journal of Consulting and Clinical Psychology, 4*, 170–173.

Hulin, C. L., Drasgow, F., & Parsons, C. K. (1983). *Item response theory: Application to psychological measurement*. Homewood, IL: Dow Jones-Irwin.

Inouye, D. K., & Bunderson, C. V. (1986). Four generations of computerized test administration. *Machine-Mediated Learning, 1*, 355–371.

Lautenschlager, G. J. (1994). Accuracy and faking of background data. In G. S. Stokes, M. D. Mumford, & W. A. Owens (Eds.), *Biodata handbook: Theory, research and use of biographical information in selection and performance prediction* (pp. 391–419). Palo Alto, CA: Consulting Psychologists Press.

Mills, C. N., & Stocking, M. L. (1996). Practical issues in large-scale computer adaptive testing. *Applied Measurement in Education, 19*, 287–304.

Schwartz, A. E. (1998, April 26). Grading by machine. *The Washington Post*, pp. xx–xx.

Scrams, D. J., & Schnipke, D. L. (1997, April). *Making use of response-time in standardized tests: Are accuracy and speed measuring the same thing?* Paper presented at the National Council on Measurement in Education, Chicago.

Segall, D. O. (1987). *Relations between estimated ability and test time on the CAT-ASVAB*. Unpublished manuscript.

Spearman, C. (1927). *The abilities of man*. New York: Macmillan.

Thissen, D. (1983). Timed testing: An approach using item response theory. In D. J. Weiss (Ed.), *New horizons in testing: Latent trait test theory and computerized adaptive testing* (pp. 179–203). New York: Academic Press.

Thissen, D., Pommerich, M., Billeaud, K., & Williams, V. S. (1995). Item response theory for scores on tests including polytomous items with ordered responses. *Applied Psychological Measurement, 19*, 39–49.

Wightman, L. F. (1998). Practical issues in computerized test assembly. *Applied Psychological Measurement, 22*, 292–302.

Wild, C. L., & Durso, R. (1979). *Effects of increased test taking time on test scores by ethnic and gender subgroups* (GRE 76-06R). Princeton, NJ: Educational Testing Service.

Yen, W. M. (1984). Obtaining maximum likelihood trait estimates from number-correct scores for the three-parameter logistic model. *Journal of Educational Measurement, 21*, 93–111.

RESEARCH AGENDA

CBT: A Research Agenda

Robert L. Linn
University of Colorado, Boulder

Fritz Drasgow
University of Illinois at Urbana-Champaign

Wayne Camara
The College Board

Linda Crocker
University of Florida

Ronald K. Hambleton
University of Massachusetts at Amherst

Barbara S. Plake
University of Nebraska–Lincoln

William Stout
University of Illinois at Urbana-Champaign

Wim J. van der Linden
University of Twente, The Netherlands

On September 25 to 26, 1998, a colloquium entitled "Computer-Based Testing: Building the Foundation for Future Assessment" was held in Philadelphia, Pennsylvania. Seven papers summarizing issues that are critical for CBT were presented by researchers engaged in work related to CBT. A wide range of topics was discussed, including models for CBT, item development, controlling item exposure and maintaining security, and alternatives for scoring and test analysis. In addition to describing the current state of the art, these papers were forward looking in that they provide a roadmap for new research needed to build a solid infrastructure for CBT. After each paper was presented, it was discussed by two distinguished psychometricians, and then the colloquium participants, some 250 strong, formed break-out groups to further consider the issues and identify research needs.

From the papers presented at the colloquium, the comments of discussants, and the ideas developed in break-out groups, it was clear that although we have made substantial progress in CBT during the past few decades, much additional work needs to be conducted. Part of this research might be considered evolutionary. A great deal of research is needed comparing various options for the test model, administrative procedure, and scoring so that test developers can make informed judgments on the basis of empirical research.

Revolutionary research is also needed. New types of assessments may present audio and video. They may involve interactive simulations that make the presentation of information to test takers contingent on their requests or actions. Automated scoring of constructed responses may enhance the assessment process. Computers may devise items on the fly; item difficulty and discrimination parameters may be approximated from knowledge of the features of the items. Costs, which are always a concern, need to be reduced.

This chapter provides an overview of the research needed to support CBT in the years ahead. Of course it is not comprehensive; doubtlessly some of the best research will result from serendipity or findings and ideas not yet imagined. Nonetheless, this chapter describes a wide variety of research needed to place CBT programs on firmer footing.

TEST MODELS

Research on CBT began with the work by Jensema (1974), Lord (1970, 1980), Urry (1977), and Weiss (1974) and others in the 1970s. In hindsight, this early work, though innovative and involving a dramatic shift of paradigm in testing, was limited in the following aspects: (a) the focus was almost exclusively on the statistical reliability of ability estimation, (b) only adaptive testing formats were studied (i.e., CATs), (c) items with dichotomous scoring were assumed, and (d) response models with a unidimensional ability parameter were used. In particular, there was no emphasis on increasing test validity or increasing the scope of constructs to be tested through the introduction of new item types and new item scoring rubrics, such new item types and scoring made possible by the computer administration and scoring of items.

The advent of cheap and powerful computers in the 1990s has helped facilitate the first operational large-scale CBT programs such as the ASVAB, certain GRE tests, and the TOEFL. Experiences with these programs have generated a host of new technical problems, many of which provide interesting and challenging research problems. In addition, the versatility of these computers and their seamless integration with audiovisual media have opened the eyes of researchers and test developers for new testing and response formats.

Interest in CBT is no longer solely in its statistical aspects and focused on increased reliability but also is in validity issues such as the need to balance test content across examinees who are being administered adaptively selected sets of test items. In addition to adaptivity, computers allow for more complex item types, often involving complex audiovisual material (e.g., simulation of processes, scenario development). Moreover, more complex interactions between examinee and item become possible; for example, the item being a simulated patient whom the test taker interactively examines, asking questions and ordering medical tests to reach a diagnosis. Computerized scoring of open-ended questions is becoming feasible, such as with the operational computerized professional architecture test developed at ETS. At the same time, however, item-pool development and maintenance for CBT seems to be more complicated and more costly than anticipated. Item security has become a source of great concern, and the testing industry might have to deal with new legislation with stringent requirements for item and test disclosure. Traditional procedures for quality control in testing (item calibration, differential item functioning, person fit, etc.) have to be revamped to deal with such statistical features of CBT as small sample sizes and incomplete data.

Research Topics

A research agenda for CBT for the next 5 years should address the following topics to achieve effective, cost-contained CBT:

1. *Item pools for CAT.* What distributions of content and values for statistical item parameters are optimal? Can item writers be helped to produce items with desirable values for their statistical parameters?

2. *Online item calibration.* Calibration data collected online are always incomplete. What sampling designs are best? Can item content and format structure be used to provide prior information about item parameters, especially about difficulty, thus allowing smaller sample sizes for item calibration?

3. *Exposure control.* What are good methods of exposure control? How can loss of information in ability estimation due to exposure control in item selection be minimized?

4. *Speededness.* In CAT examinees get different selections of items. How can differential speededness of these selections be prevented?

5. *Quality control.* In CAT less data are usually available to test, for instance, for possible differential item functioning, parameter drift, or aberrant response behavior. Can existing methods of quality control in testing be adapted for use in CAT? What new methods are possible?

Breakthrough Research

Research on the topics listed must be conducted to achieve effective and financially feasible CBT. Work on more futuristic topics will lead to the next generation of CBTs. Here, topics include the following:

1. the synthesis of CBT and psychometrically modeled cognitive diagnosis;
2. new psychometric modeling notions of information that address the complexity of item type and examinee's responding (e.g., in testing based on computer simulation);
3. methods of focusing the enormous flexibility of CBT to improve test equity (e.g., using different items depending on cultural background—a sort of portfolio approach);
4. improved multidimensional psychometric modeling, probably with a more cognitive emphasis;
5. research on the interaction between information-based adaptive item selection and large ability-estimation error due to few administered items; and
6. automatic generation (sometimes required to be parallel) of test items.

TEST ADMINISTRATION

CAT research in the 1970s and 1980s focused on topics such as IRT model selection, item-selection algorithms, stopping rules, and statistical approaches for estimating item and ability parameters. Now, CBT and CAT research is focused on new technical problems: (a) item development, item replacement, or, more broadly, item bank maintenance; (b) pretesting to obtain item statistics; and (c) item and test security. These new problems have arisen as testing agencies have attempted to implement CBT and CAT programs and discovered the threat to test score validity of item exposure to examinees before their taking the tests.

The three new technical problems are highly related: Item and test security is enhanced by the availability of large numbers of test items in an item bank. But large banks of items can be expensive to produce; therefore, cost-effective approaches for item generation and the compilation of item statistics are needed. At the same time, the compilation of item statistics means item exposure through item administration and potential threats to item and test security arise. Clearly, substantial research is needed to expand item banks and minimize item exposure. A discussion of this research follows.

Research Needed for Effective Implementation

Effective implementation of CBT and CAT will be enhanced if answers can be found to some important questions. These questions are organized into eight areas: item production, item statistics, item bank maintenance, item exposure, cost–benefit analysis, fairness, examinee behavior, and delivery options.

1. *Item production.* As a starter, how can the training of item writers be improved? Can items be cloned, and will these cloned items have similar item statistics? Can item algorithms be developed for item generation? Will automated scoring permit the use of constructed-response items in CBT? What are the practical difficulties of moving away from a focus on multiple-choice testing in CBT to more use of constructed response item formats? Does the use of cloning increase susceptibility of items to coaching (i.e., increase test scores without corresponding increases in examinee knowledge or ability)?

2. *Item statistics.* How large do sample sizes need to be to produce item statistics with sufficiently small estimation errors, and how much do these errors affect ability estimation? Can item writers be used to assist in the estimation of item statistics, and, if so, what are the most effective ways to obtain the estimates from them? Is it possible to use item statistics from paper-and-pencil administrations to obtain item statistics for CBT administrations? With which types of items will item statistics from paper-and-pencil administrations be the least useful with CBT administrations? And, finally, are there ways to motivate examinees to perform to the best of their abilities on field-test items?

3. *Maintaining a valid bank of items for test construction.* How can banks be structured and organized to create optimal pools of items from which tests are drawn, and for how long should these pools be operational? Do scores from a pool need to be equated to scores from a reference item pool? What exposure rates are tolerable? How can items be rotated in and out of a bank to maintain test security and maximize the life of test items? How can items be spotted that may have been exposed to examinees, and, if this occurs during testing, are there ways to salvage the validity of these tests for the examinees? Another question concerns the maximization of usage of items in a bank: Are there item-selection algorithms that can insure that all items in a bank are used without major effect on errors in ability estimation?

4. *Item exposure.* How consequential is it for examinees to have exposure to some fraction of the item bank? Exactly how should item disclosure be measured, and what does it mean to have high and low item exposure? Could or should exposure be defined in terms of when items are seen, as opposed to how often they may be seen? How well do

test forms retain the content representativeness of the item pool when algorithms governing exposure rate are employed?

5. *Cost–benefit considerations.* Are the extra costs associated with CBT worthwhile from the perspective of test score validity and other advantages of CBT? Does the extra cost of CBT significantly affect special populations? Are there any new ideas for reducing the costs of CBT? What is the value added of CBT and CAT over paper-and-pencil test administrations?

6. *Fairness.* Are tests that are based on different sets of items, different numbers of items, and different levels of difficulty equally fair to all examinees? How comparable are scores over time if the content specifications are changed? How might differential item functioning be detected in CAT designs? What methods are being used by examinees to cheat on tests, and how can these methods be detected when they are used?

7. *Behavior of examinees under different types of test administration conditions.* In particular, guessing at many items, answer changing, and skipping hard questions are less viable with CBT. How do the test-taking strategies of examinees differ under CBT, CAT, and pencil-and-paper testing conditions? How do these differences affect scores? Are there differential test-taking strategies for CBTs favored by examinees from different demographic groups or developmental levels? Can differential strategies lead to exposure to longer tests?

8. *Delivery options.* Stand-alone personal computers or a series of personal computers connected to a local area network have been the delivery mechanism for the early implementations of CBT. Web-based testing offering delivery through the Internet is also being used, but it raises new challenges. How can security be maintained? How can test-taker identity be verified? How can the quality and comparability of delivery be ensured?

Breakthrough Research

Several breakthroughs in CBT technology are needed. First, cheaper and faster ways must be found to produce assessment material of high quality. Valid test items are the center of any quality assessment, but to produce valid items cheaply and quickly is not the professional norm. Superficial or cosmetic changes to items may be useful, especially for memorable problems such as performance tasks. Another possibility is algorithmic item writing. These are easy to imagine in some aspects of mathematics. It is trivial, for example, to automate the generation of arithmetic problems involving use of any of the basic operations with a predefined range of integers. Slightly more complicated generation rules can also be developed with relative ease for skills requiring the use of a standard mathematical algorithm to solve well-formulated and highly structured problems.

It is less obvious how algorithms might be used to generate items to measure higher level cognitive skills and content areas such as, say, history. Cloning or milking good items to produce more items like them appears to be a promising direction for item production. The production of items in a cost-effective way must come for CBT to be feasible for many testing agencies.

Second, a balance needs to be found between the need for precise item statistics in a CDT (requiring large examinee samples) and the need to minimize item exposure. It may be, for example, that item statistics can be inferred from already calibrated items that are similar in content and that measure the same or similar skills. Another possibility is that expert judgments about item statistics might be combined with empirical data to reduce required examinee sample sizes for a desired level of precision of item statistics. Here, research is needed to identify factors that may be predictive of item statistics, and the information needs to be passed onto item writers in training sessions. Yet another possibility is that of optimal examinee sampling designs to minimize sample sizes to obtain a desired level of precision of item statistics. Such designs have been proposed by Berger, van der Linden, and Stocking, but more research is needed on possible optimal designs and their effectiveness.

Third, there are many test designs for CBT, ranging from a full adaptive test design at one extreme to a linear CBT at the other. In between are multistage designs, randomly equivalent test form designs, and others. But are there better designs, and how do these designs interact with item bank size and assessment purposes, and do these designs respond to the common criticisms of CBT (e.g., examinees want the flexibility of revising their answers during the test administration)?

Fourth, CBTs offer potential for reducing test time, increasing test security, and providing scores immediately following a test administration, but they also offer the potential to assess new skills and assess some skills better than paper-and-pencil tests. A needed breakthrough is new formats for assessing skills such as those that permit free responses, items that incorporate video and audio stimuli, and so on, and that can be computer administered and scored. We have only scratched the surface of possible new item formats to enhance the validity of test scores. But these new formats may create the need for automated scoring of free responses and use of testlets, and they may affect CBT designs.

Finally, a major breakthrough would be the development of a set of practical guidelines for designing and implementing a CBT system. Many small testing agencies have neither the resources to carry out research in the area nor the technical expertise to conduct sophisticated research. At the same time, many of these agencies want to know how to implement CBT programs. Guidelines for design and implementation, as well as guidelines for reporting psychometric characteristics of test forms taken by examinees, not just for larger item pools, would be valuable.

TEST ANALYSIS

Research on test analysis, scoring, score reporting, and additional factors that may relate to student performance on CBT is needed to establish a foundation and psychometric infrastructure for the current generation of CBTs, as well as to provide breakthroughs for the next generation of CBTs. Research that can inform current and future generations of CBT is described next.

Development of Methods for Scoring CBTs That Use Raw Scores, as Opposed to Pattern of Item Responses

Examinees should be able to understand how their scores are derived. Explaining pattern scoring can be challenging, even to a person astute in the principles and mathematics of IRT. Furthermore, when IRT-based proficiency estimates are based on a 2PL or 3PL model, item responses are weighted so that more able examinees who answer a difficult item correctly are given more credit than a less able examinee who answers the same item correctly. This may seem inherently unfair to some practitioners, parents, and members of the legal community. In an attempt to circumvent these issues, several alternative scoring methods have been examined, and this direction for research should continue. Some possible areas for research in this topic include the following:

1. Investigate whether use of item discriminations as fixed weights in Stocking's procedure would improve its accuracy.
2. Investigate Green's procedure under more realistic simulation conditions and with real data.
3. Examine the utility of Thissen's or Stocking's procedures to obtain a theta estimate from the sum of testlet scores as opposed to total raw score.
4. Examine the interpretability of various scoring methods by constituent groups.

Automated Scoring of Complex Item Types

In the past decade there has been a dramatic increase in the popularity of constructed-response or open-ended performance tasks in education. The cost and additional time required to score performance assessments is considerably greater than those associated with selected-response or multiple-choice items. Scoring of such performance tasks has traditionally been completed by human readers. Substantial time and cost are associated with many facets of the scoring, including reader travel to a scoring site; specification of rubrics (for holistic or componential scoring); reader training and monitoring; actual scoring of papers; standard setting; and score reporting, which often involves specifying more descriptive levels of performance (e.g., proficiency statements).

Performance tasks introduce added complexity when incorporated into CBT programs. The most visible advantages of current CBTs—immediate score and increased efficiency—are in conflict with complex item types. Automated scoring of complex item types can help current generations of CBT meet the demand by educators for more constructed forms of assessment and increased contextualization of tasks, while reducing costs and permitting immediate score reporting under some models. Automated scoring is also required to support new types of items that may offer additional cognitive features that can expand the information provided by assessments.

Additional research questions that can inform these issues include the following:

1. What are the most efficient and effective methods to develop algorithms for automated scoring systems? How many experts are required to develop algorithms and determine the accuracy of the system? Can this be done remotely or must experts work together? Can the number of performances that must be scored by humans in rule-based approaches be reduced, and in what other areas can costs and effort be reduced? How does the score scale (e.g., number of score points, continuous versus interval scale) affect the precision and efficiency of algorithms? Finally, how are these issues moderated by the item type, and how is the content or skill domain being assessed?

2. What additional criteria should be used to evaluate the accuracy and precision of scores? Is comparison with reader reliability the most important criteria? Can automated-scoring models score more consistently than human readers; if so, what observable criteria can be established that will be accepted by test users? Are classification trees or other methods able to automate the identification of cases likely to produce disparate scores or cases that can be accurately assessed without human readers? Similarly, with more open-ended essays and item types, can automated classification trees be used to assign responses with certain features to particular readers to maximize scoring precision and reader expertise?

3. What hybrid approaches involving a combination of automated scoring with human judgment yield the highest validity and reliability? For example, is the paired scoring by a machine and a human reader better than a machine alone or than two readers? What approaches are most cost effective? What approaches are most credible and acceptable to the public? What rules might be put in place in machine scoring to determine when a review by a reader is needed?

4. Would regression-based, complex rule-based, or some other type of algorithmic application be best for scoring complex performance assessments? Can the precision and utility of automated scoring models be improved by alternative methods, which combine

components of regression- and rule-based approaches? What level of measurement precision is appropriate for different types of complex items, domains, and proposed uses of tests (e.g., high stakes, diagnostic)? What are the optimum type and number of features, and do they generalize across tasks within the same domain?

5. For which types of current and new items are automated scoring procedures most accurate and valid? To what extent can algorithms for scoring an item in a specific domain generalize across other items, reducing costs associated with development of algorithms for each item? Other issues of generalizability by item type must also be addressed.

6. Can diagnostics be more efficiently employed with automated scoring models to provide test users with additional information? Can procedural components, as well as grammatical components, be scored in written essays to provide a potential context for an enhanced validated model of writing? Can essays and other more structured item types be scored on multiple dimensions to permit several valid uses of scores (e.g., placement, diagnostic, remediation)?

Response Time

Research is needed to explore how we can make better inferences about examines' abilities and competencies from evidence provided in assessments. Additional ways of using response time to make inferences about examined behavior are one example of how we can use such additional information. However, other components may also inform our inferences and description of examined behavior. Examples of important research in this area include the following:

1. Examine the added value of response time in estimating ability and the usefulness of differential time use when reading or responding to test questions to inform of processing skills of examinees. Is response time useful in eliminating noise from data when estimating psychometric properties of tests? Does response time differ among different examinees in terms of high versus low ability, gender, and race group differences?

2. Investigate alternative models, such as response time, that can inform inferences about cognitive strategies employed by test takers in domains such as mathematical reasoning, writing, and domain knowledge (e.g. biology, history). Do response time models advance our understanding of strategy in these domains, and what additional factors might moderate the relationship between response time and strategy? Can response time and other models of strategy detect differences across subgroups and domains?

3. Support additional research employing response time as a dependent measure that examines speed and pacing behavior in ways that can increase the validity of individual scores. That is, what can we learn by examining patterns of response time (including rapid guessing, pacing, etc.) that would reduce construct-irrelevant influences (e.g. anxiety, strategy) associated with test validity? Are certain response time patterns associated with maximum performance, and do these findings generalize across domains? Do sub-

group differences in response time, pacing, and speediness partially account for subgroup differences?

REFERENCES

Jensema, C. J. (1974). The validity of Bayesian tailored testing. *Educational and Psychological Measurement, 34*, 757–766.

Lord, F. M. (1970). Some test theory for tailored testing. In W. H. Holtzman (Ed.), *Computer-assisted instruction, testing, and guidance* (pp. 139–183).

Lord, F. M. (1980). *Applications of item response theory to practical testing problems.* Hillsdale, NJ: Lawrence Erlbaum Associates.

Urry, V. W. (1977). Tailored testing: A successful application of item response theory. *Journal of Educational Measurement, 14*, 181–196.

Weiss, D. J. (1974). Strategies of adaptive ability measurement (Research Report 74-5). Minneapolis, Uniberaity of Minnesota, Psychometric Methods Program.

Author Index

Subject Index

A

AAMC, *see* Association of American Medical Colleges

Ability
  characterization of, 247–248
  pacing and, 284
  qualitative changes in, 247–248
  response times and, 258
  testlets and multidimensional, 48–49
  time limits and, 283–284

Ability distribution, 133–134

Ability estimation
  for computerized adaptive testing, 111
  item parameter estimate errors and, 196
  item response theory and, 42–44, 216–217
  methods of, 216–224, 229–231
  multistage test scoring, 94, 97, 117, 199, 221–223, 230–231, 269
  non-item response theory, 223–224
  number-correct scoring, *see* Number-correct scoring
  see also Scoring

Ability estimators, 98–101

Ability groups, pacing differences across, 256–257

Accuracy
  pacing and, 255

  vs. speed, 213, 237–239, 241, 242, 244–247, 251–252, 261, 283

Achievement tests, 242

ACT, *see* American College Testing

Adaptive mastery testing (AMT), 52–53, *see also* Computerized mastery testing

Adaptive testing, *see* Computerized adaptive testing

Admissions decisions, test scores and, 118, 208

Advanced Placement, 281

African American examinees, 260

Algorithmic item writing, 117, 198, 201, 294–295

α-trimmed mean, 186

Alternate test designs, 199

American College Testing (ACT), 150, 168

AMT, *see* Adaptive mastery testing

Analogical reasoning
  accuracy and response-time data and, 261–262
  cognitive theories of, 262
  performance, 262
  problem solving, 256, 262

Analytical-reasoning skills tests, 246–247, 256

Anchor items, 132–133

Anxiety
  measuring, 214
  response times and, 258, 259